This Notebook Belongs To:

_____

Copyright notice:
Published by **POD Only Publishing**

Without your input we don't exist.
Please, cheer us and leave a review!

Thank you!

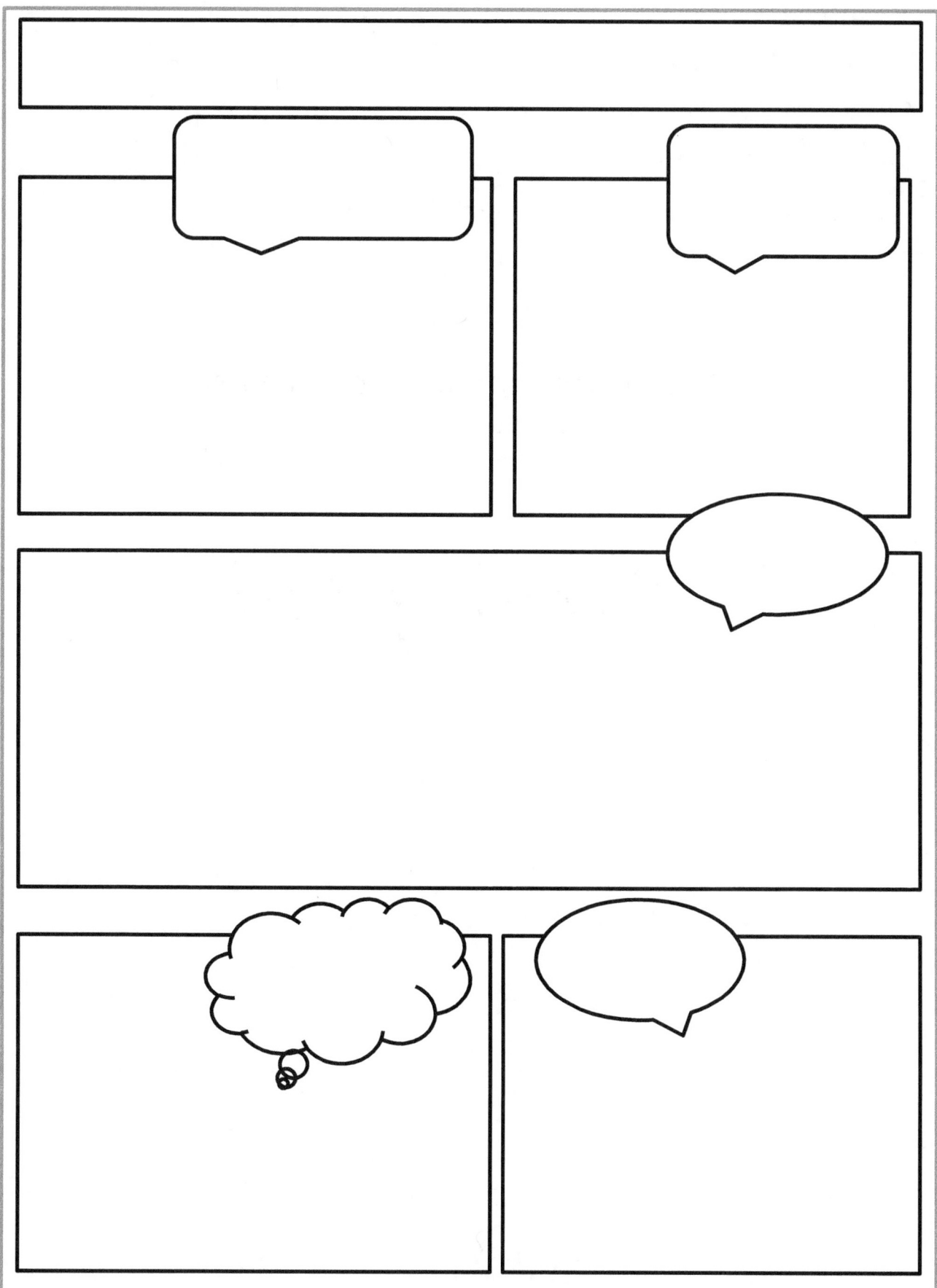

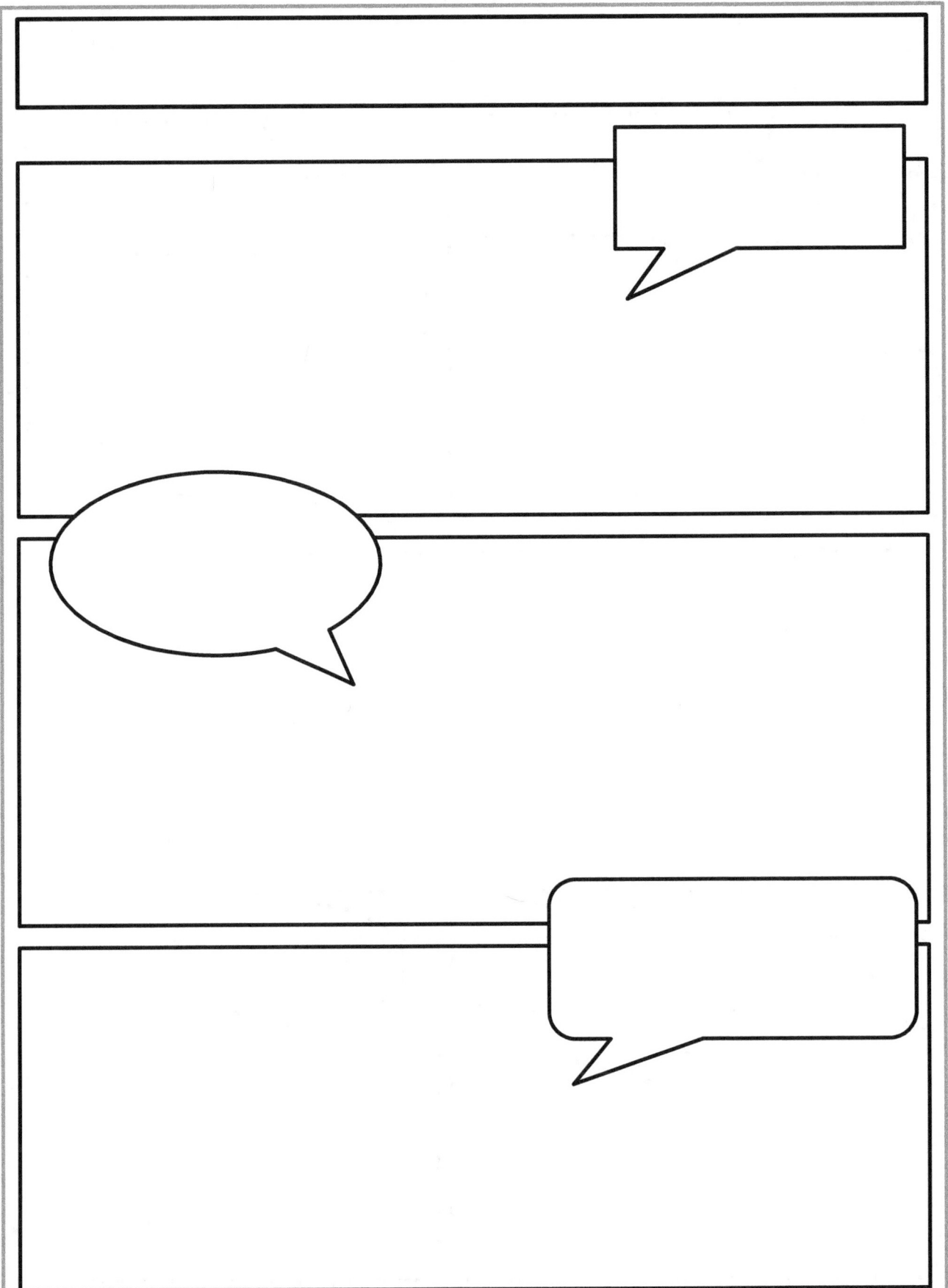

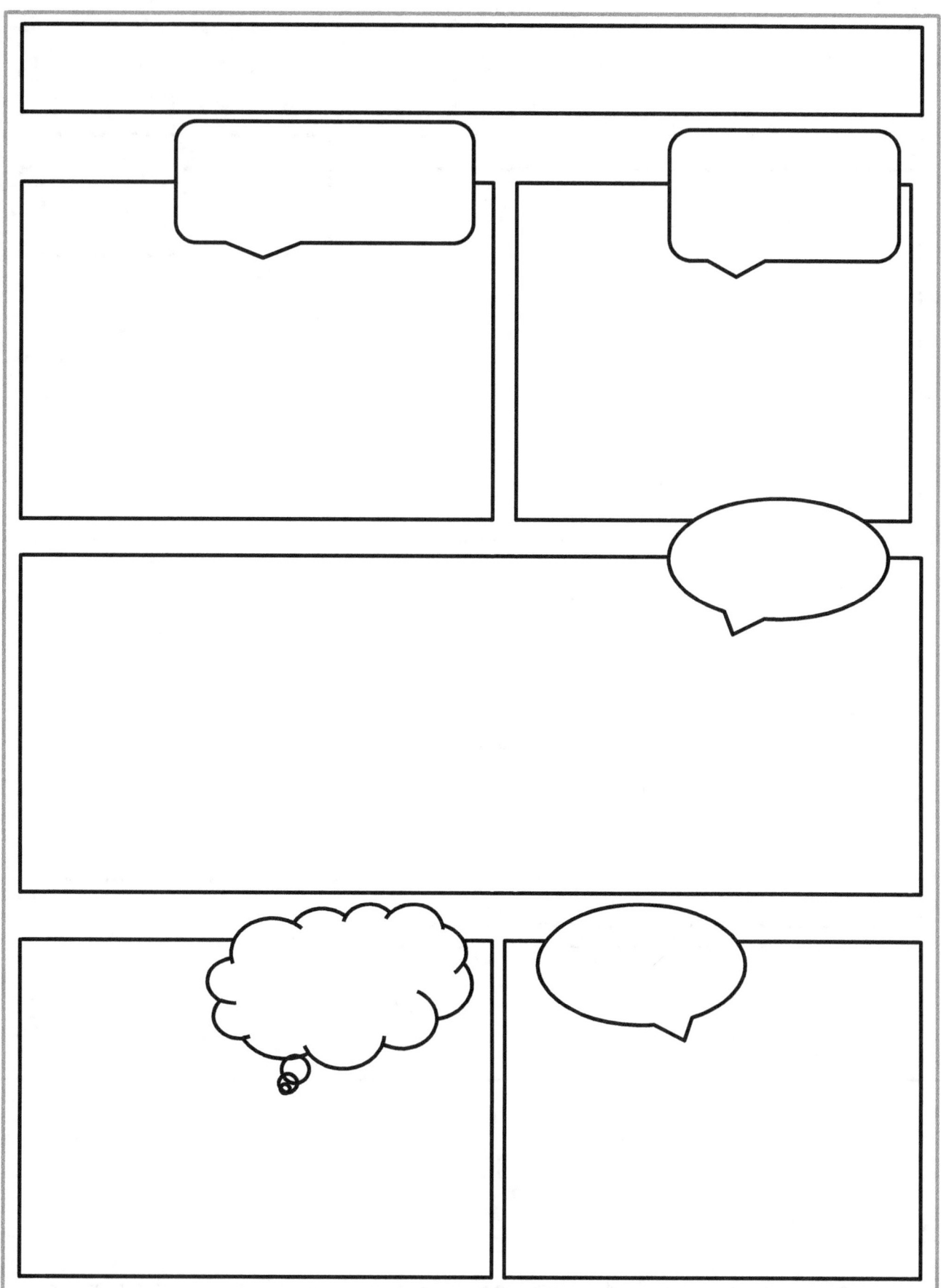

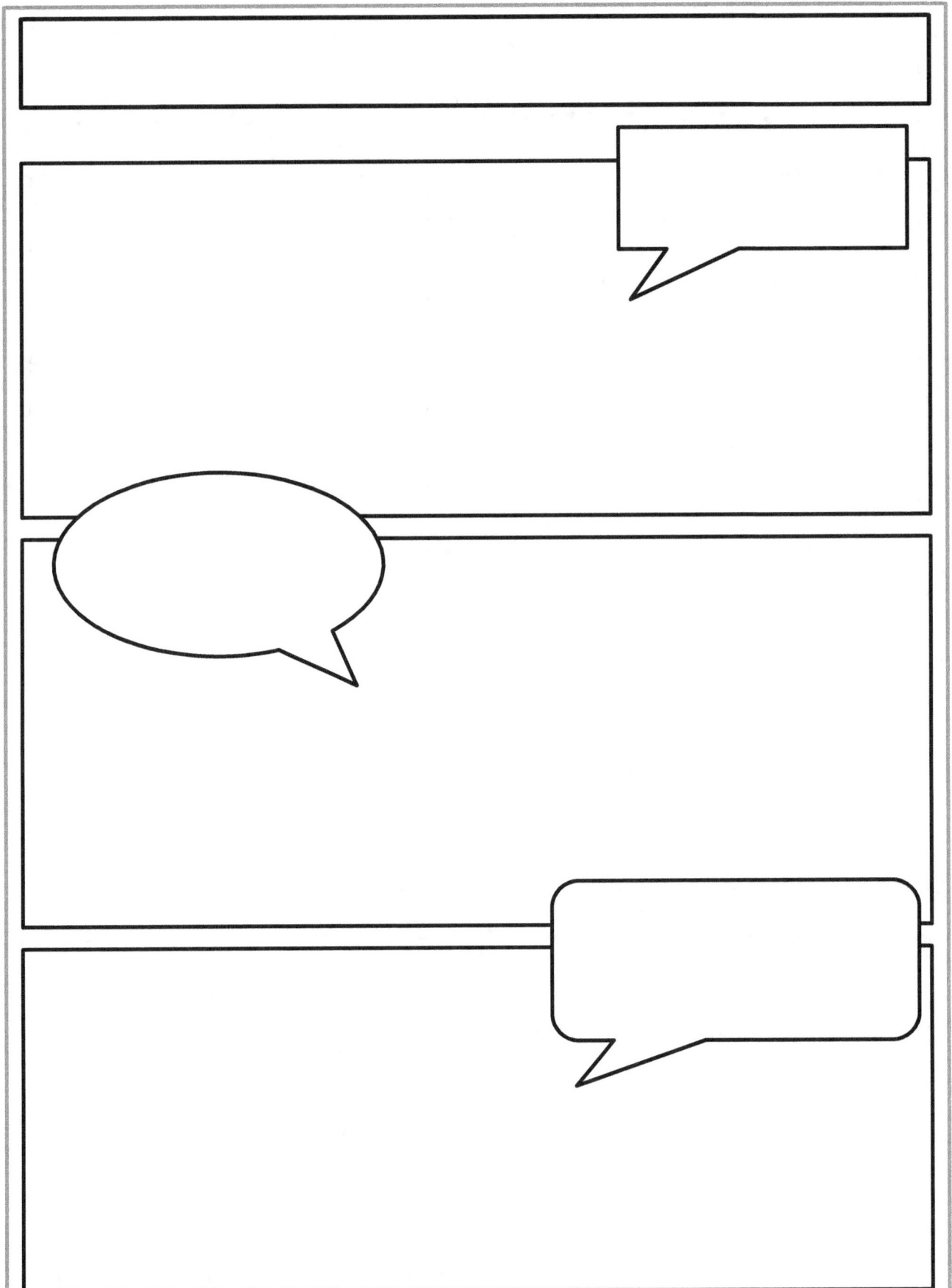

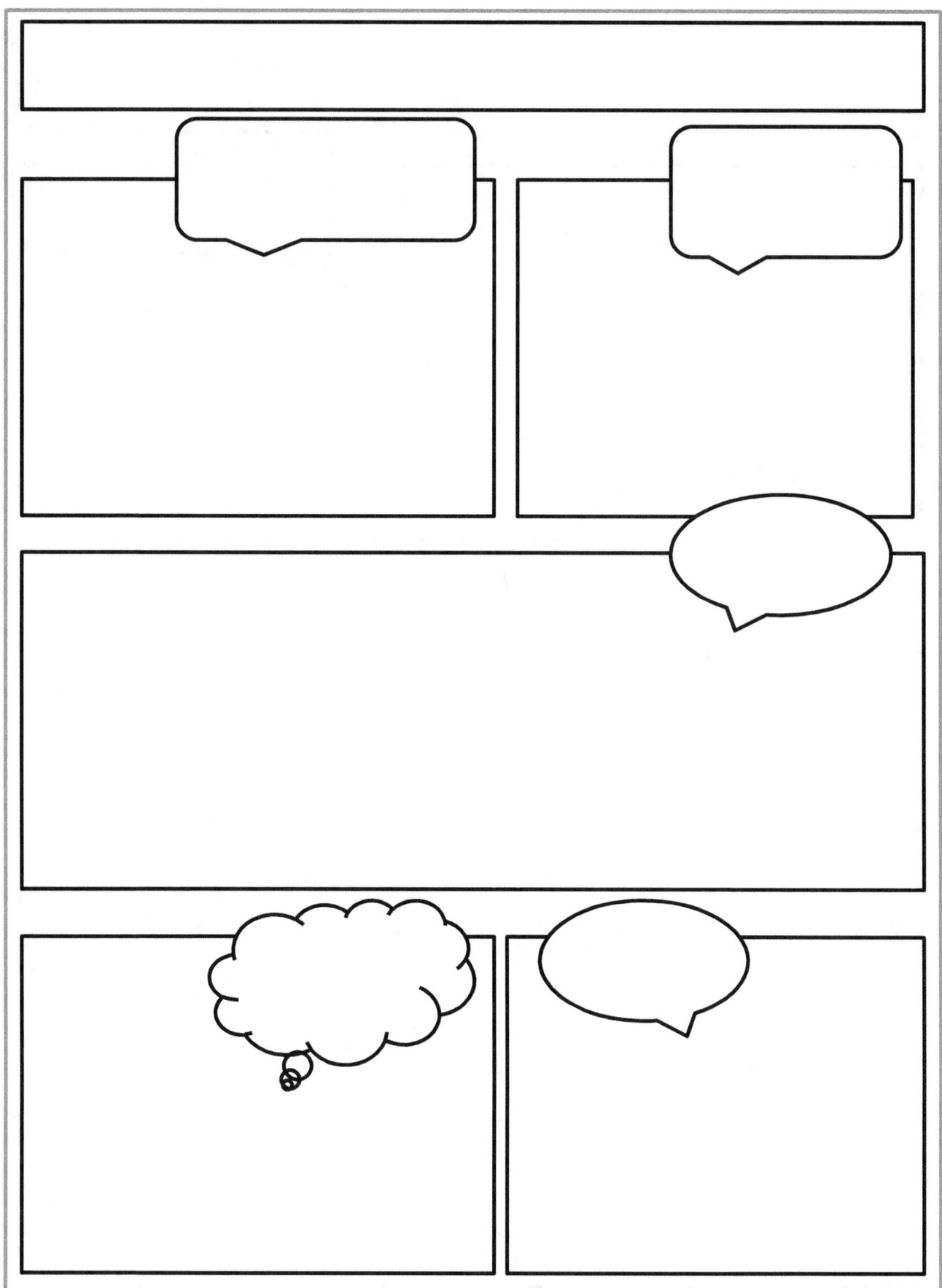

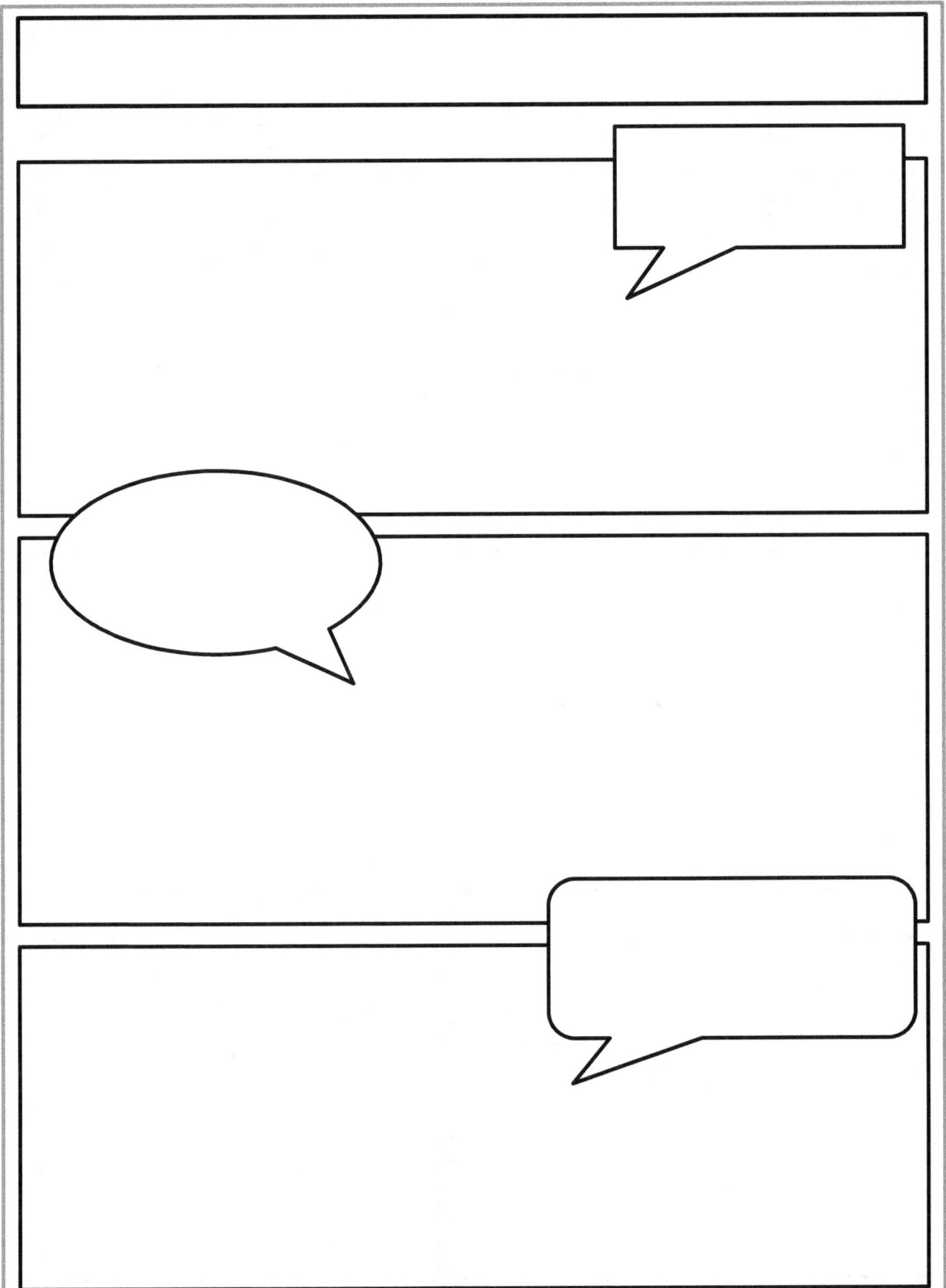

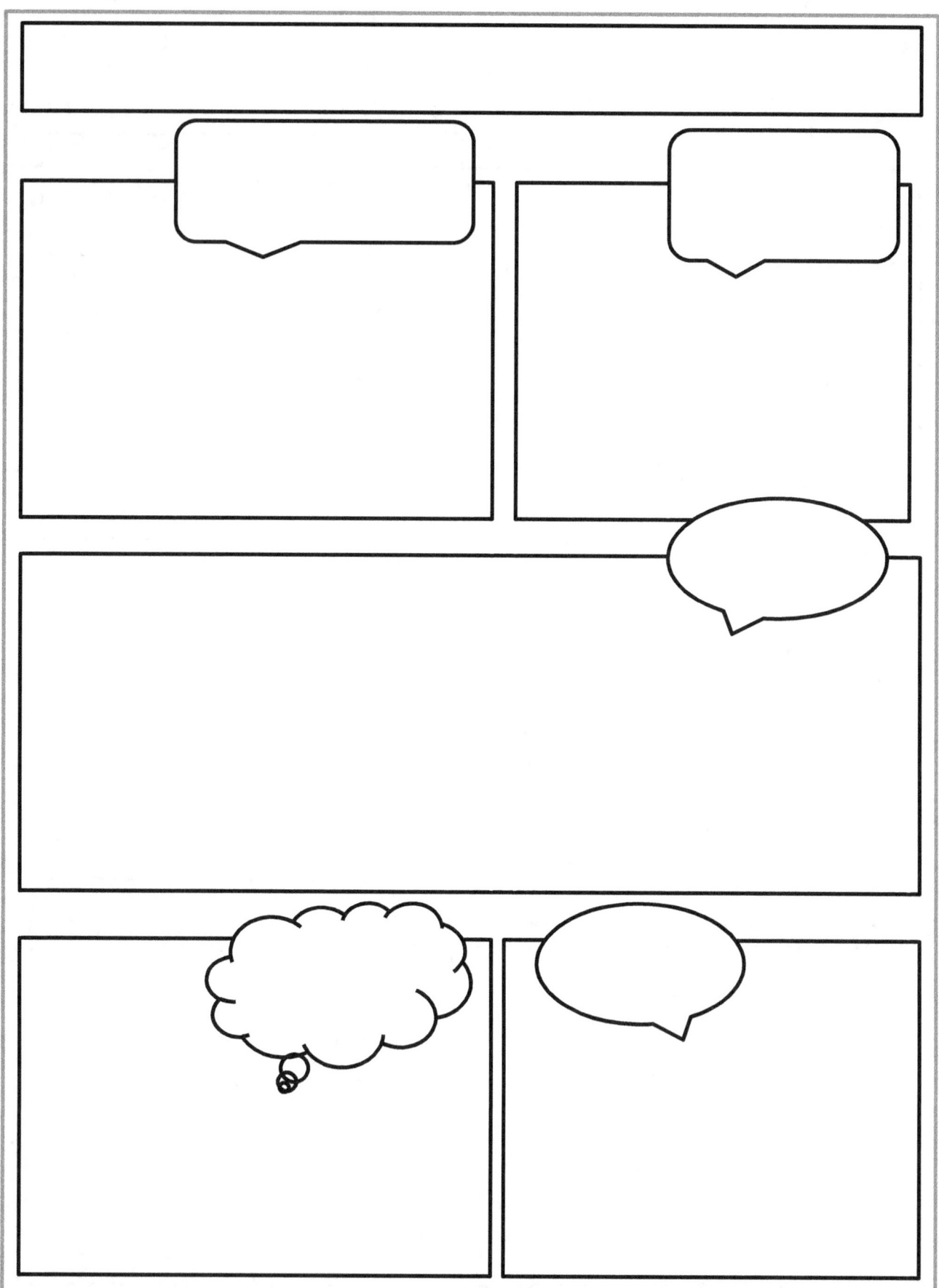

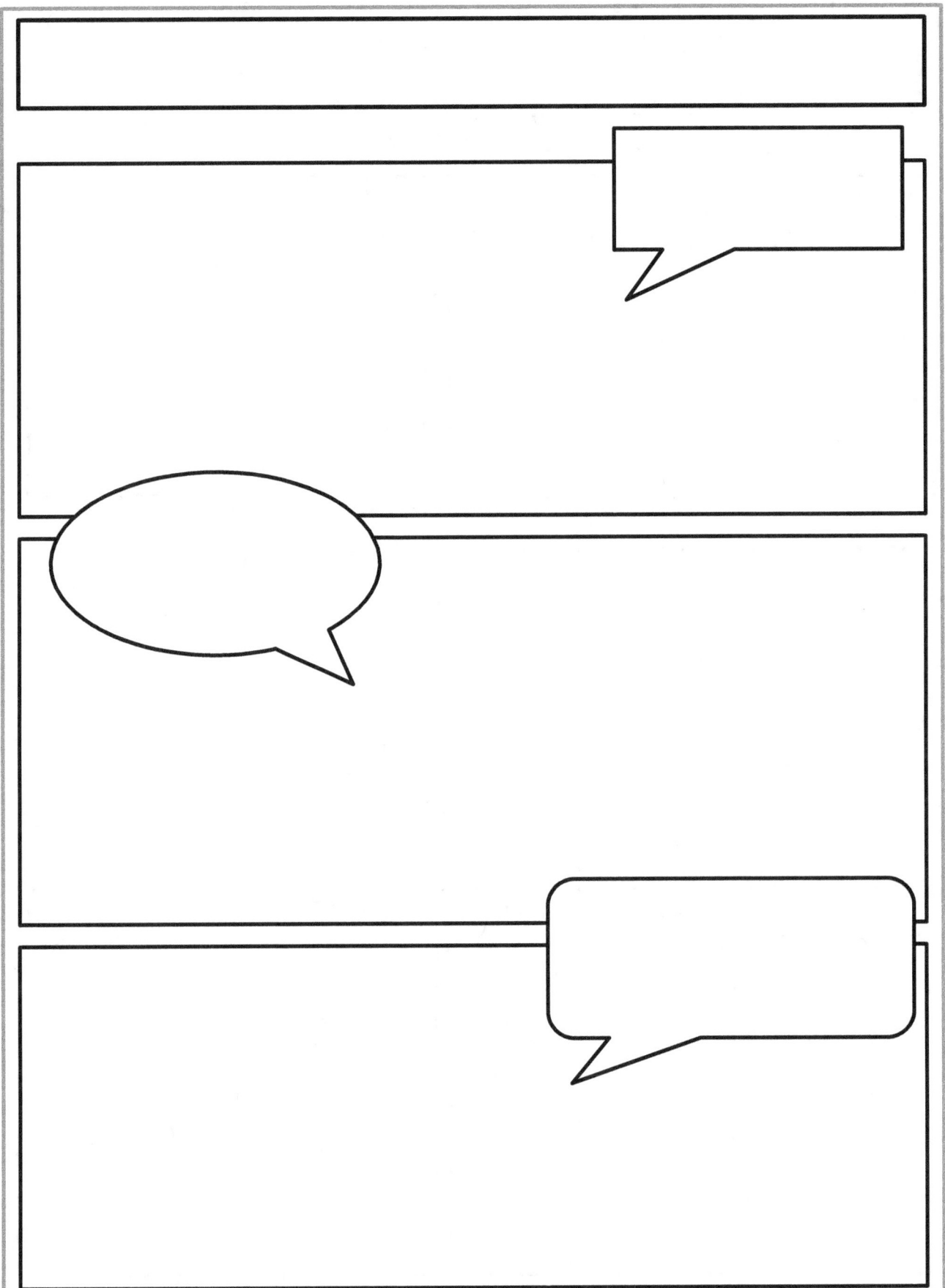

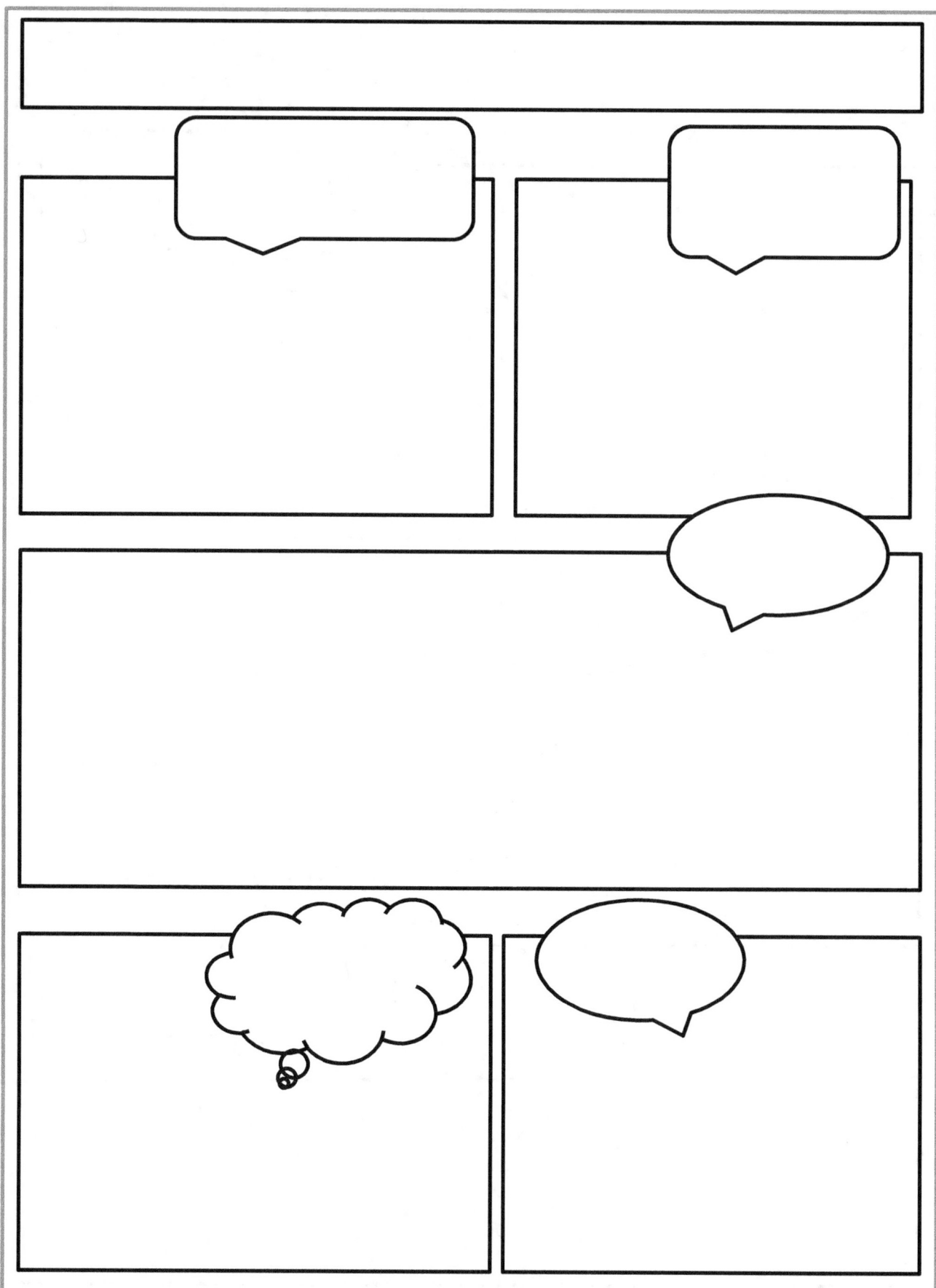

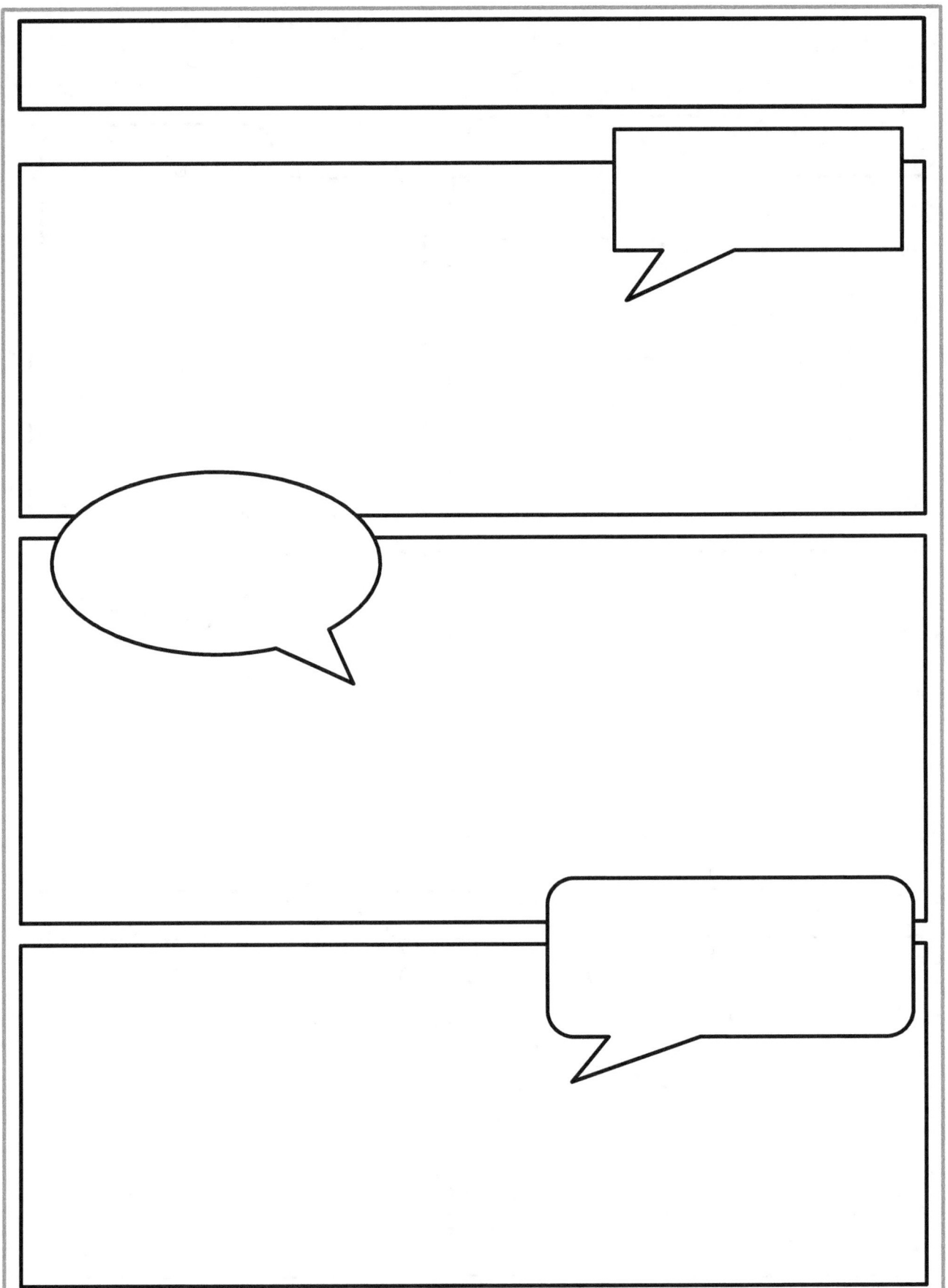

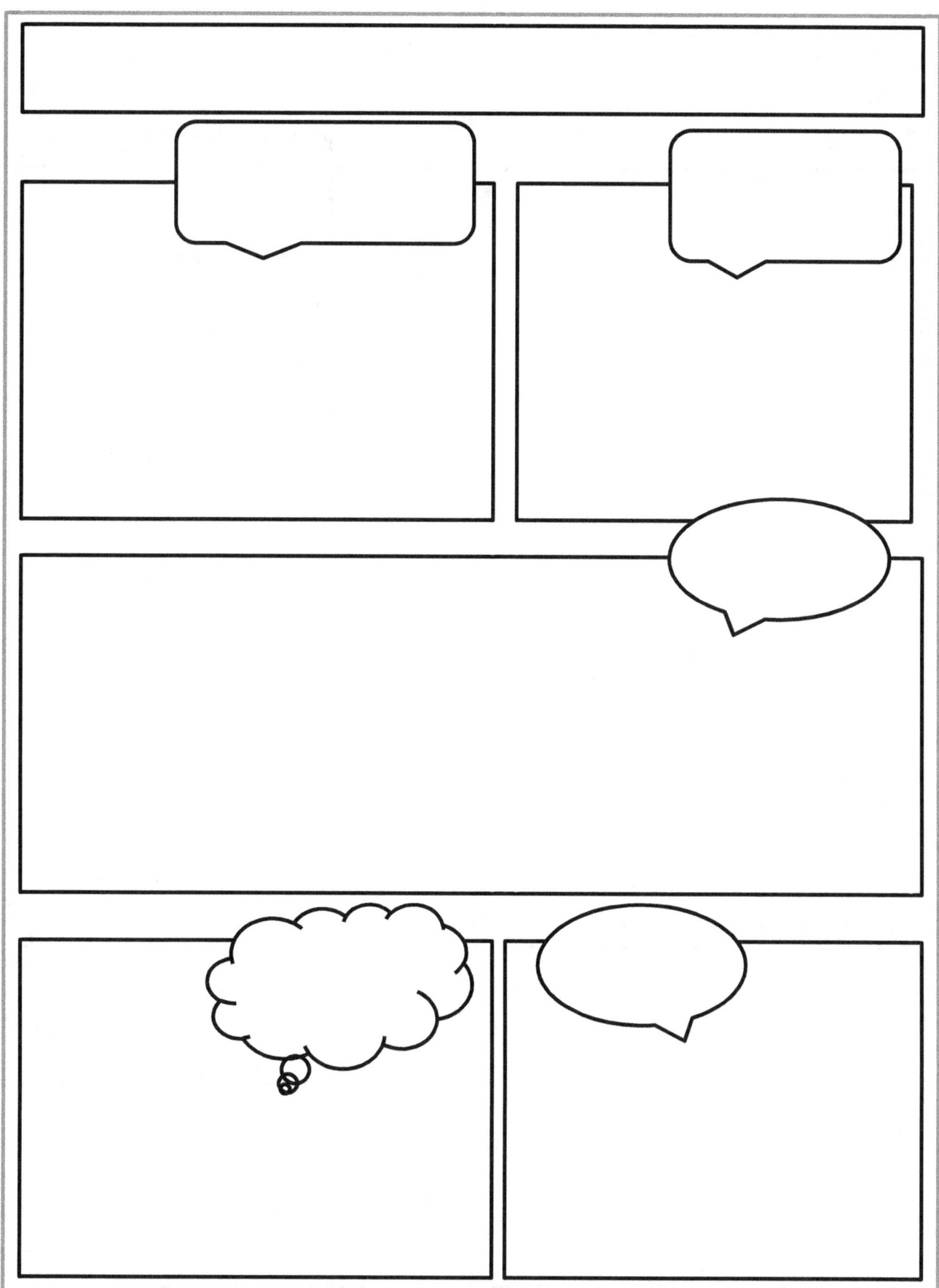

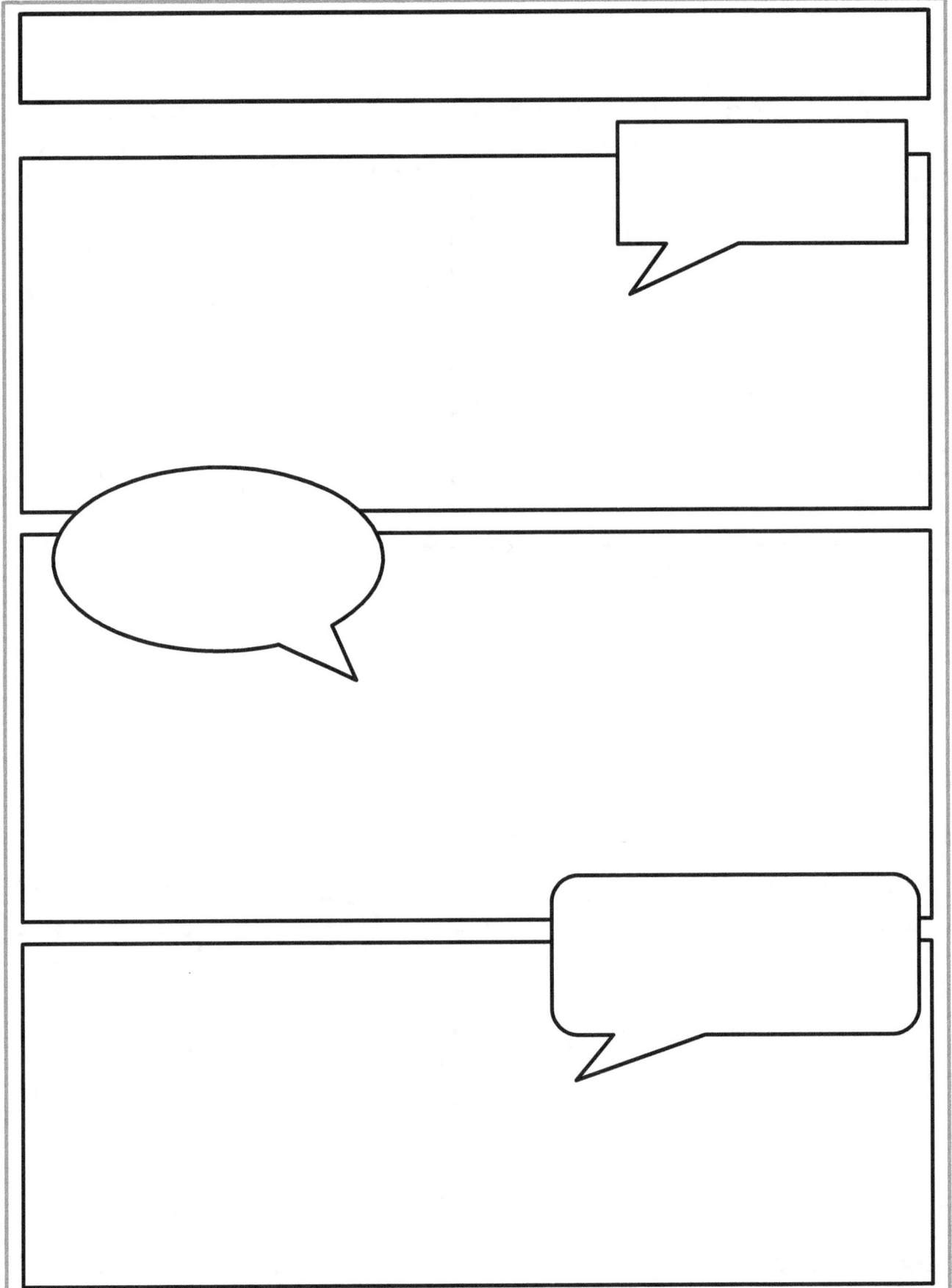

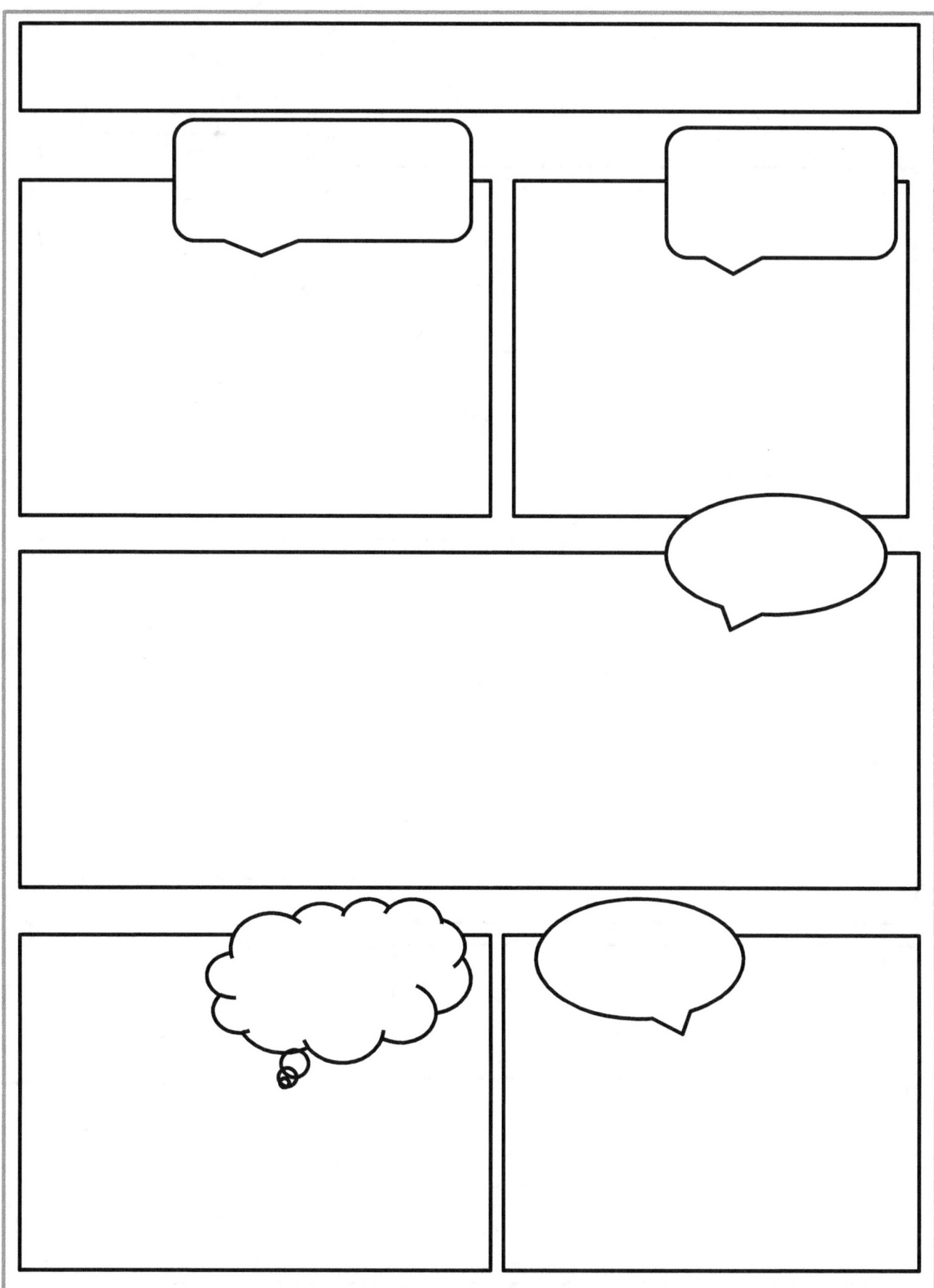

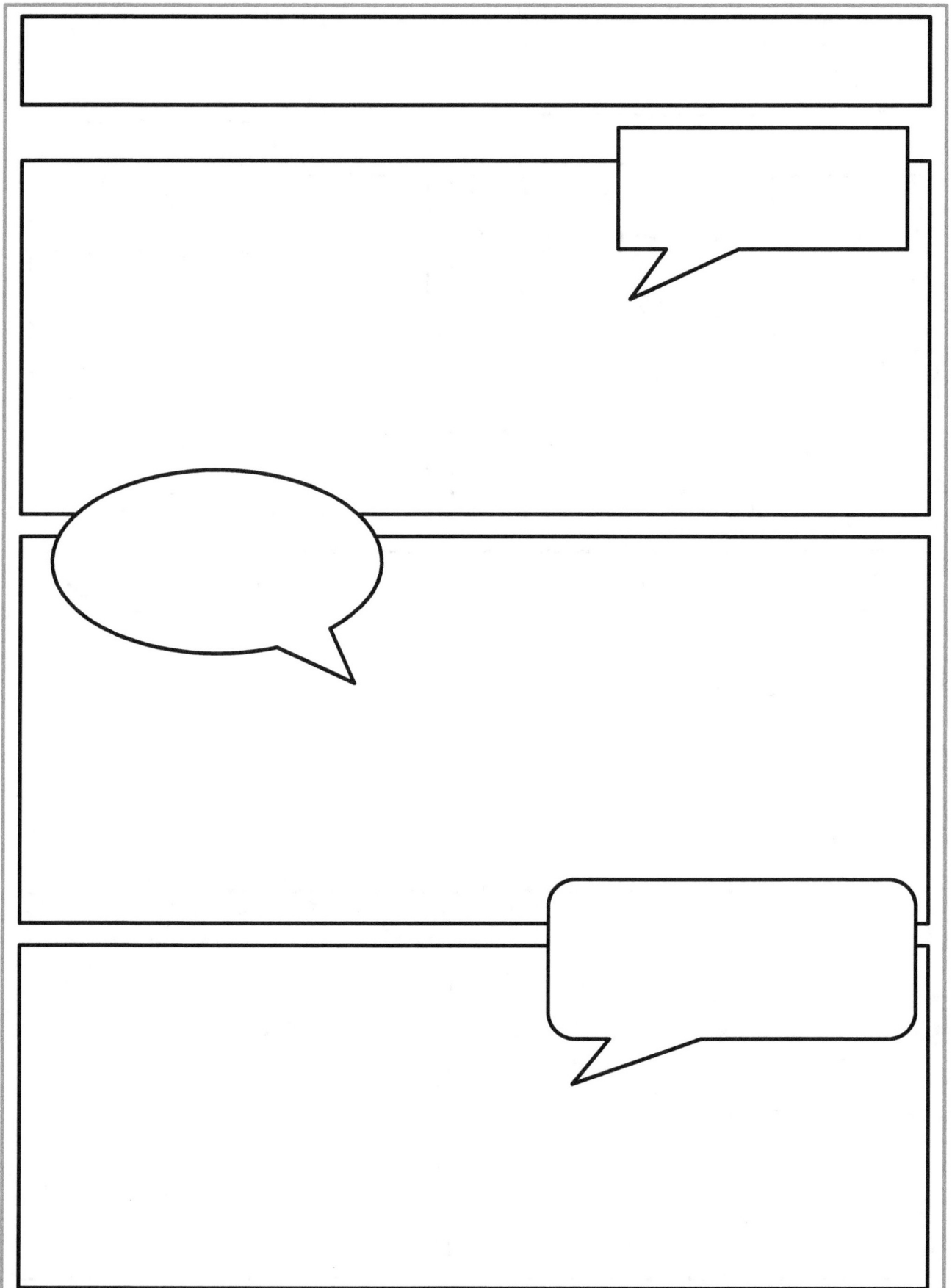

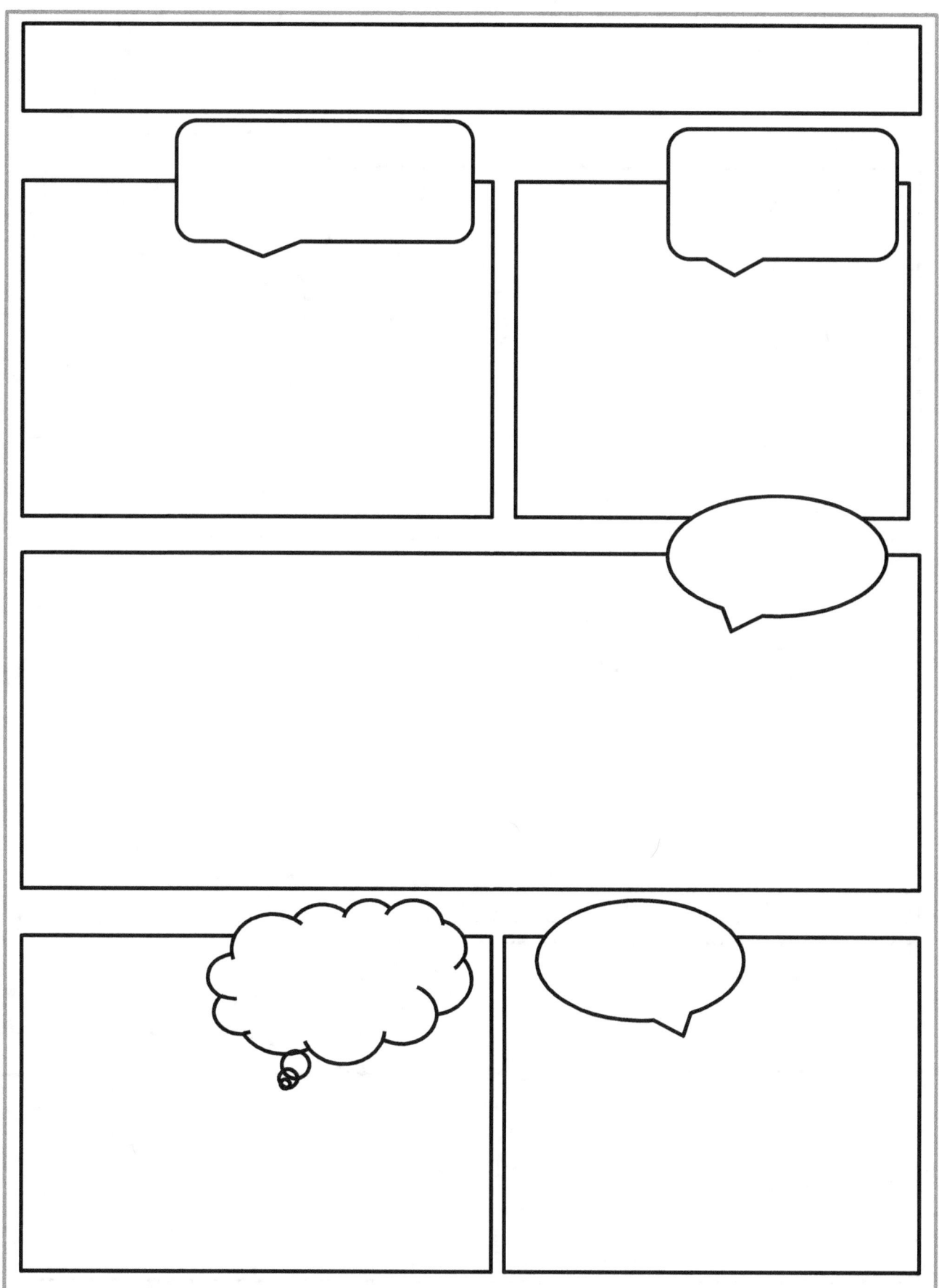

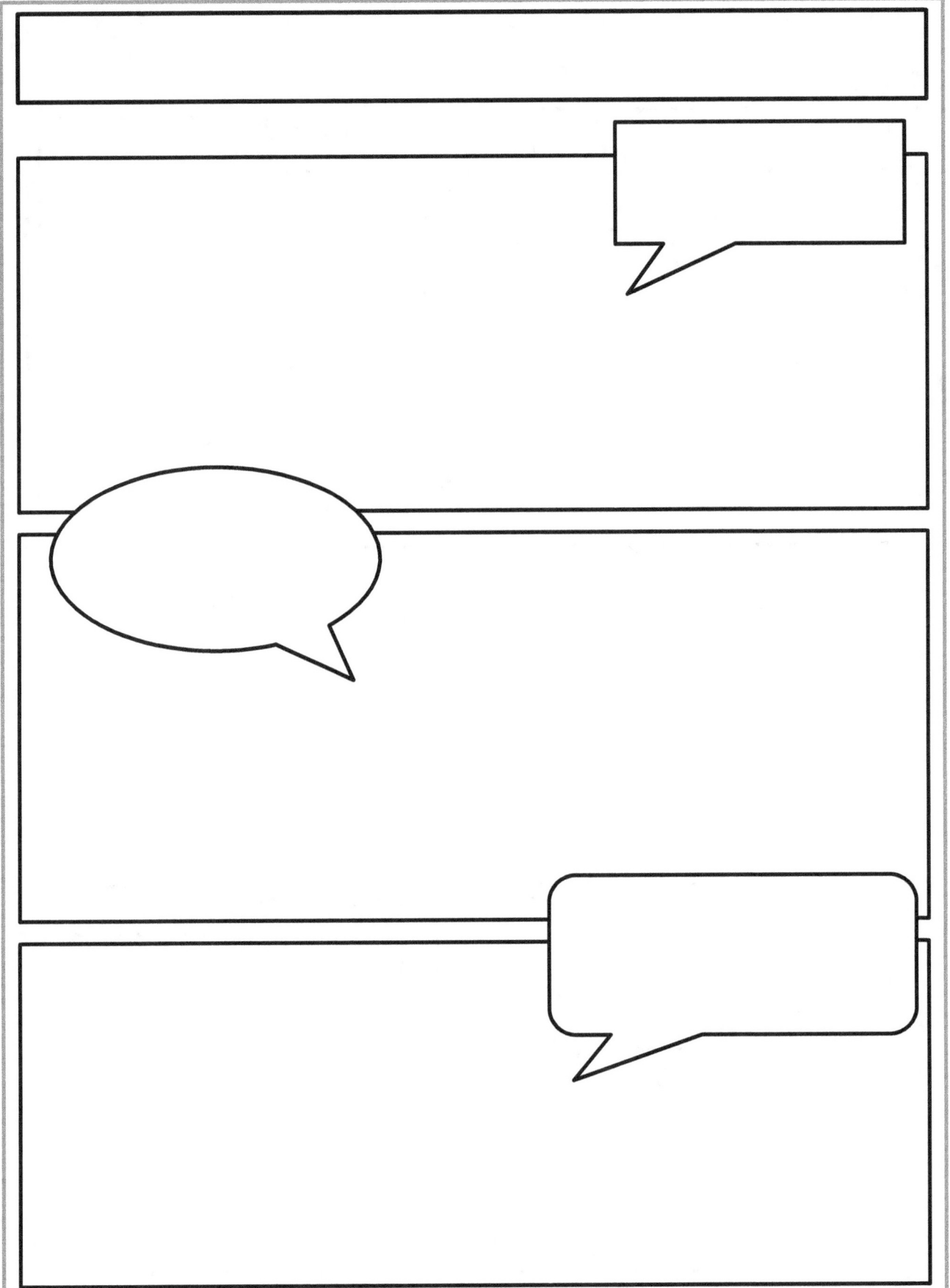

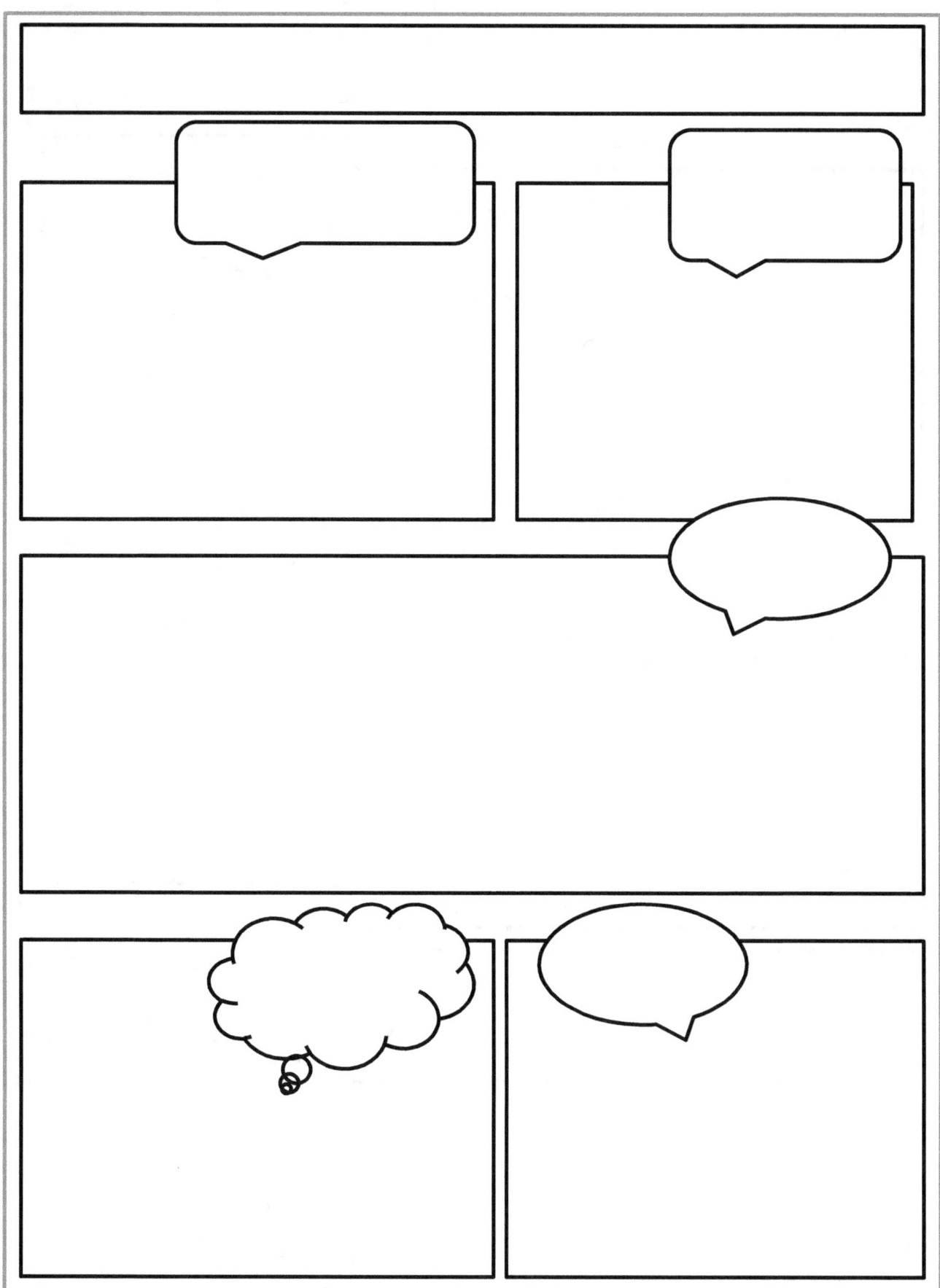

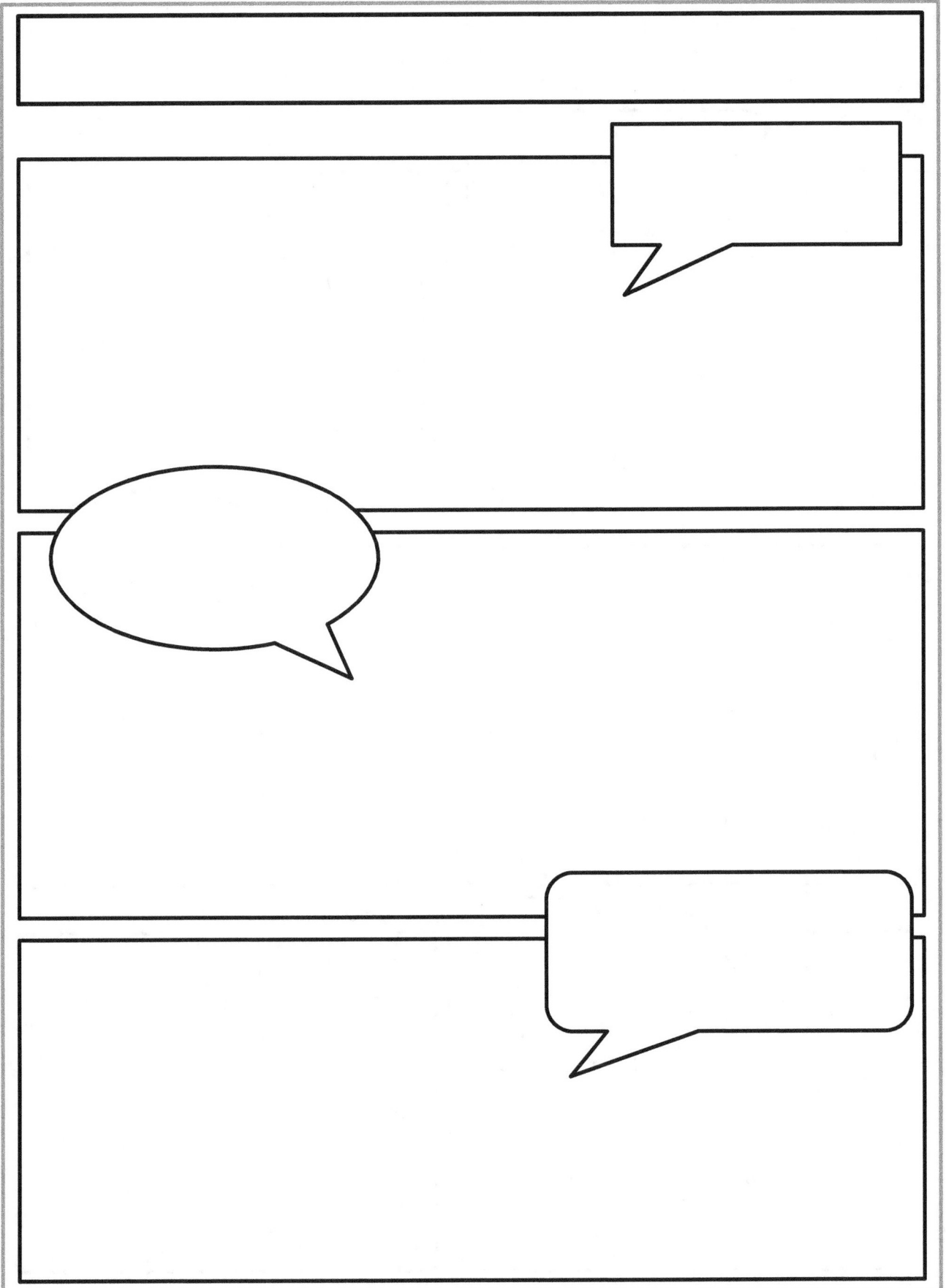

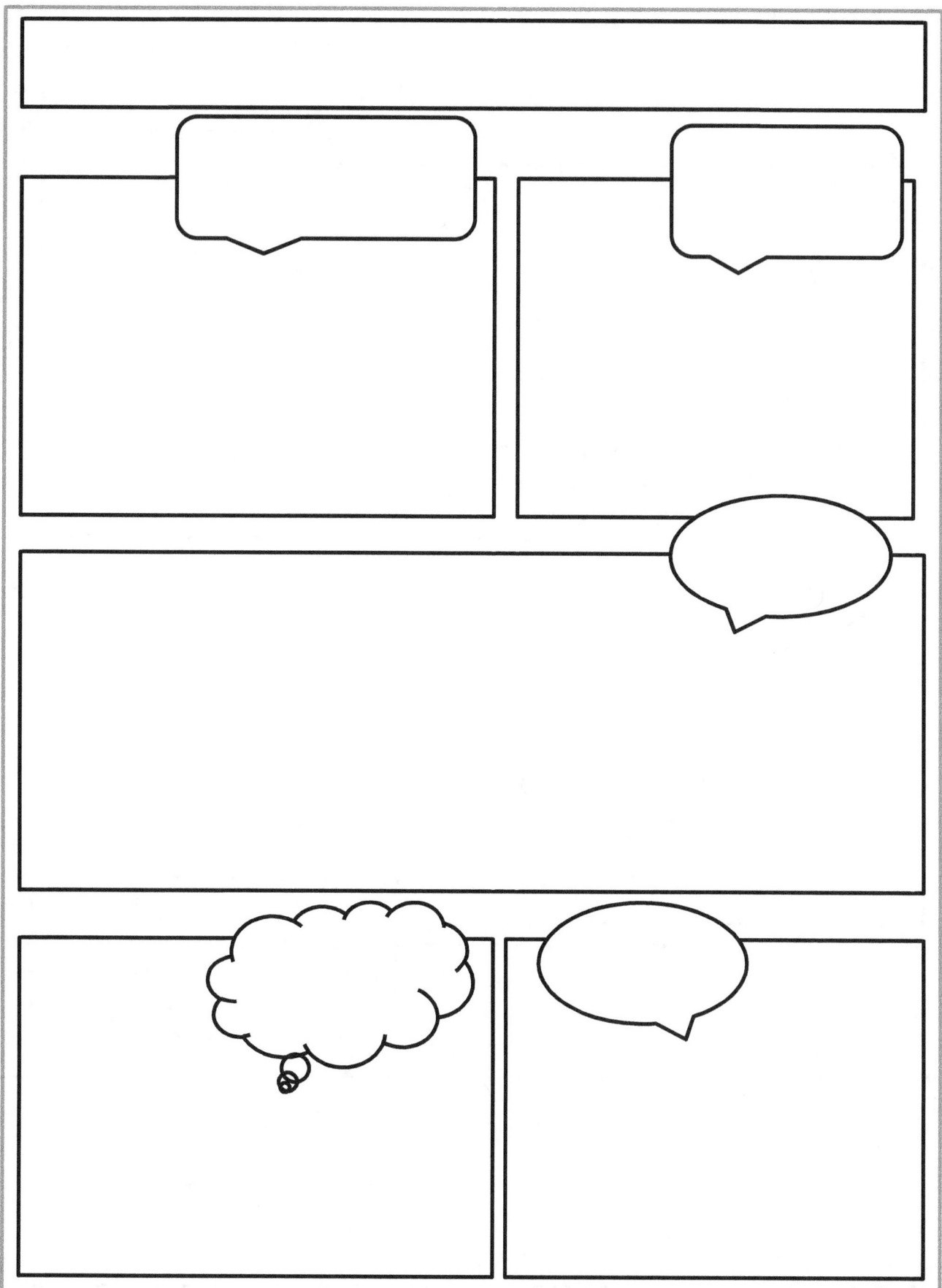

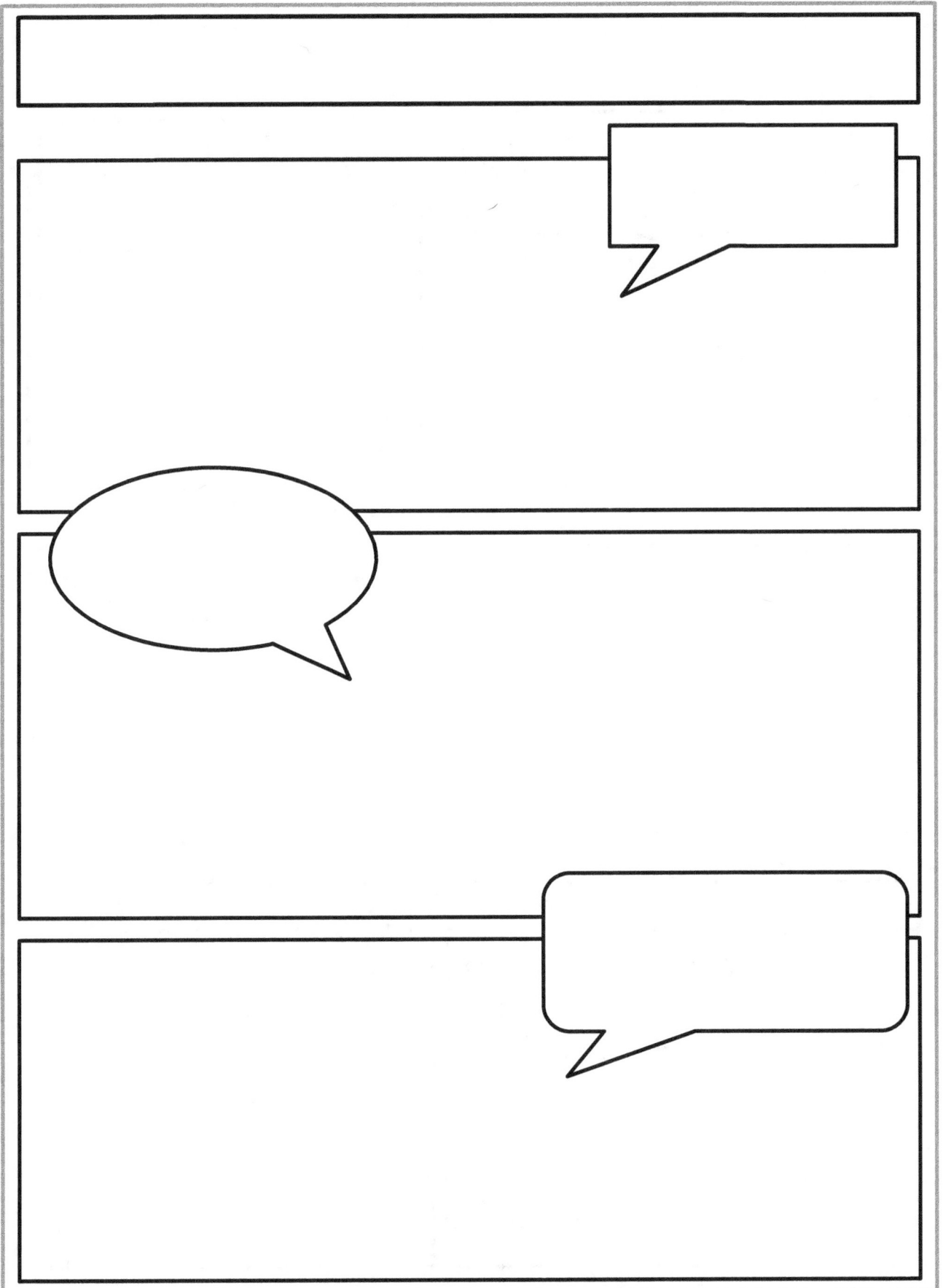

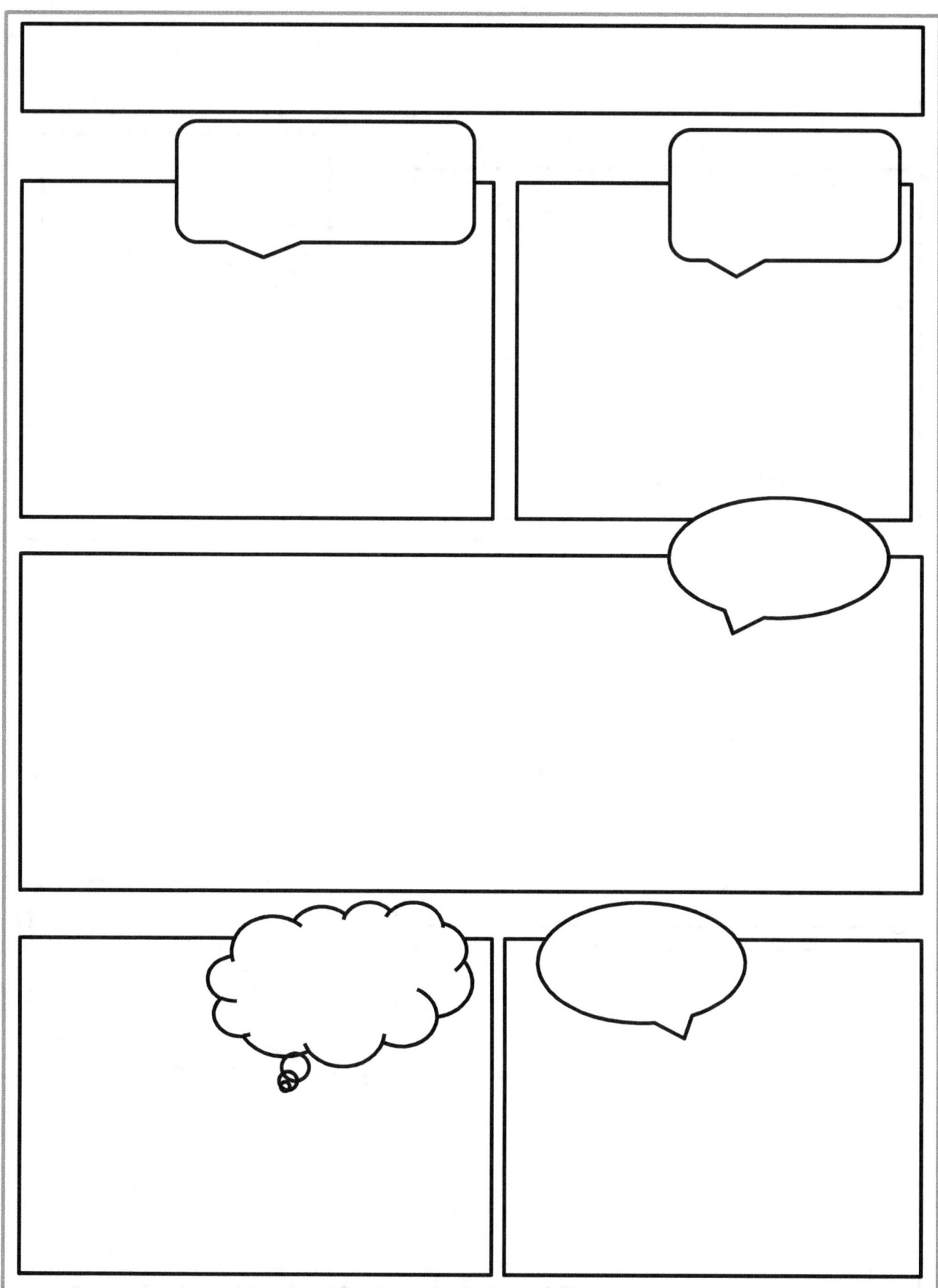

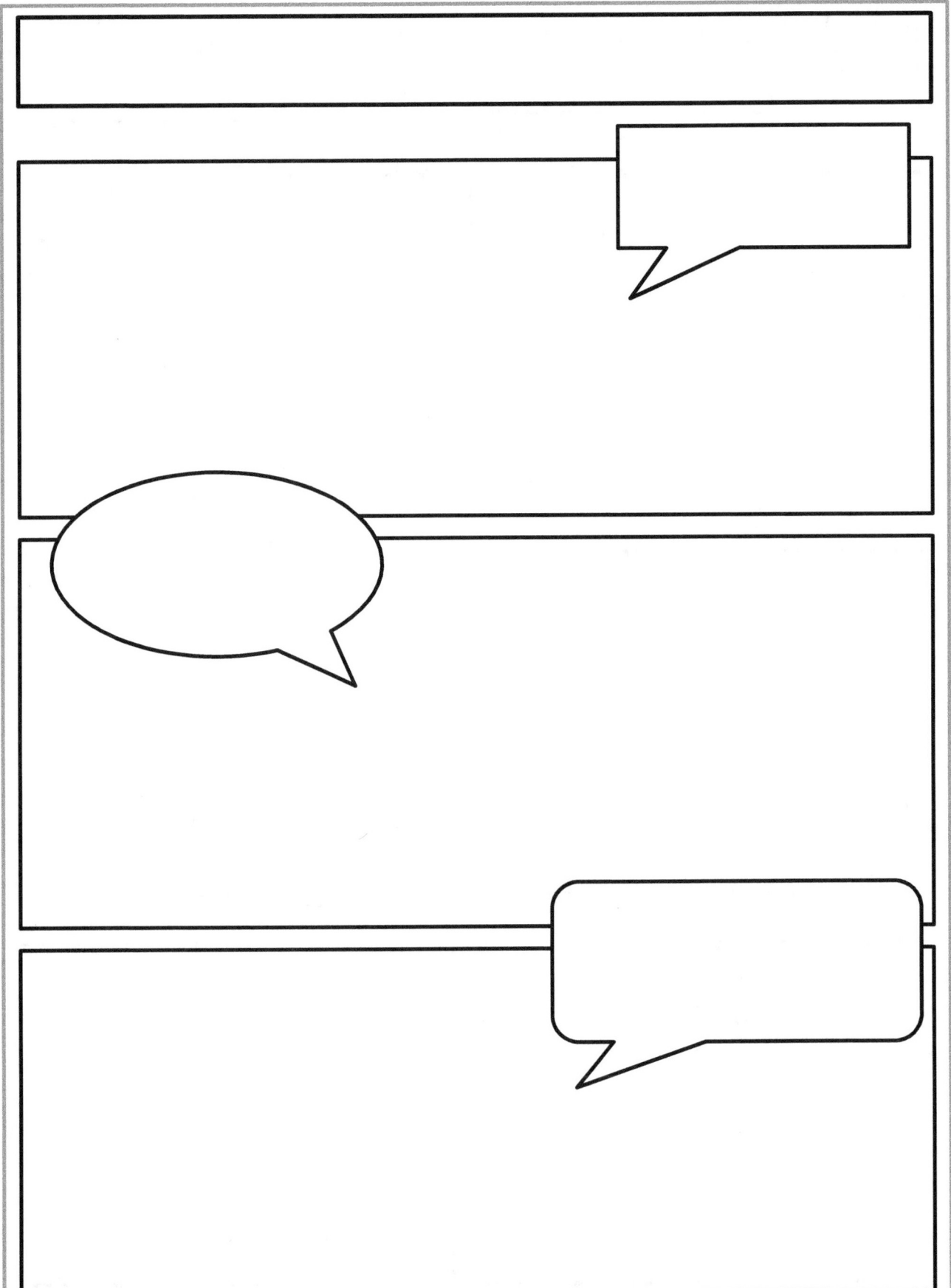

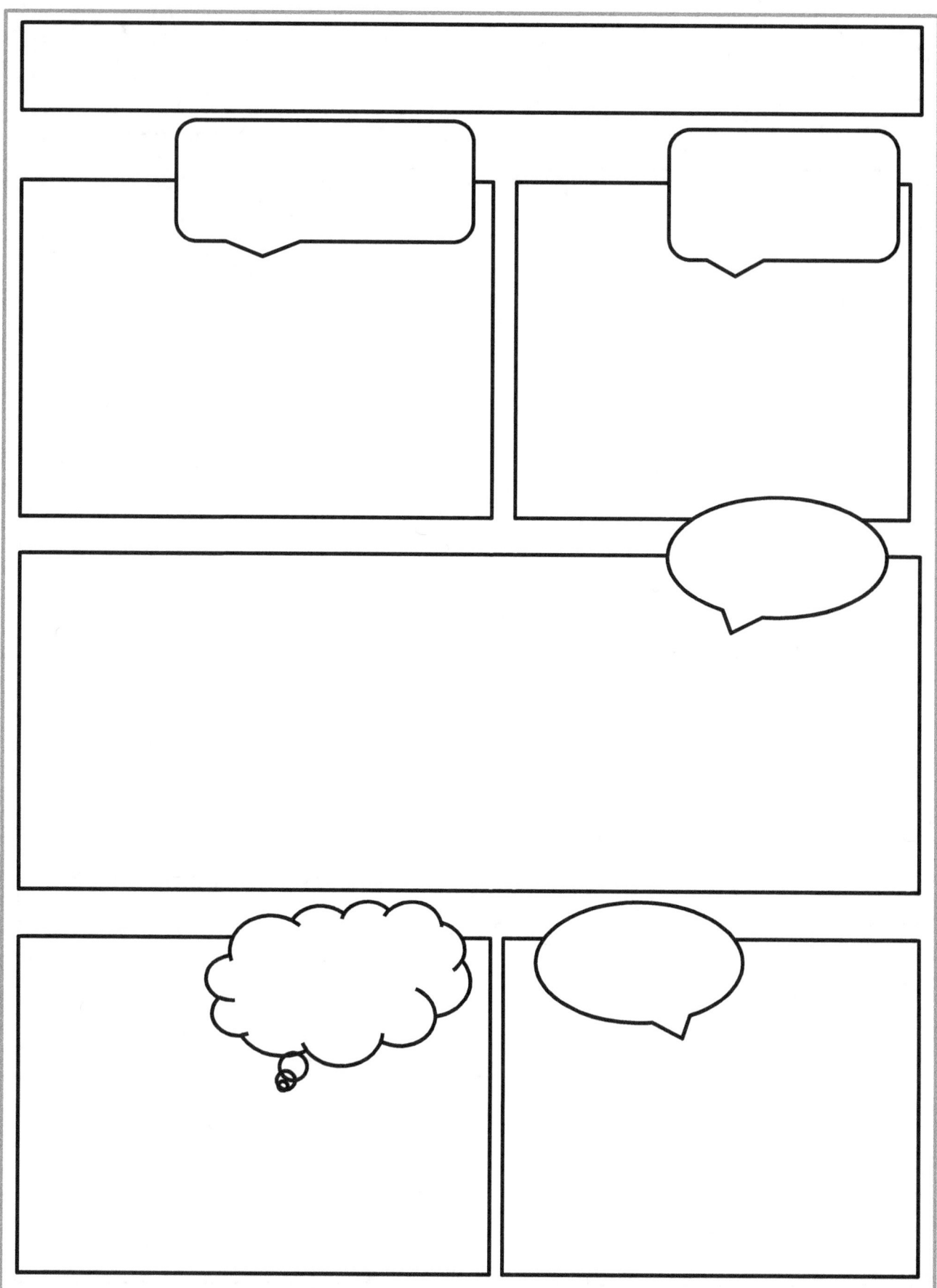

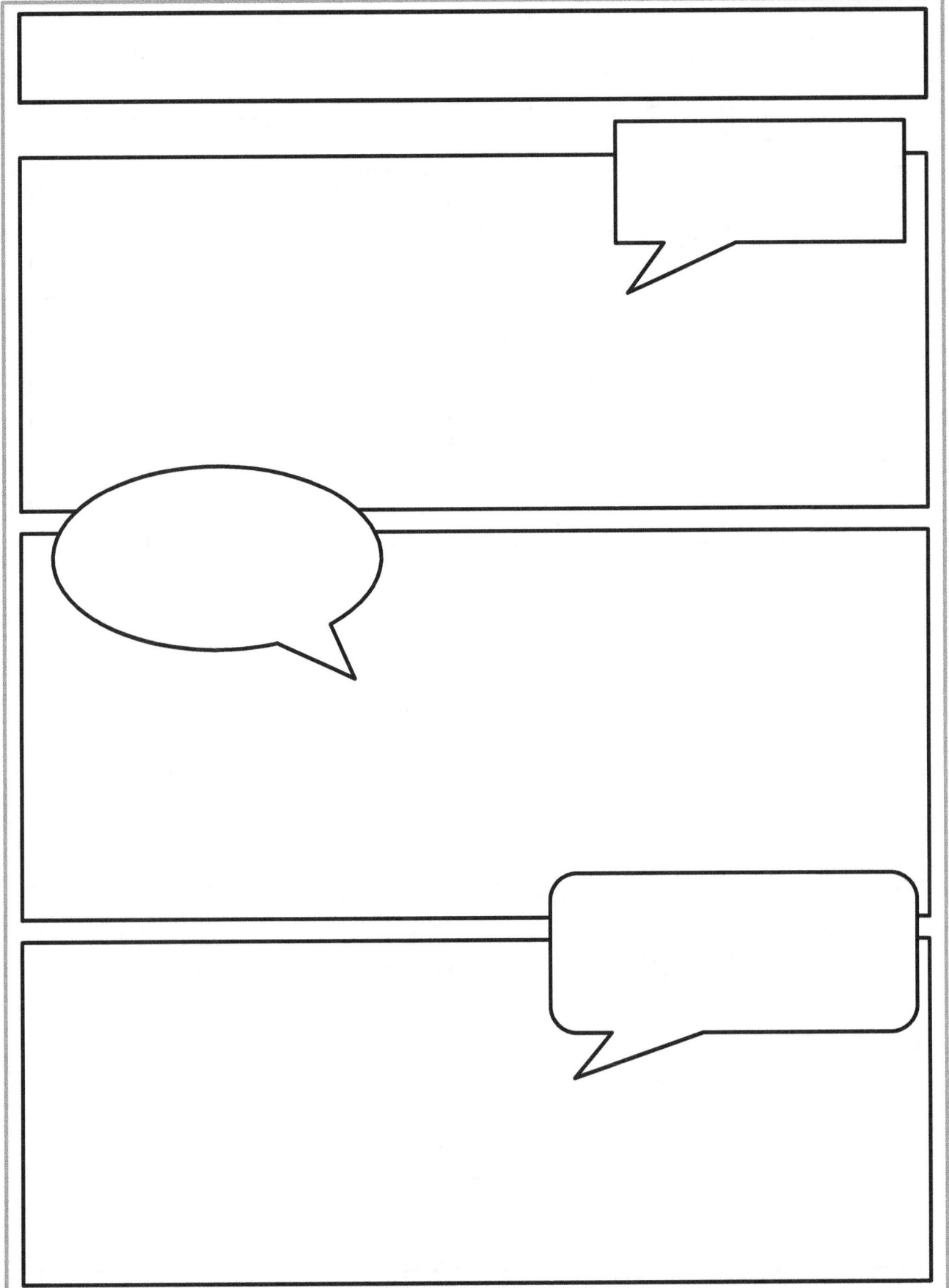

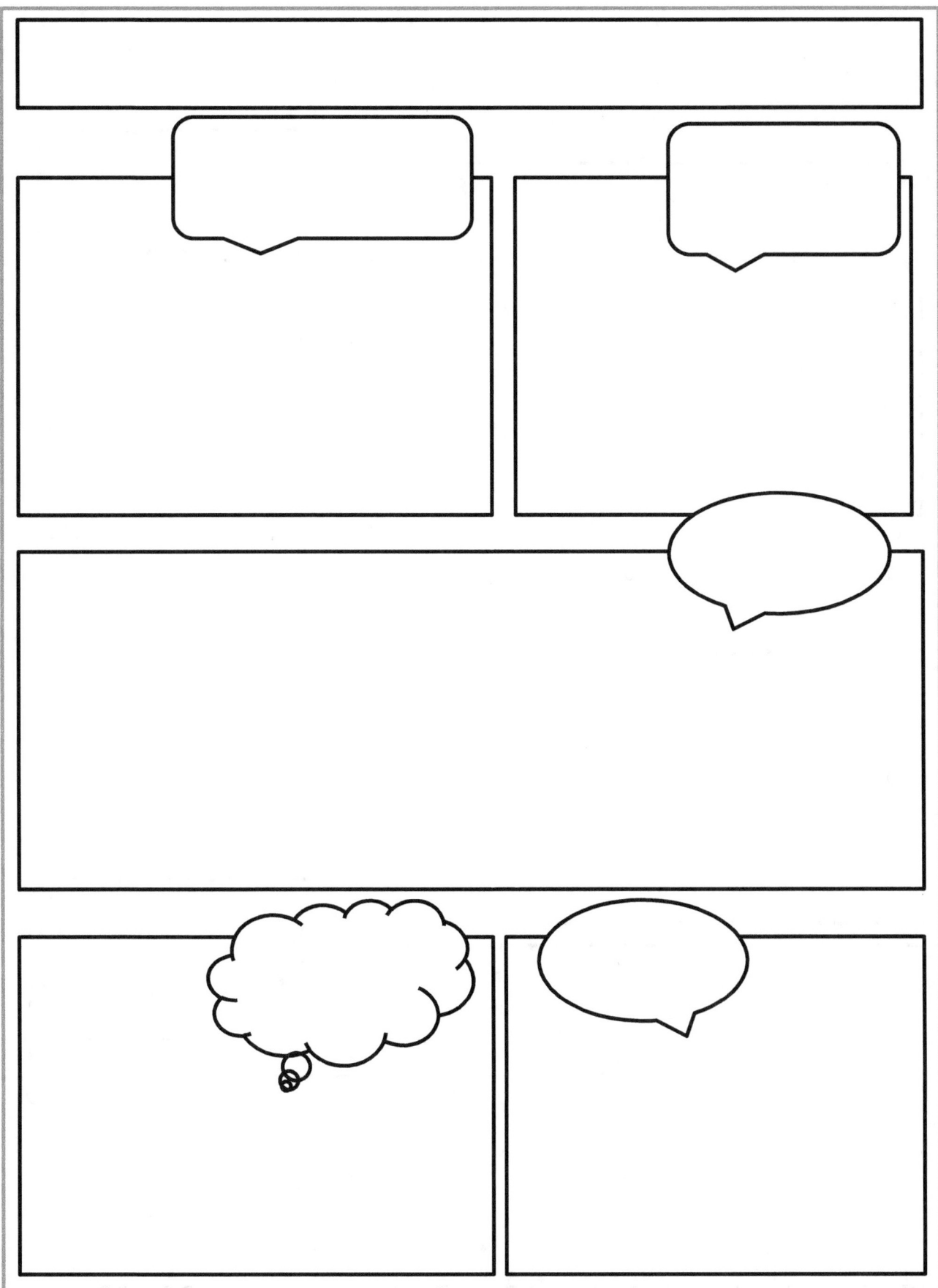

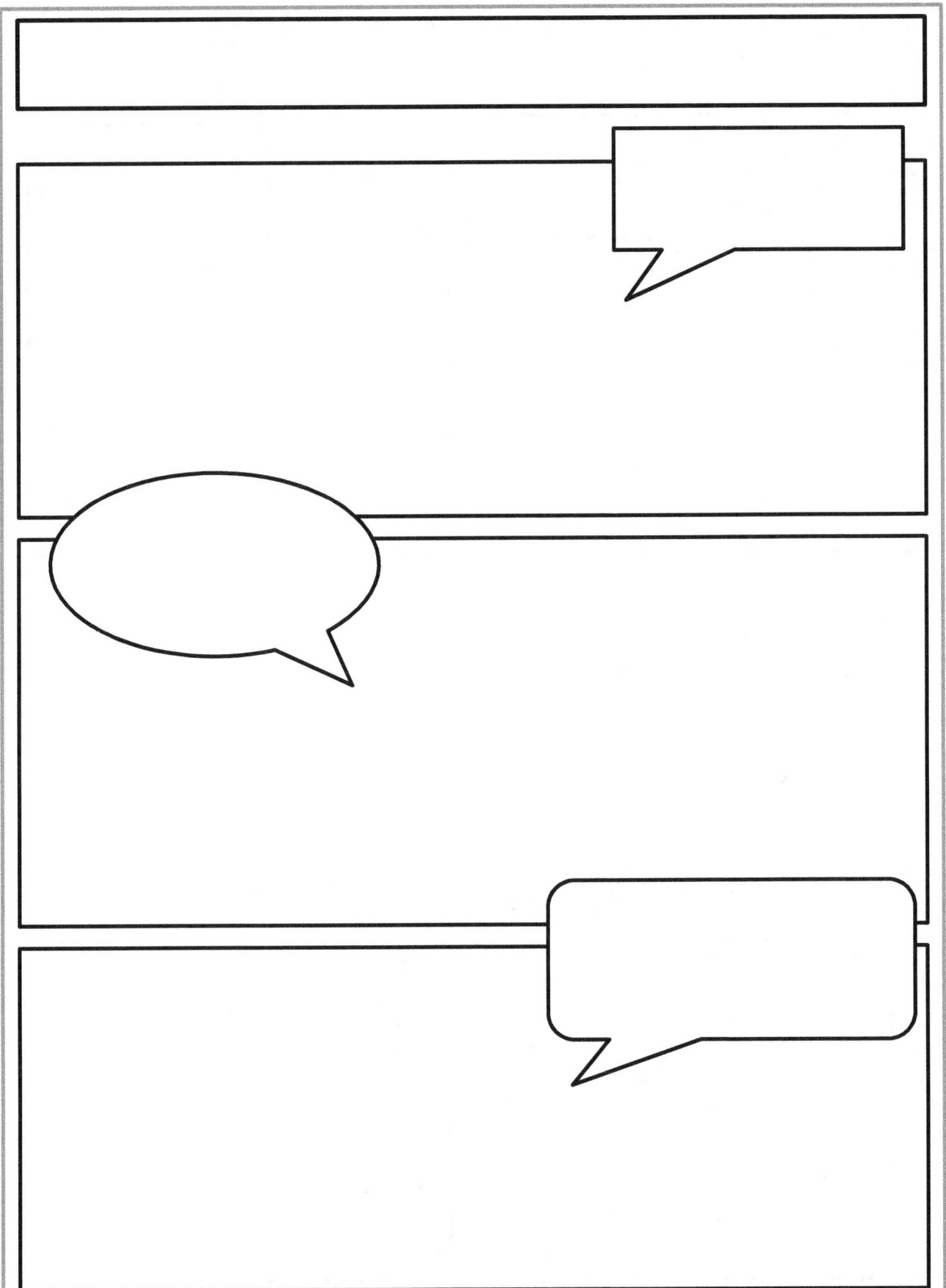

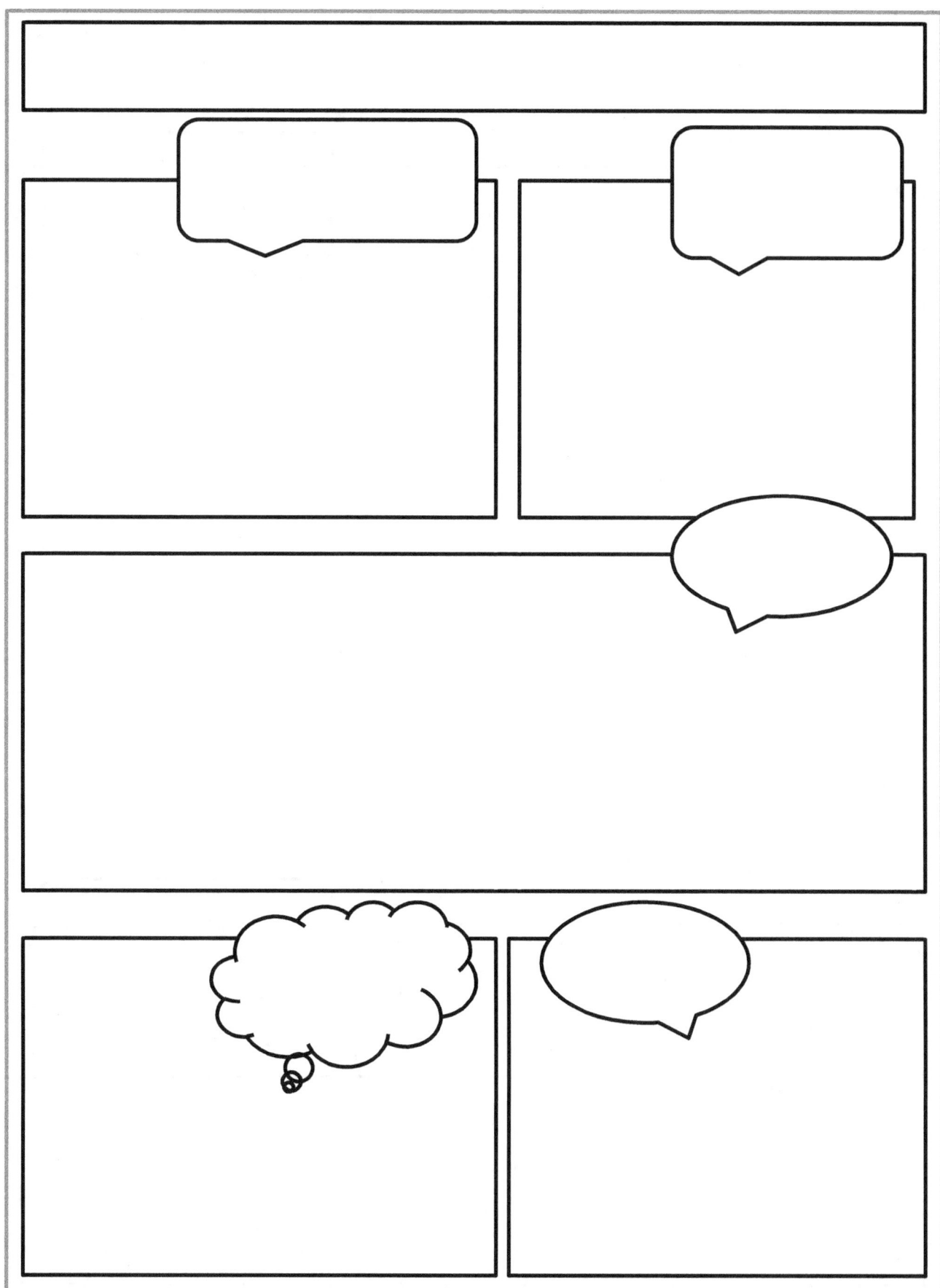

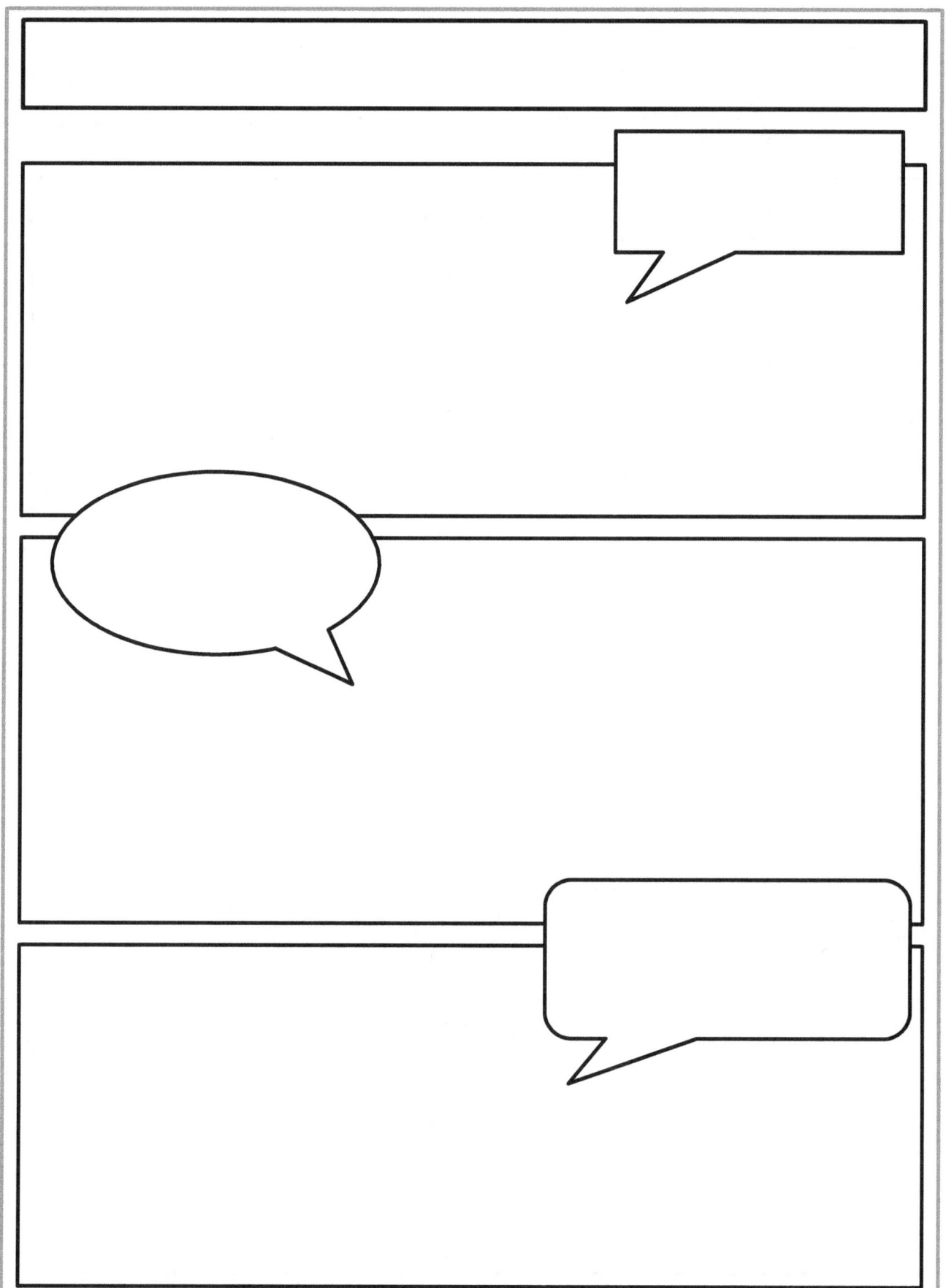

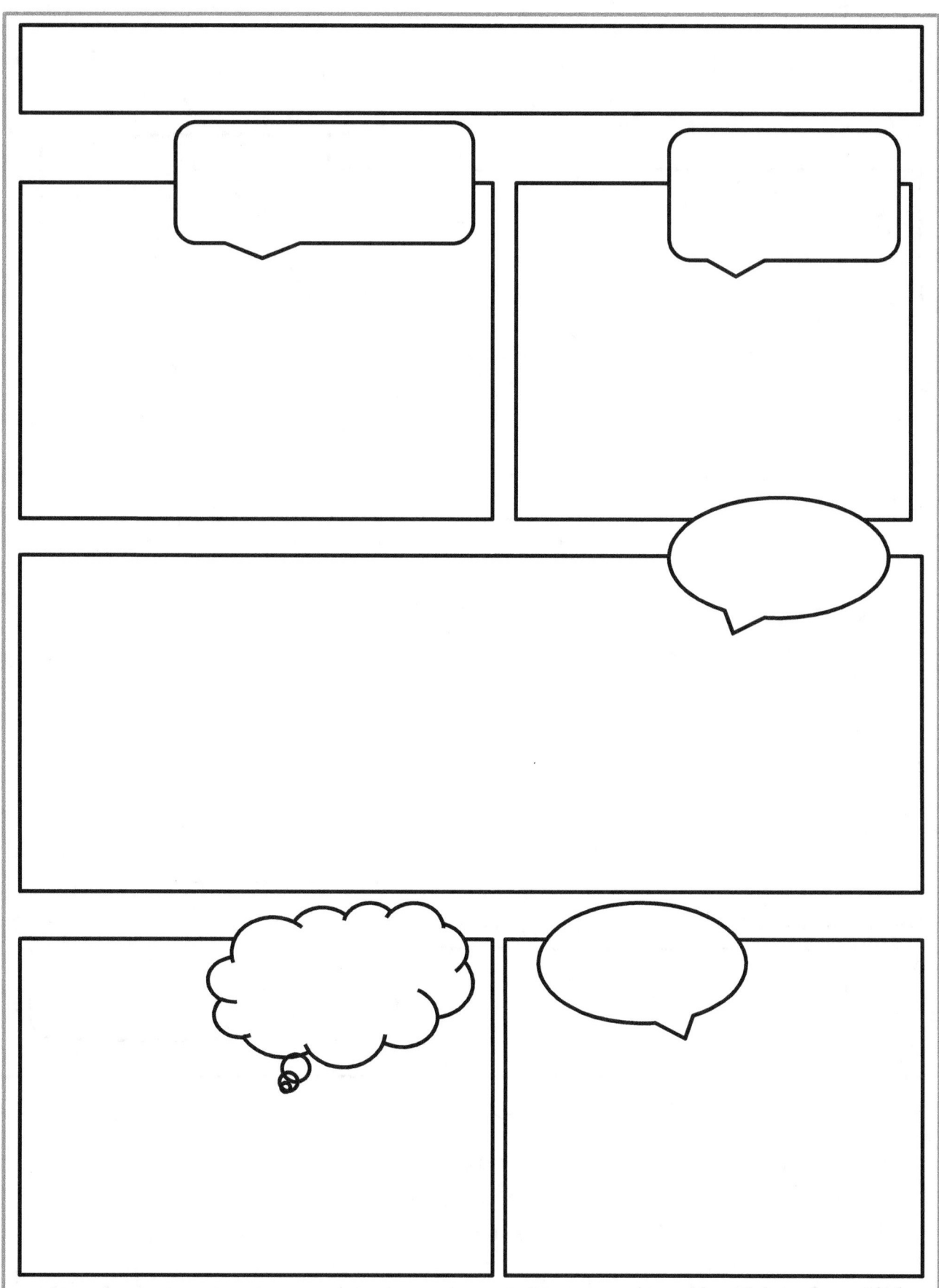

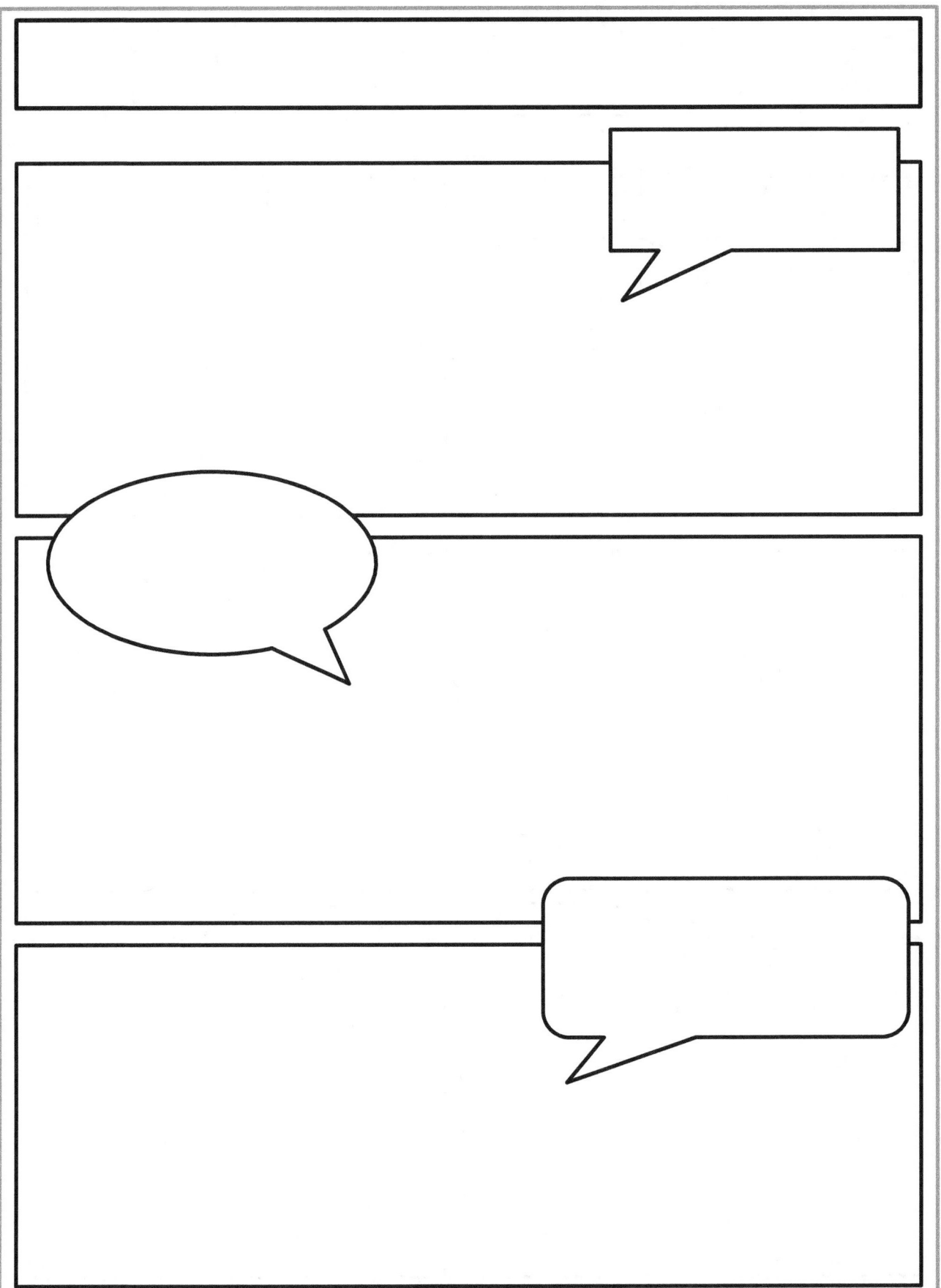

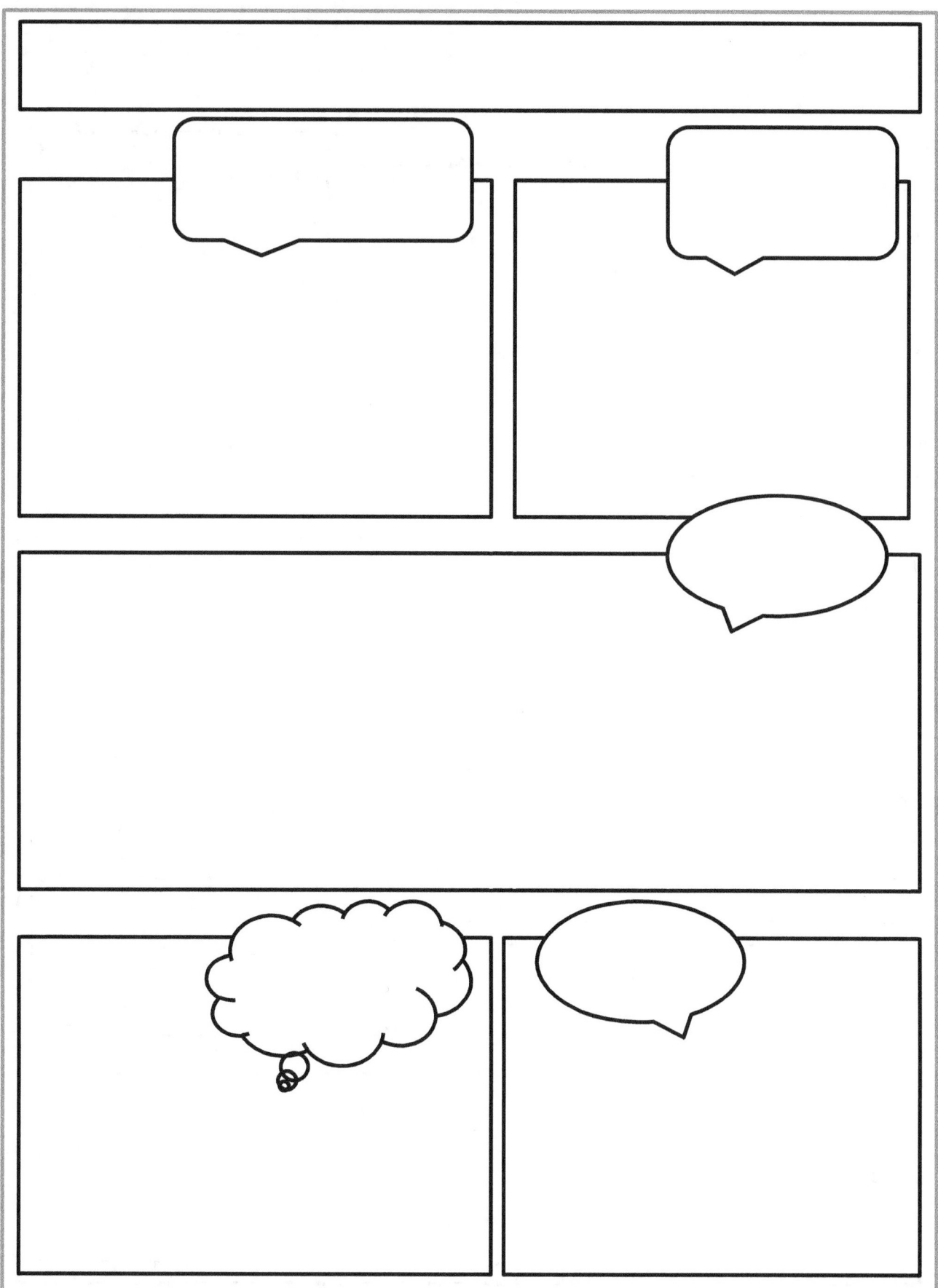

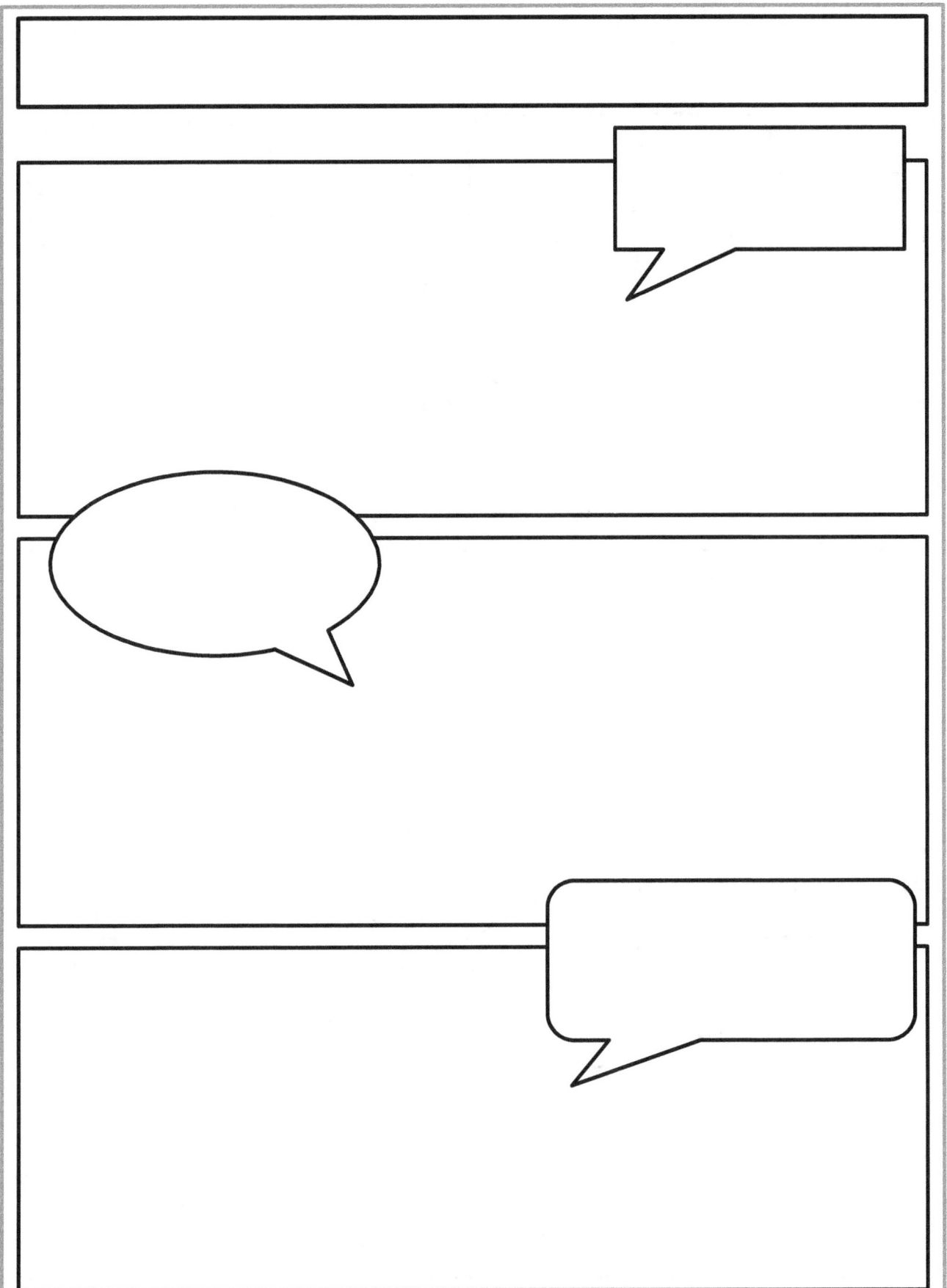

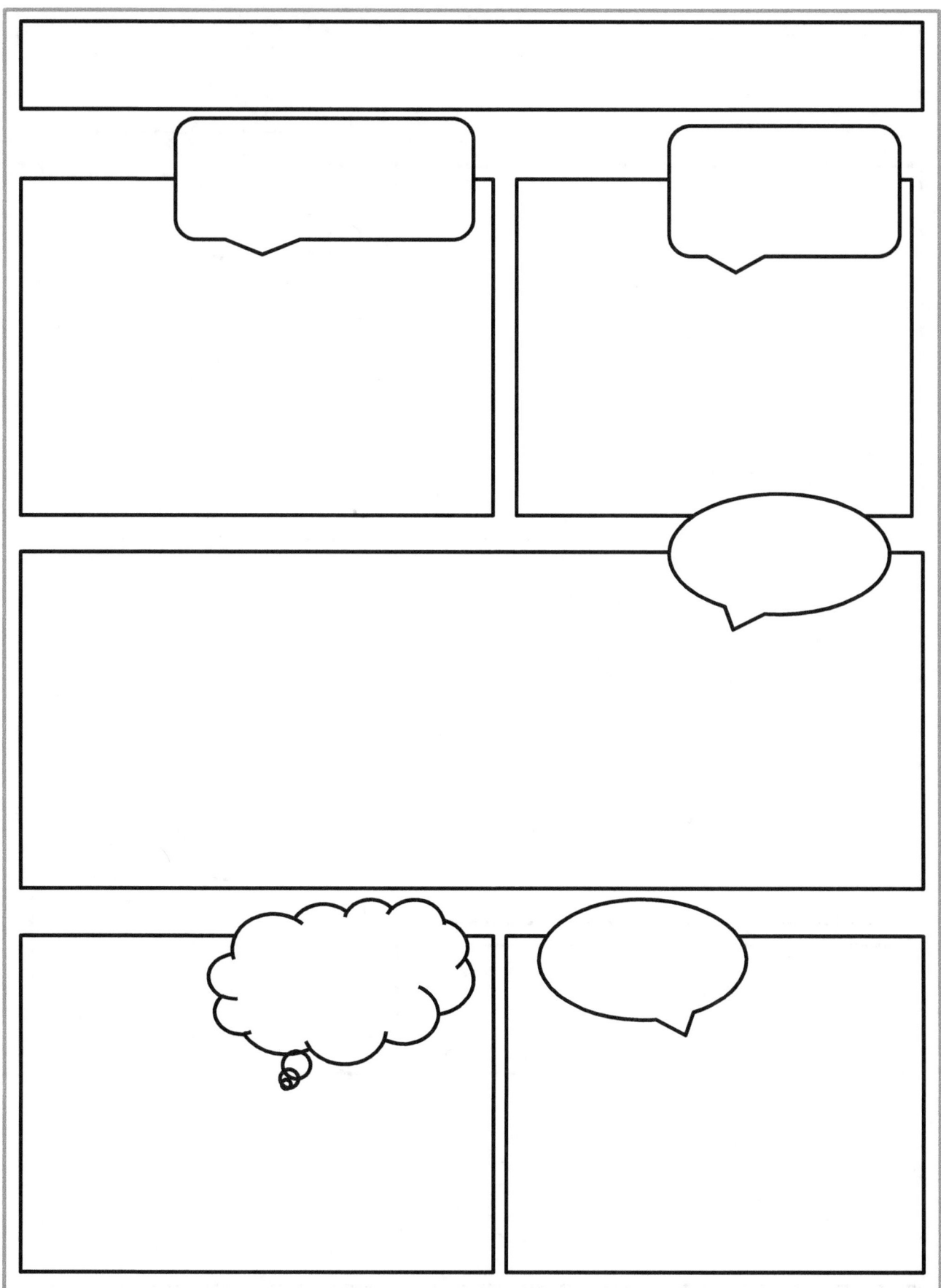

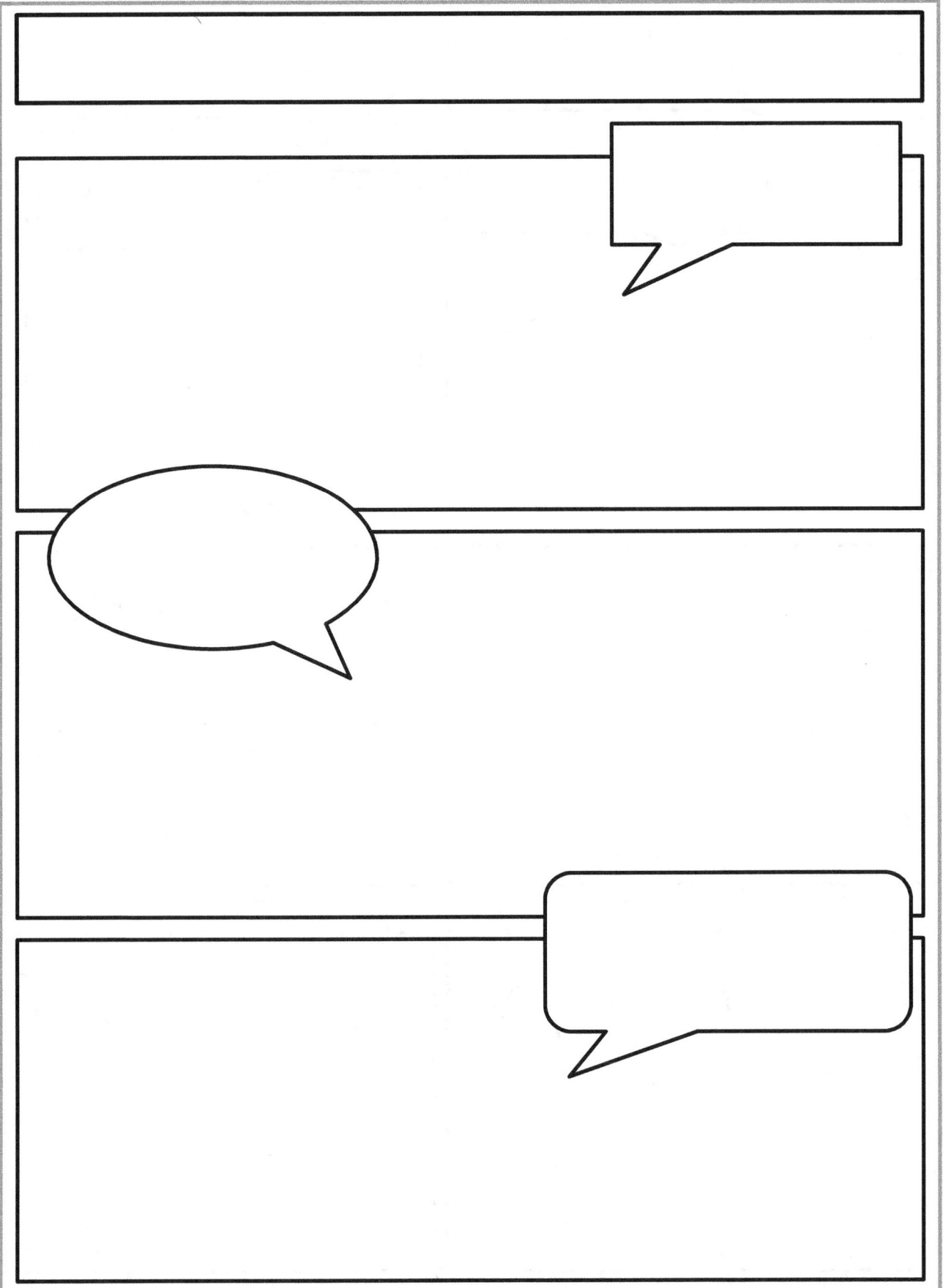

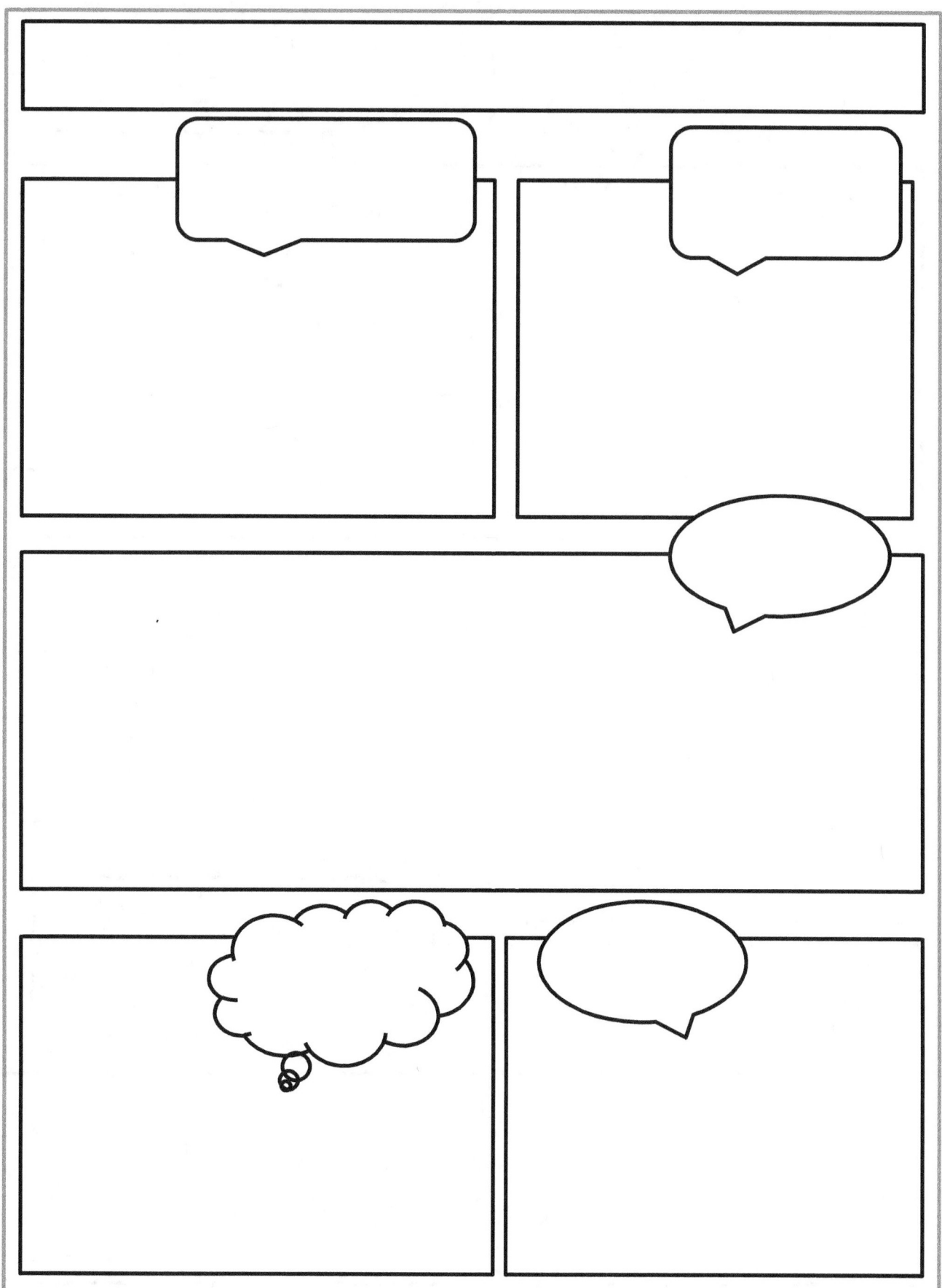

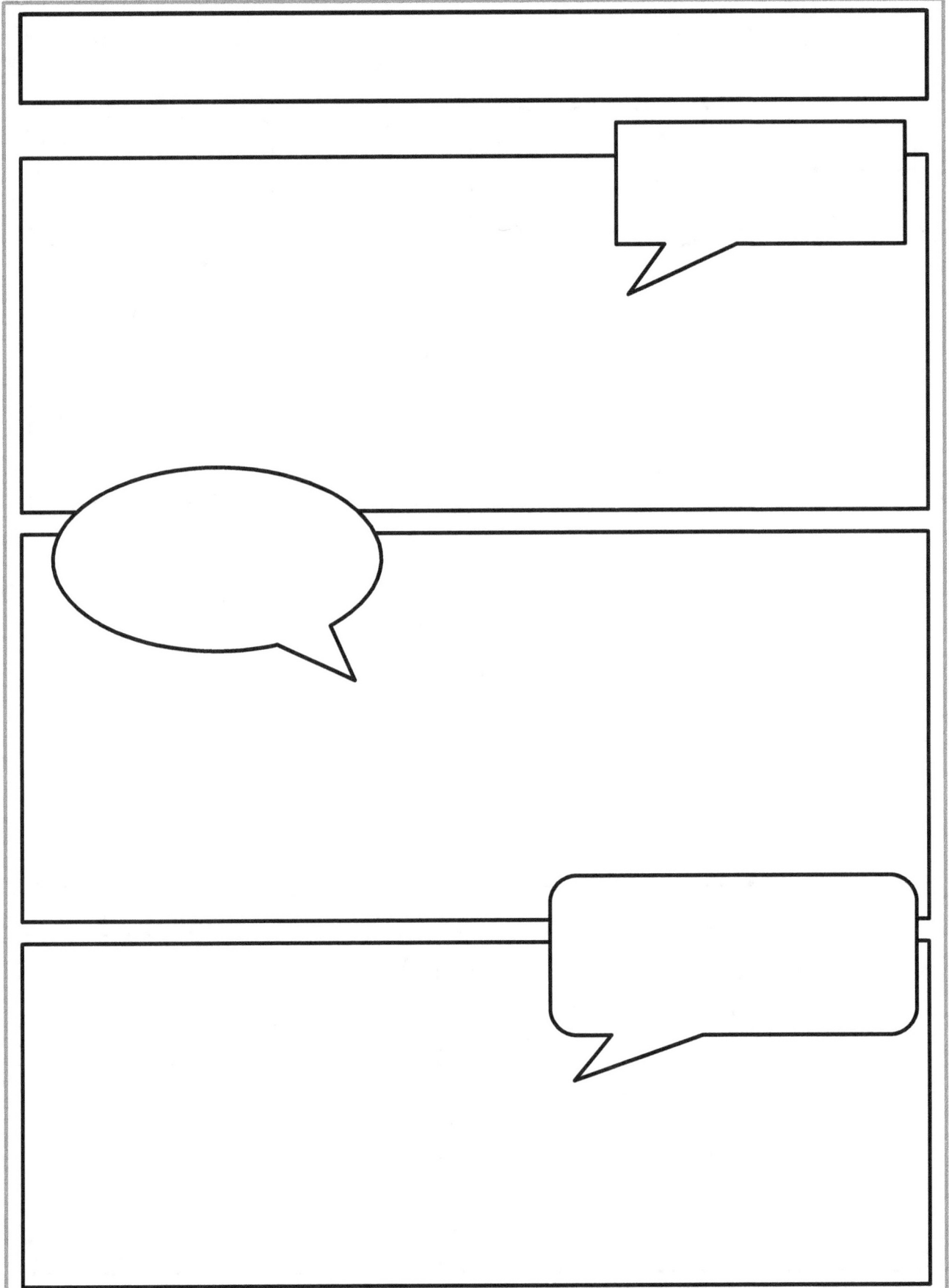

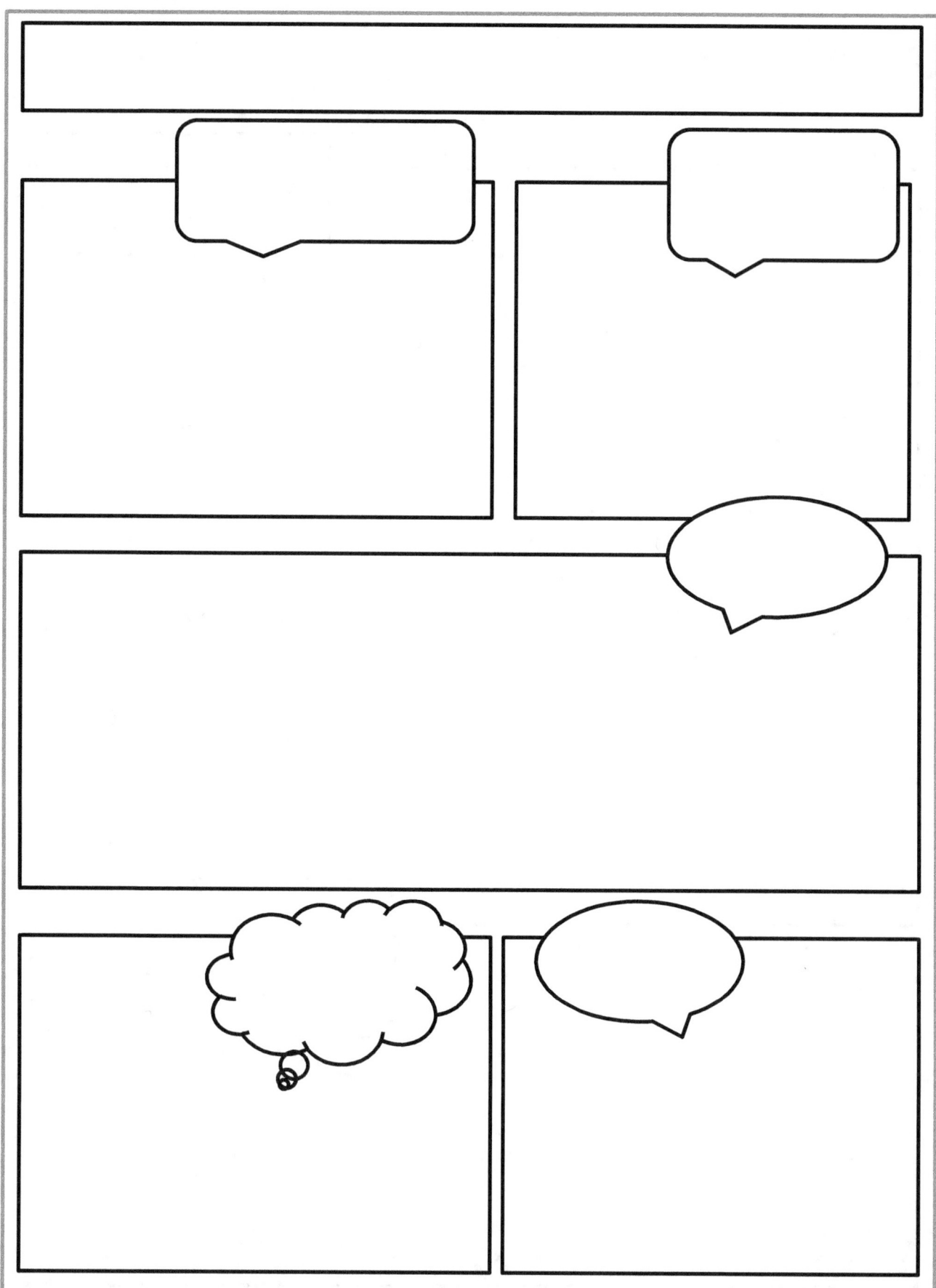

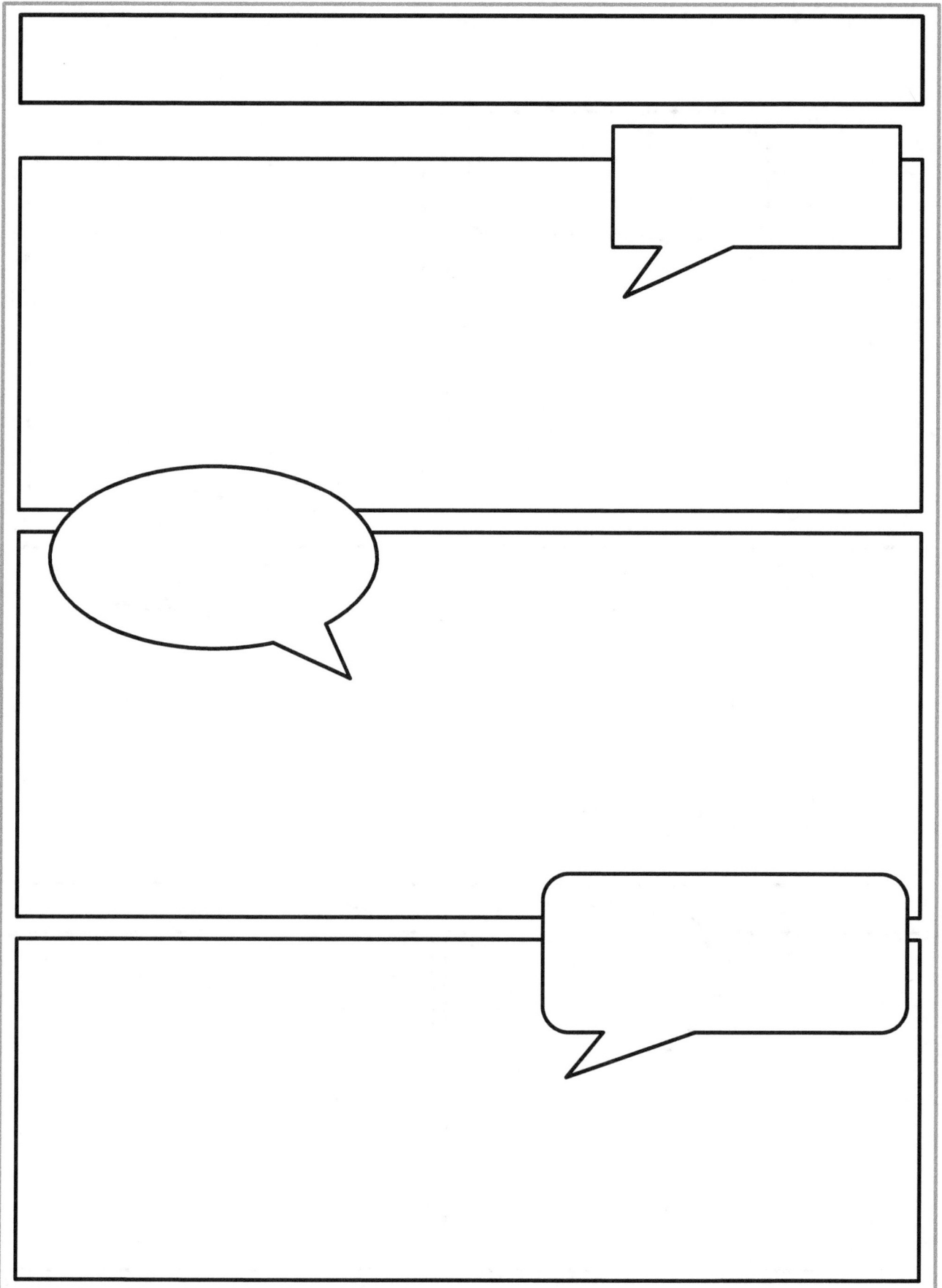

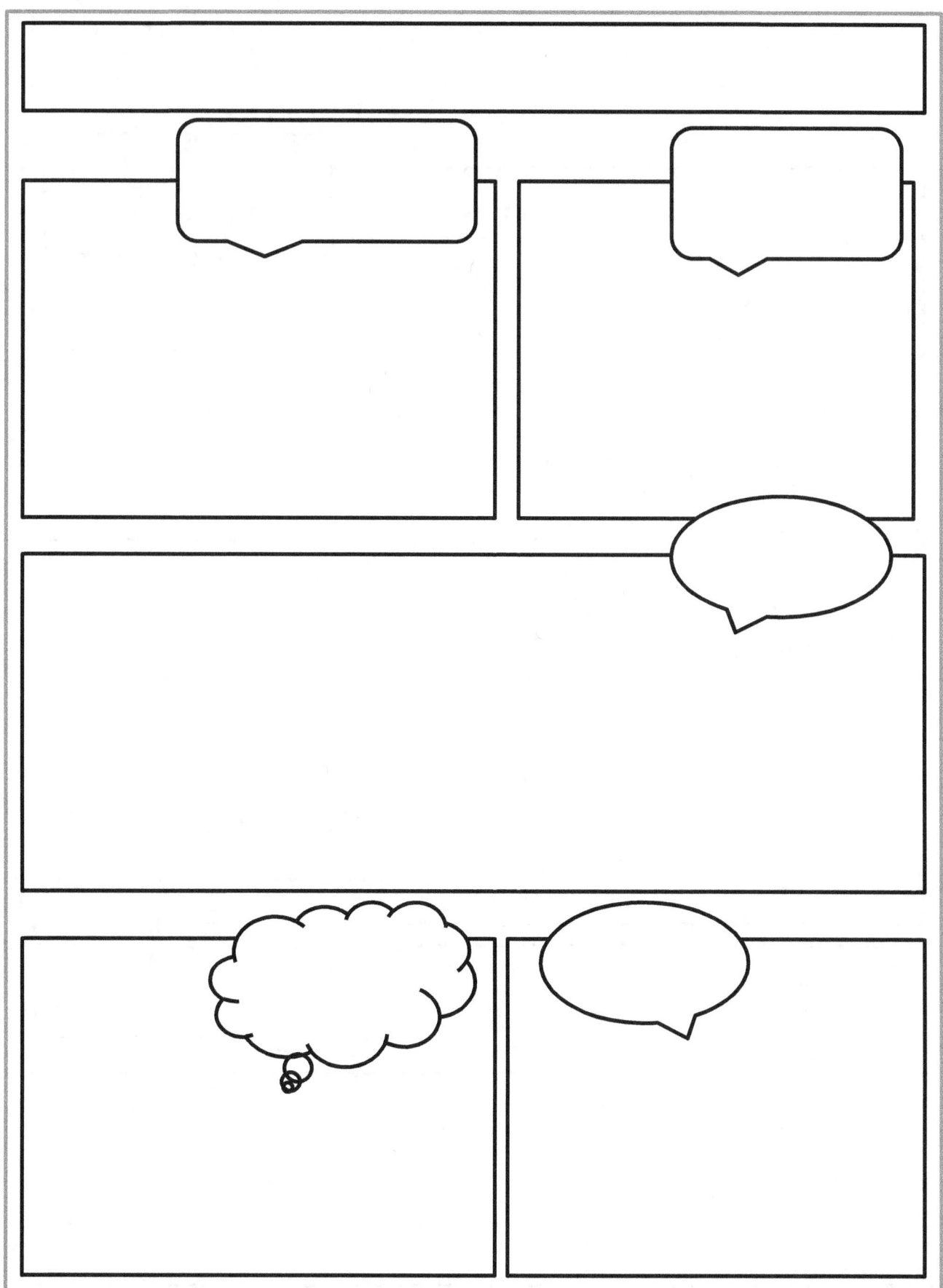

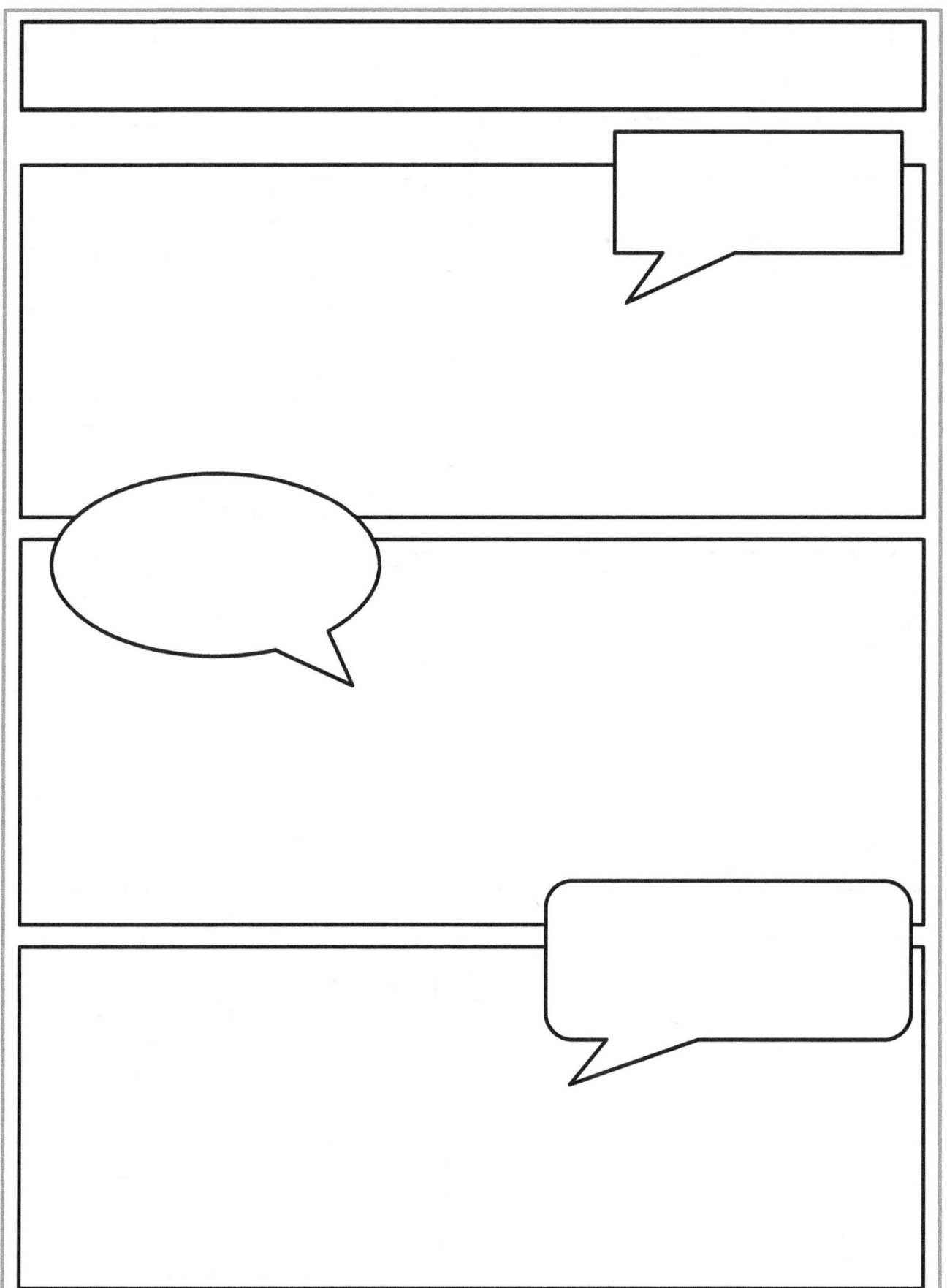

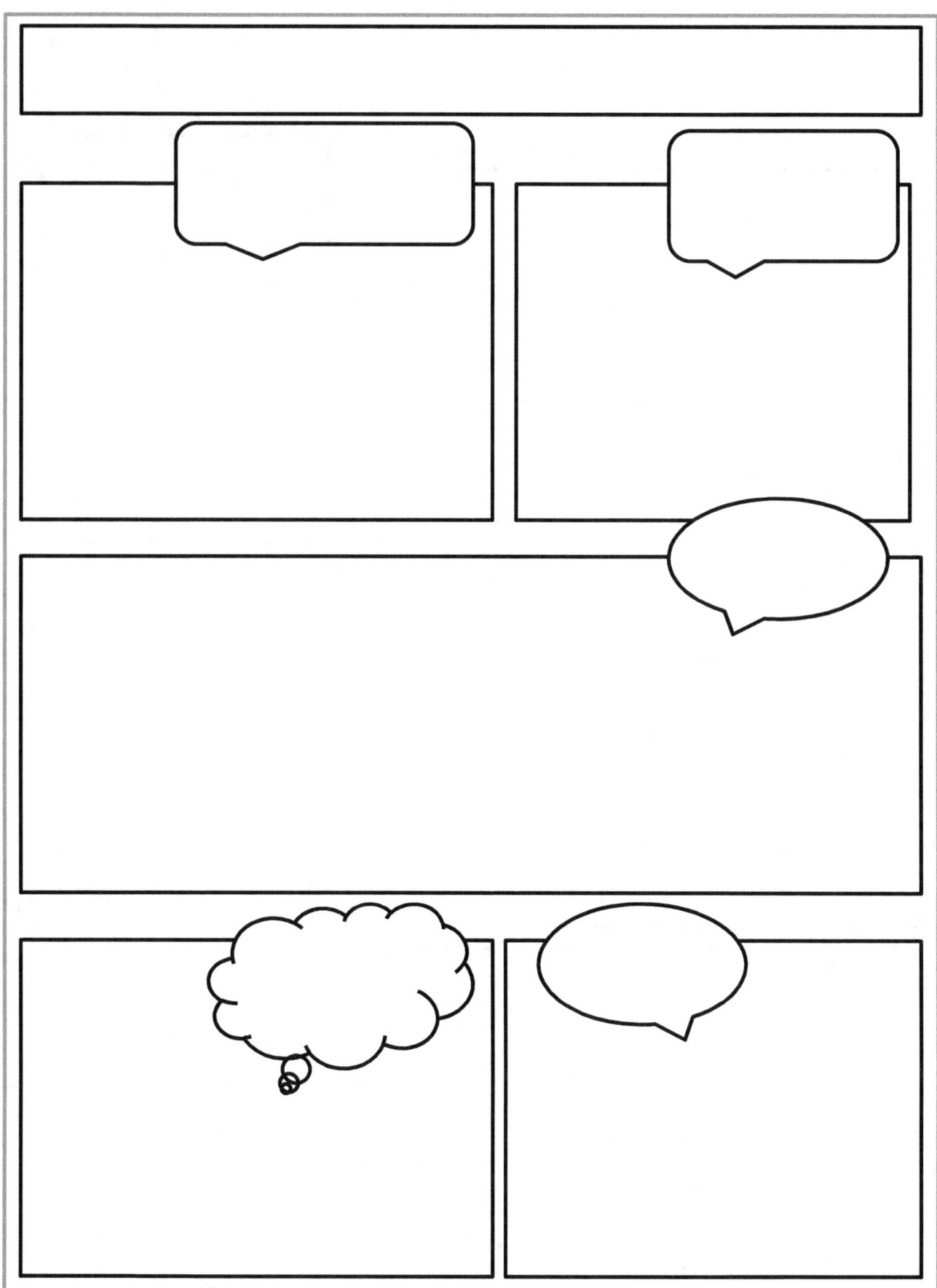

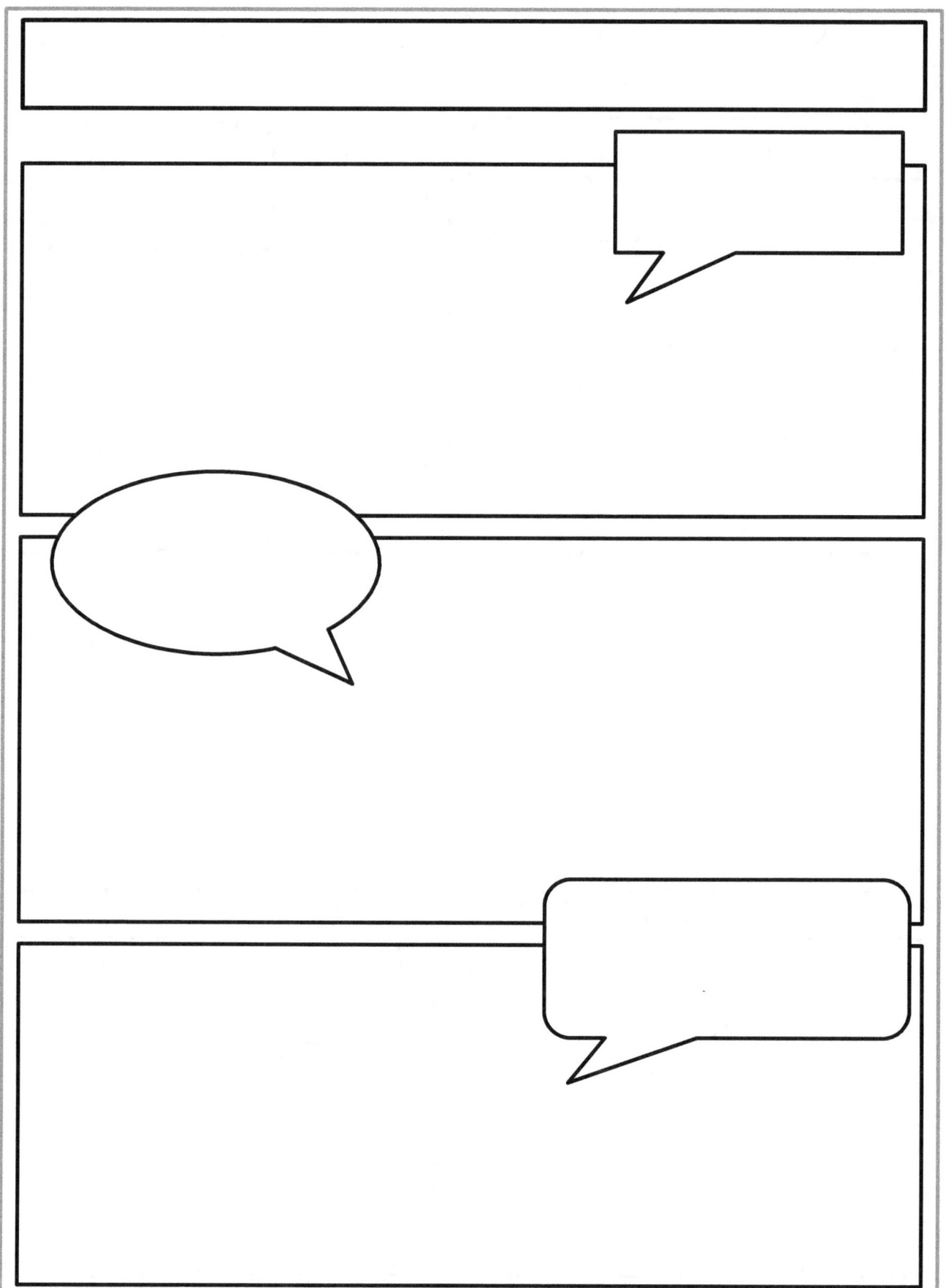

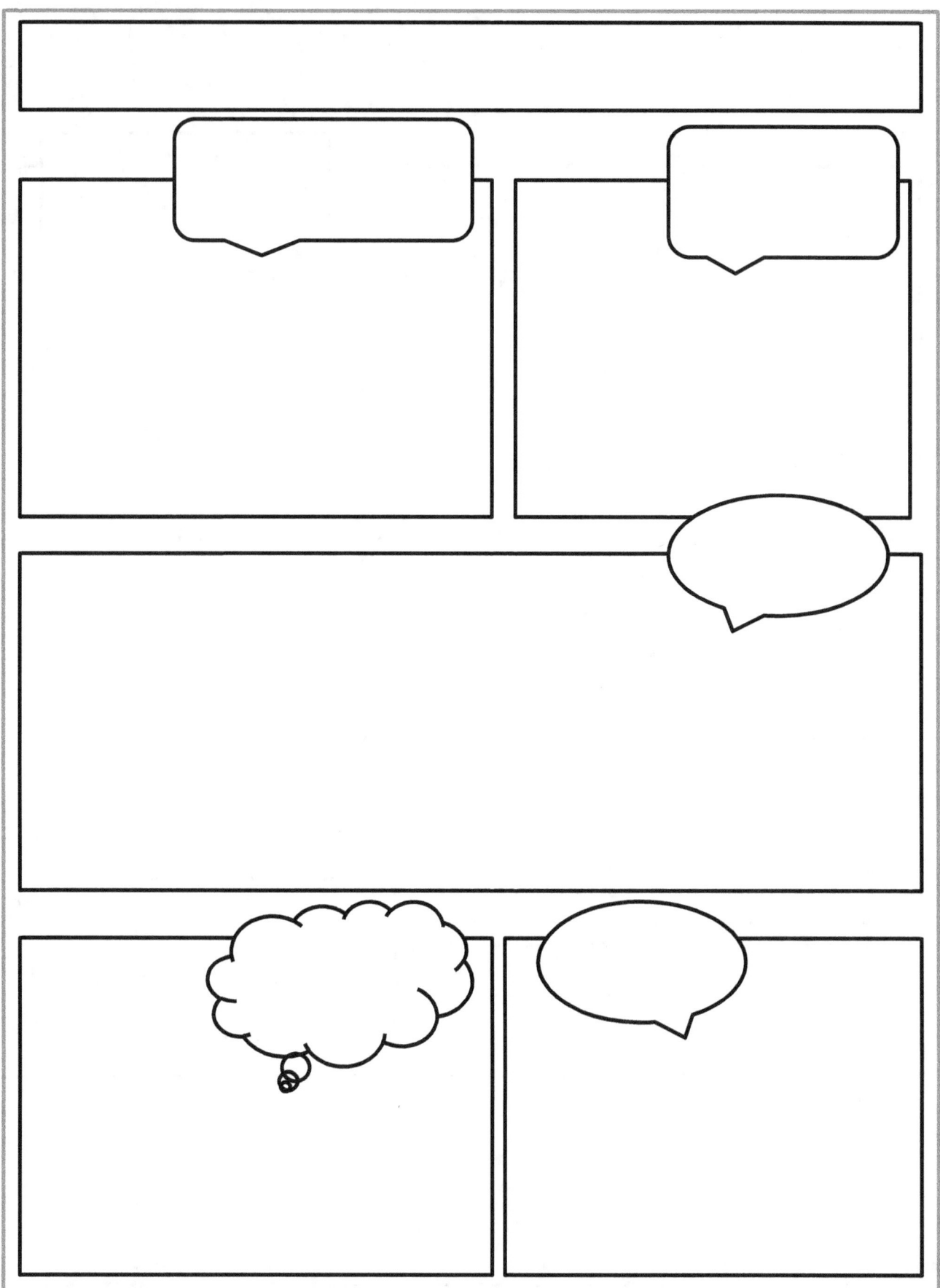

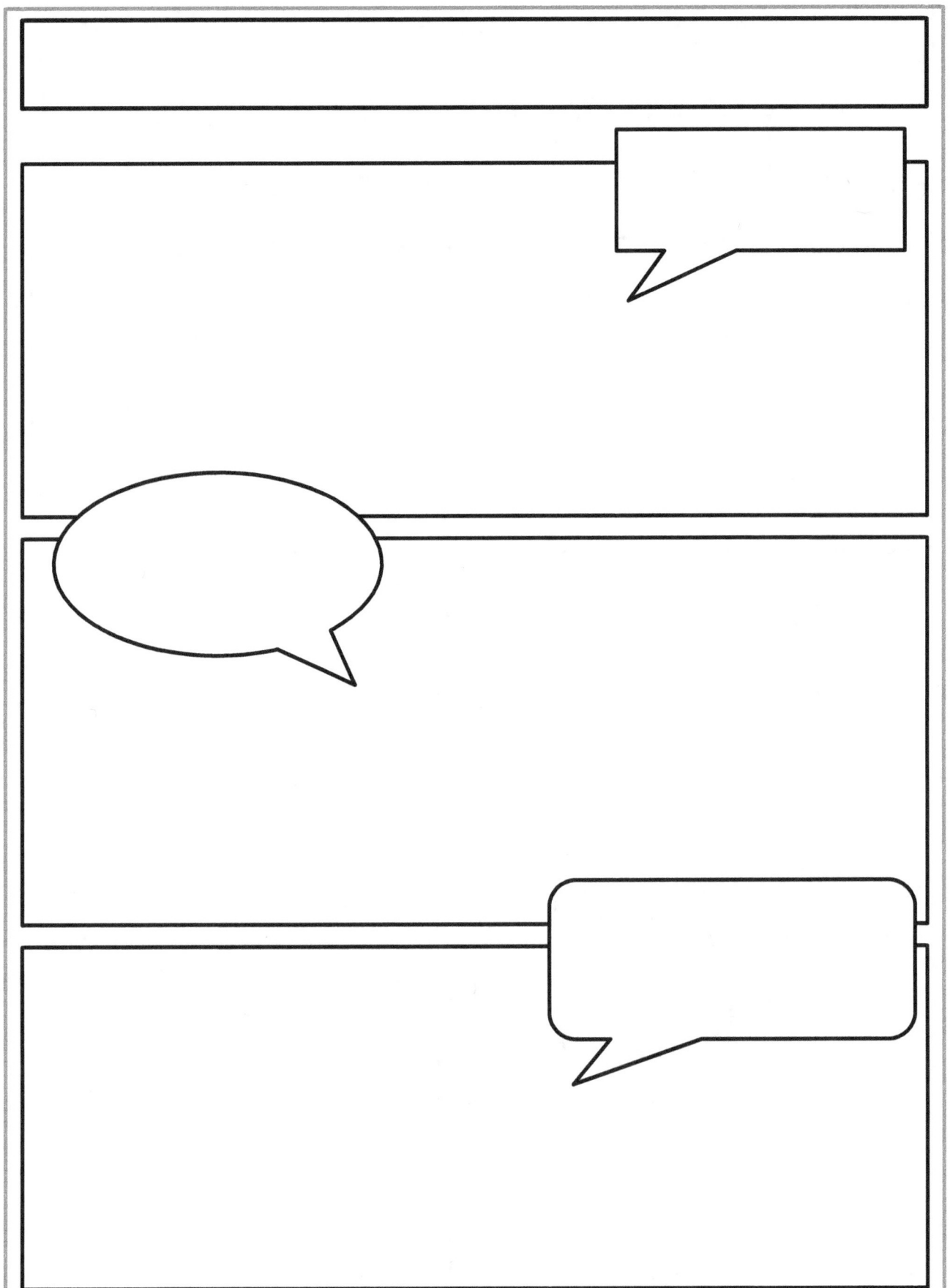

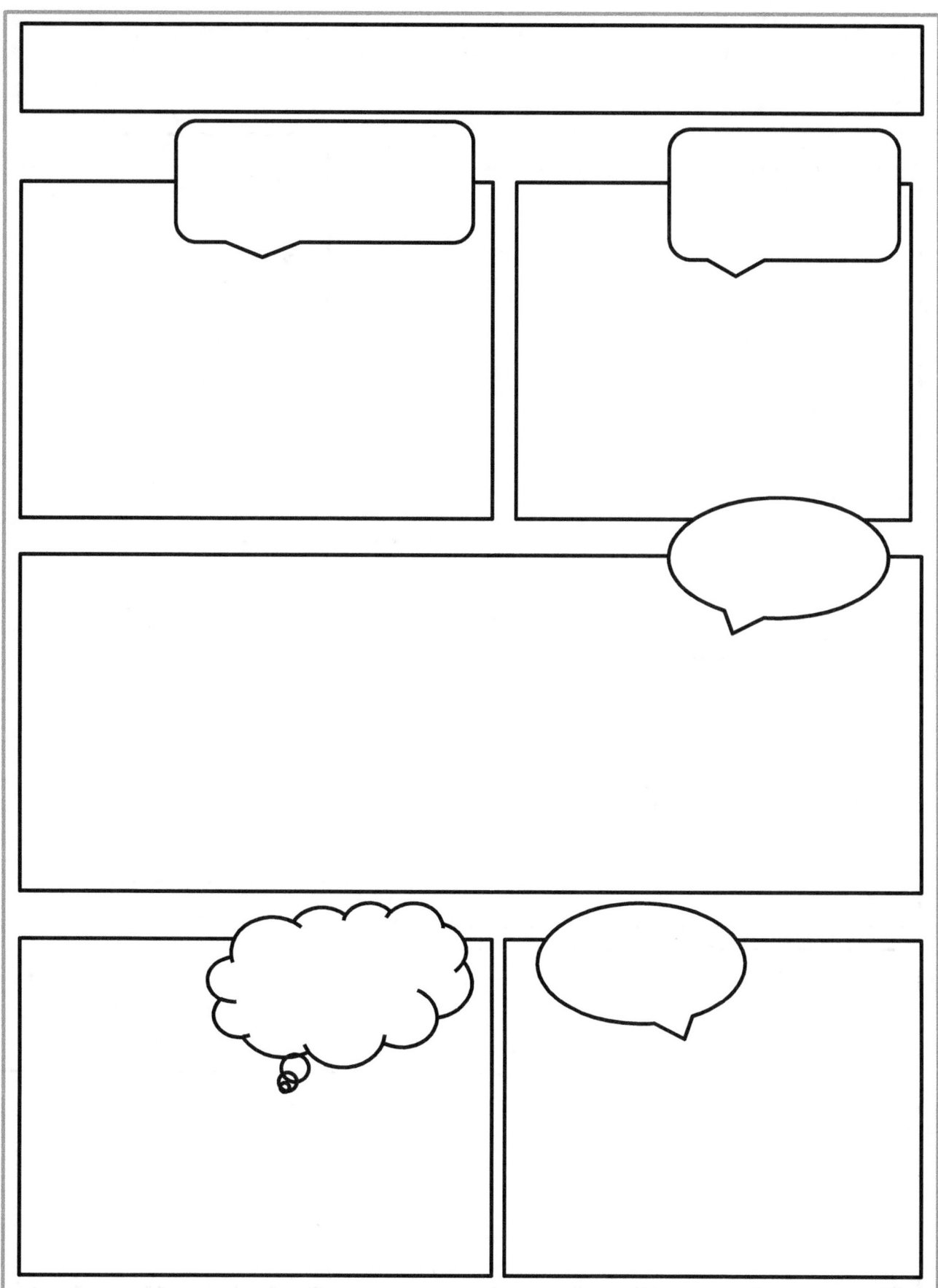

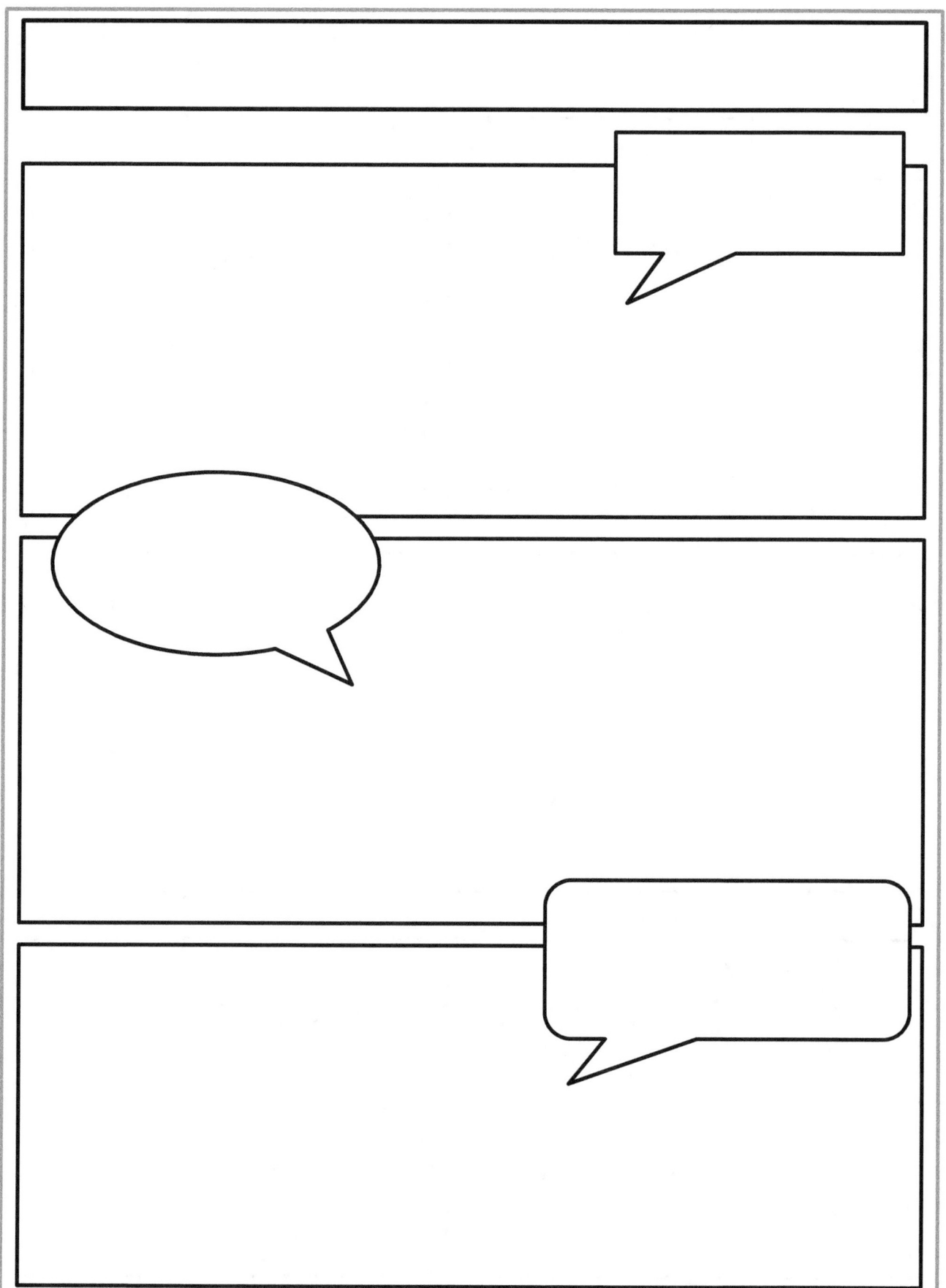

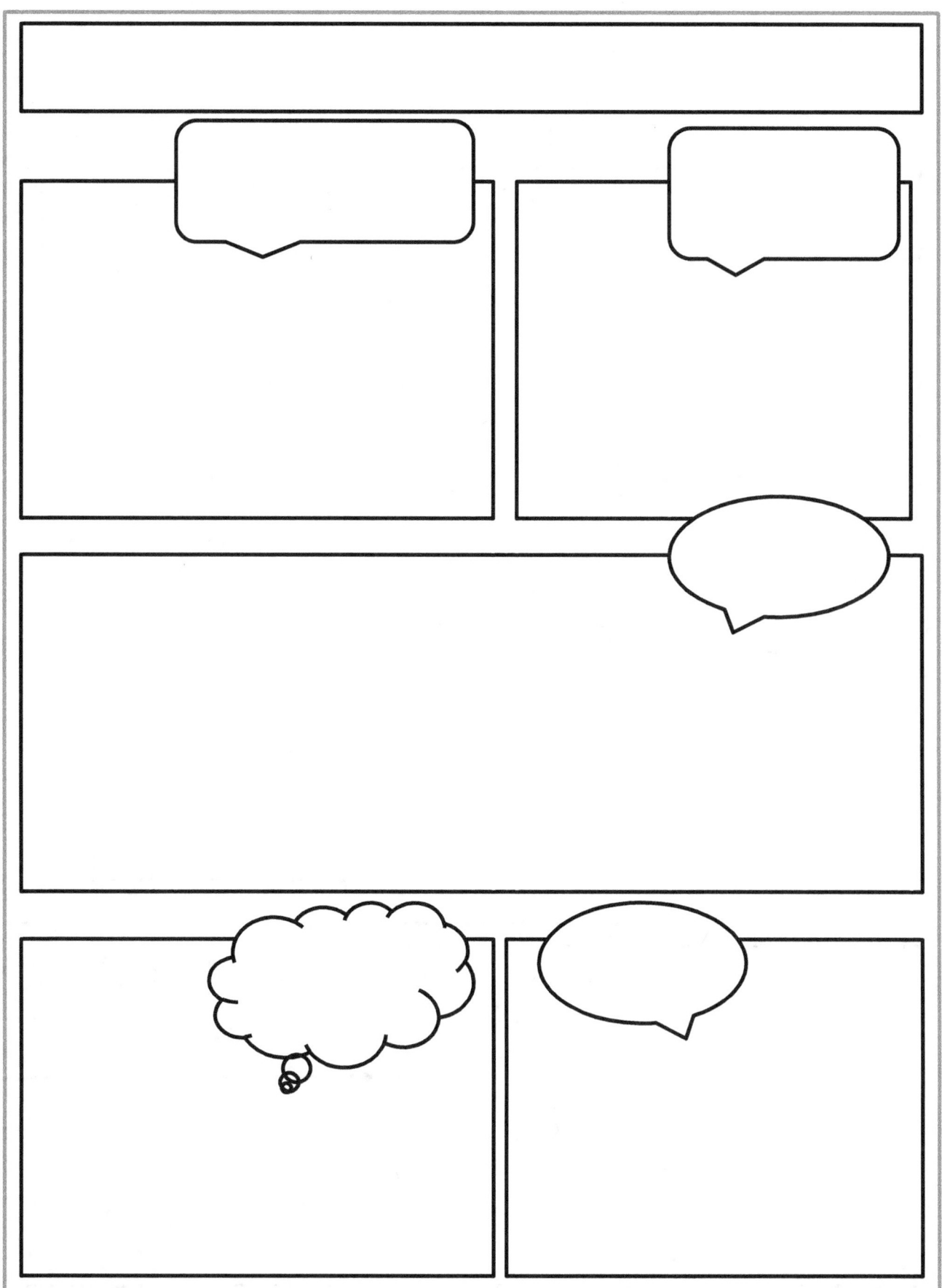

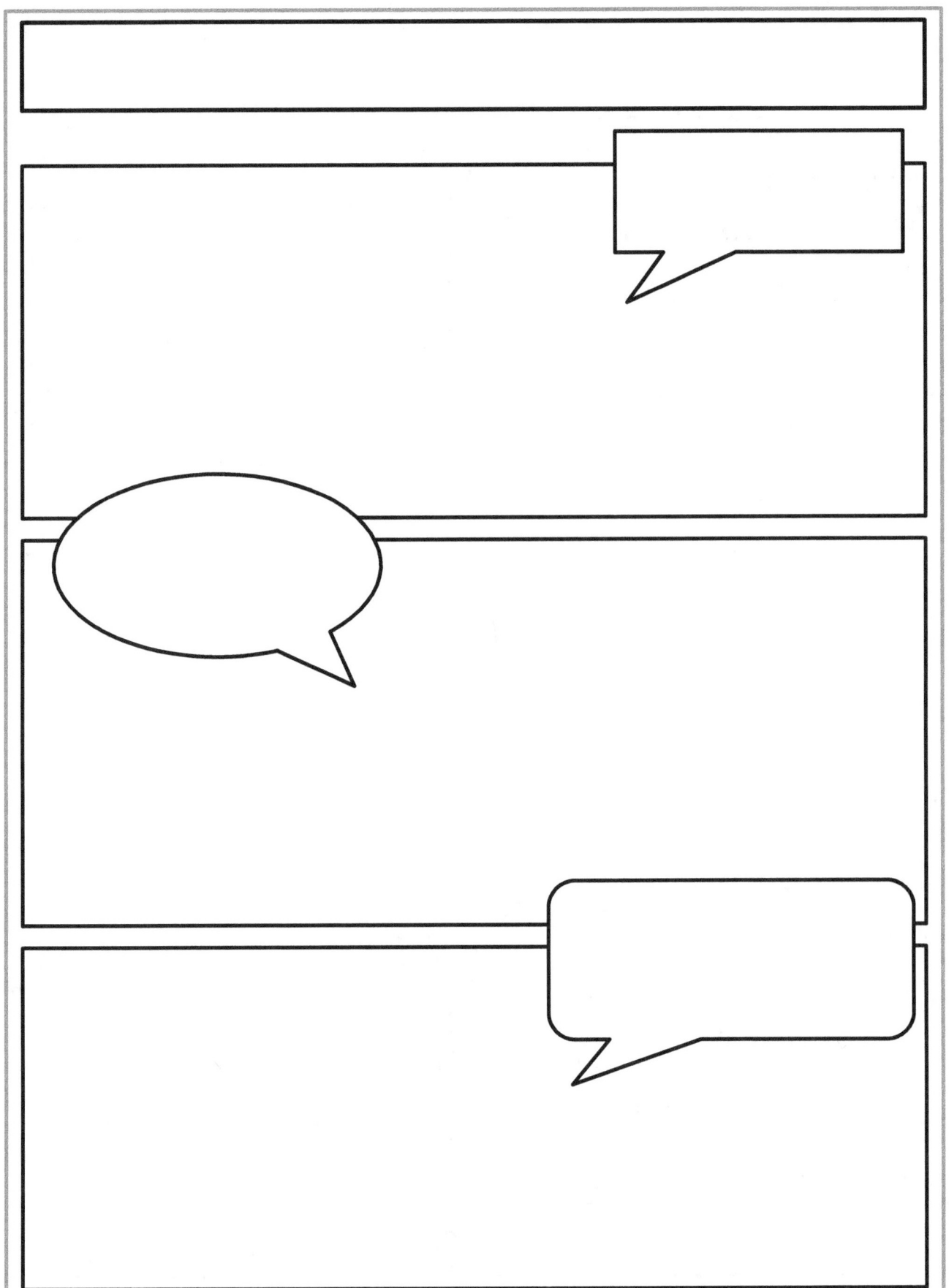

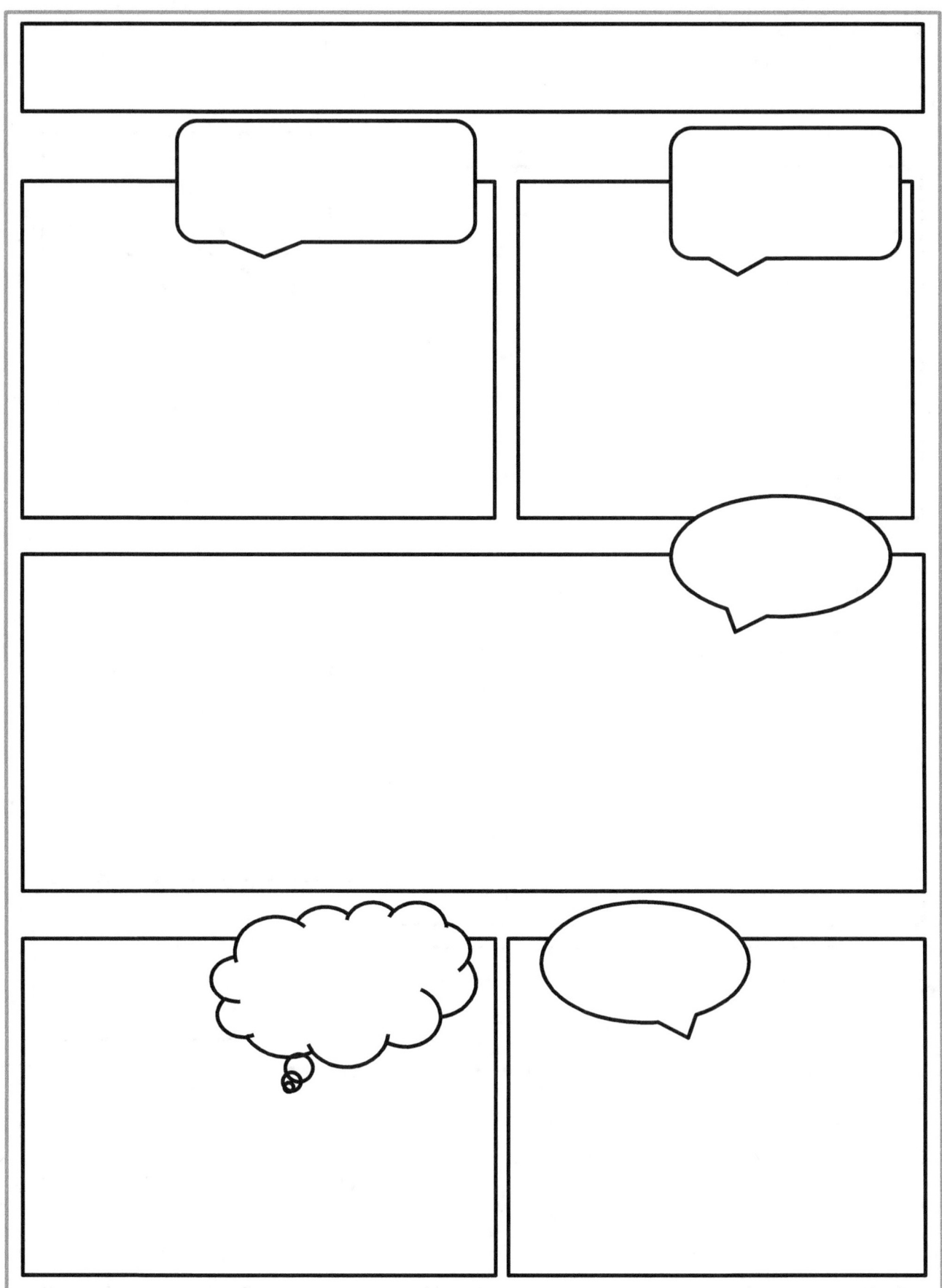

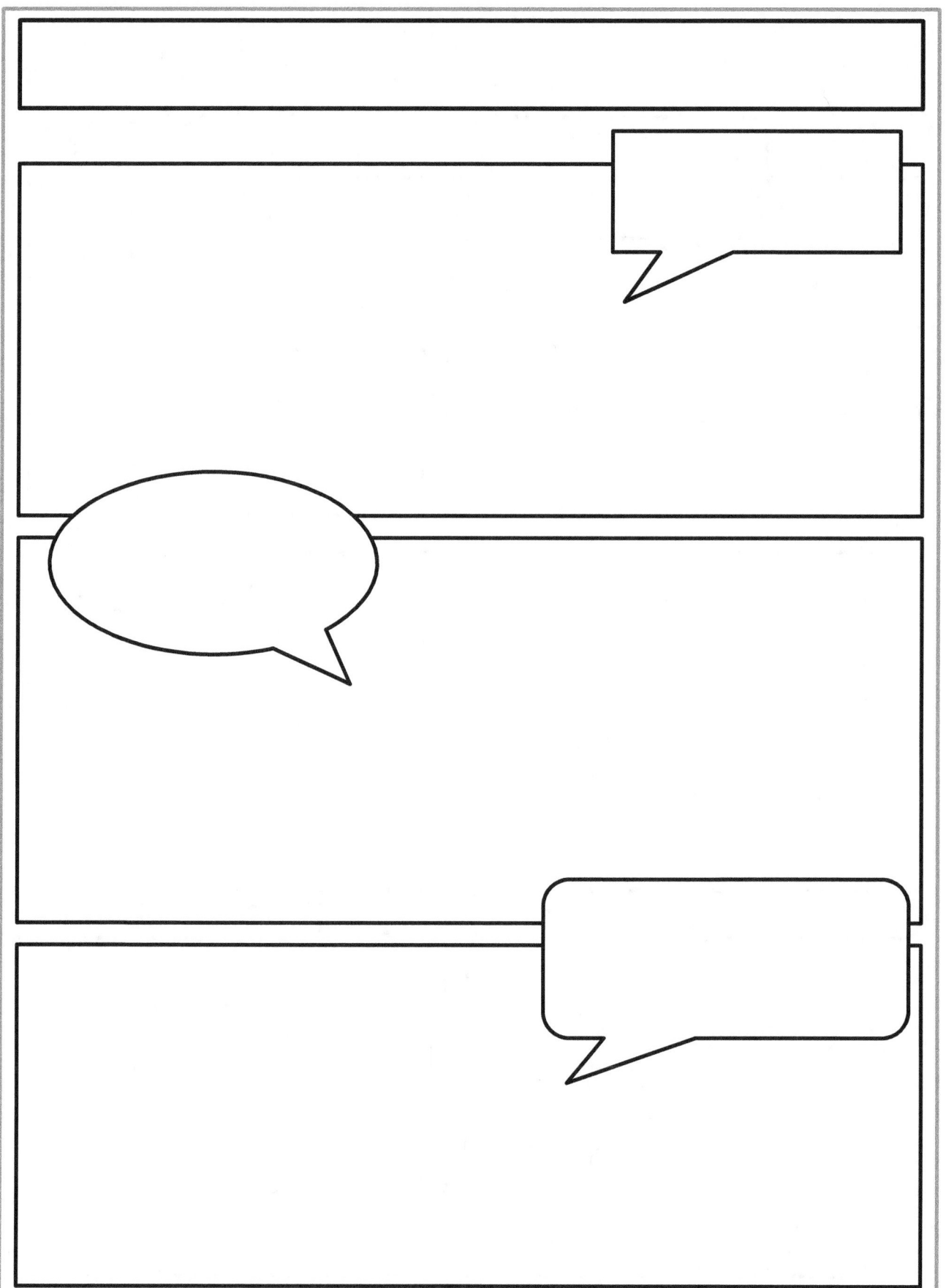

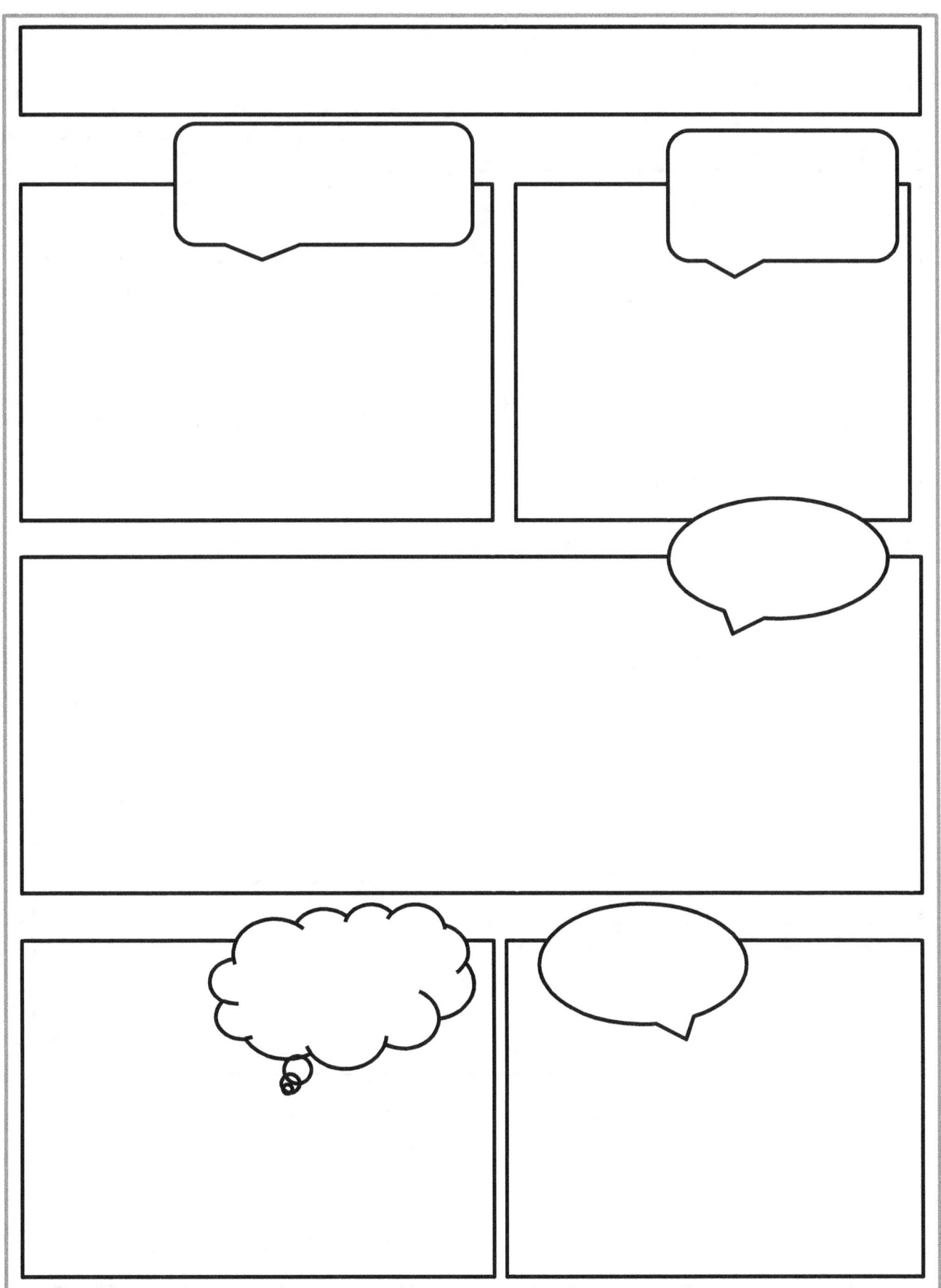

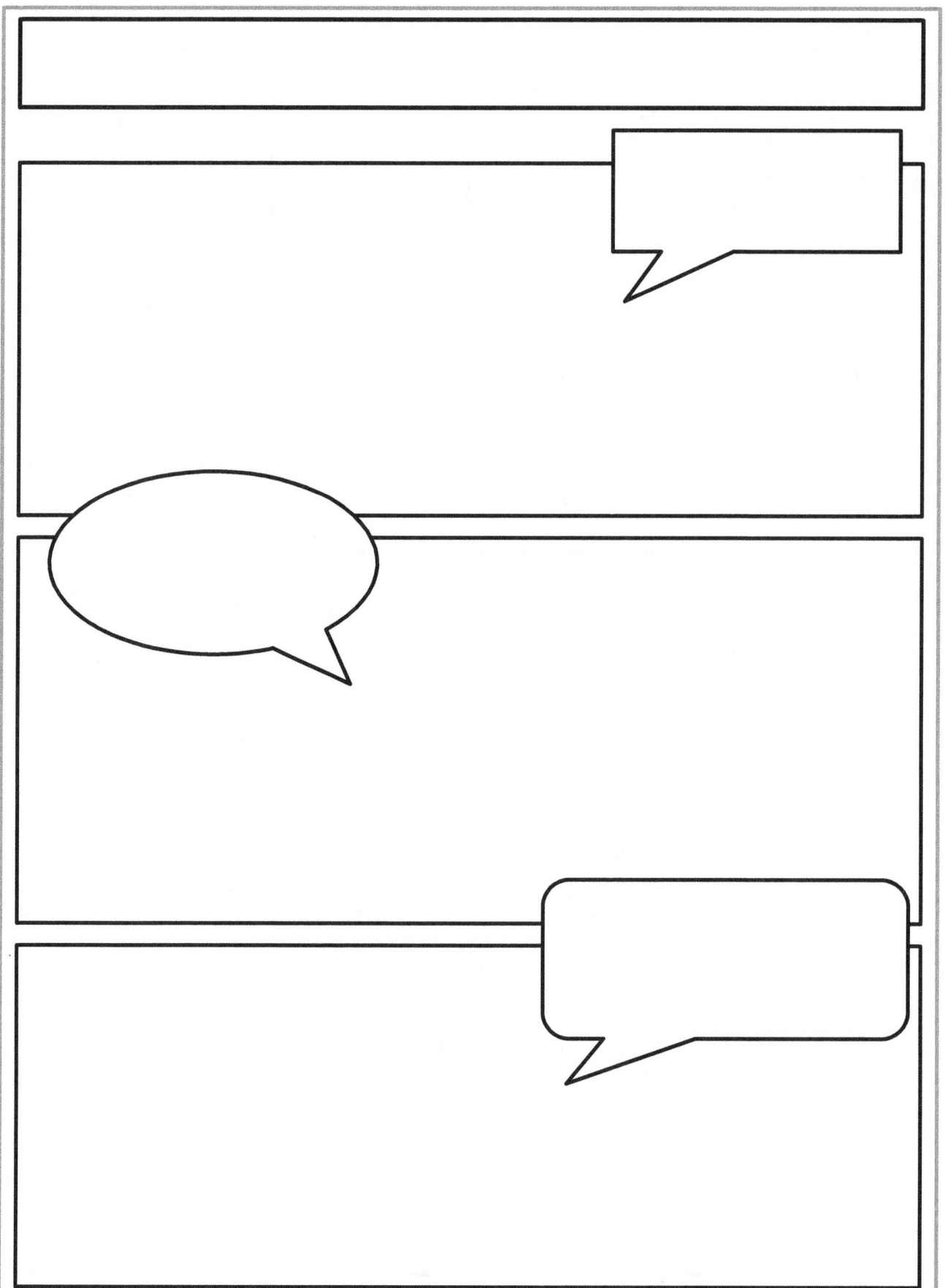

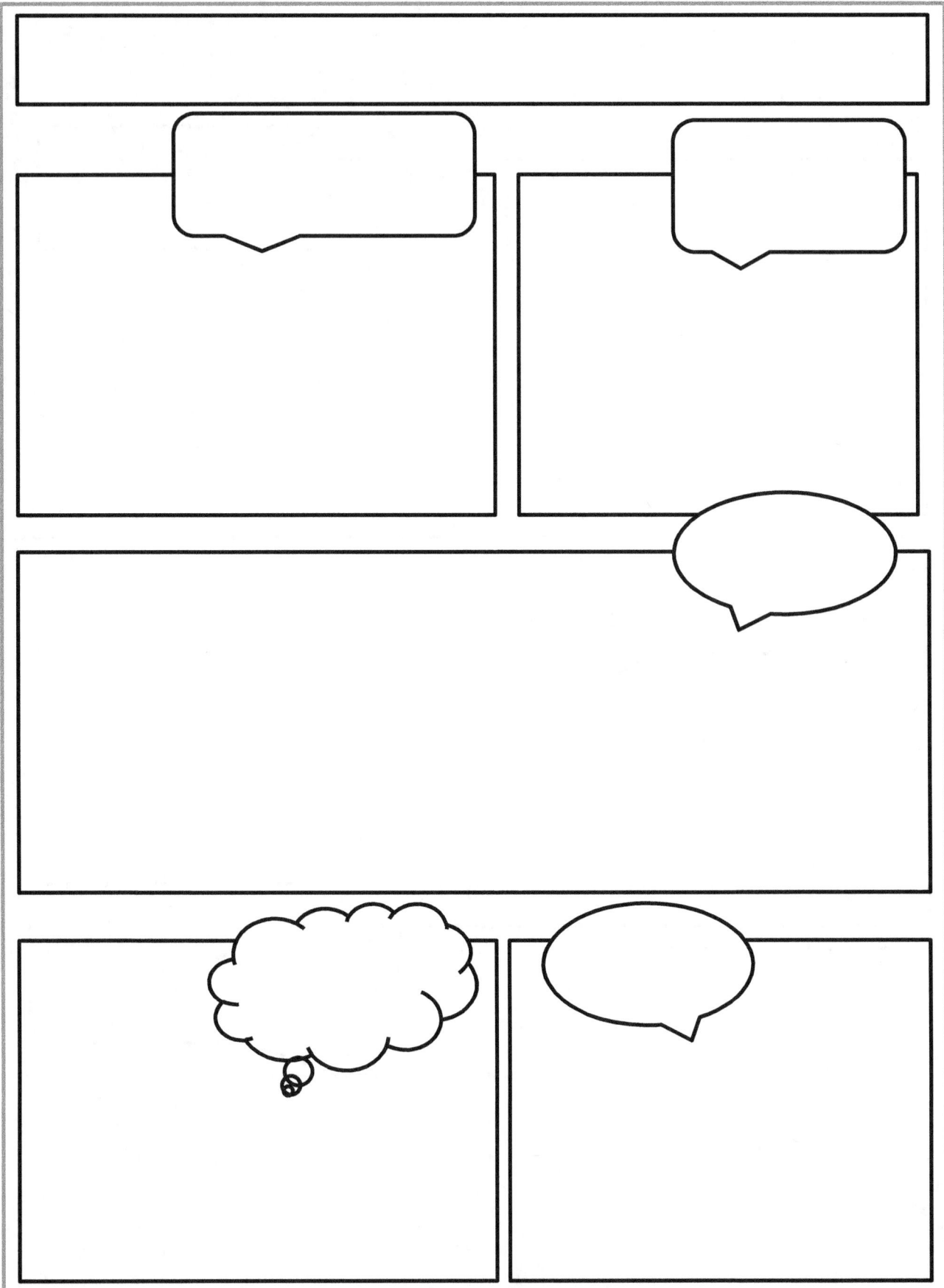

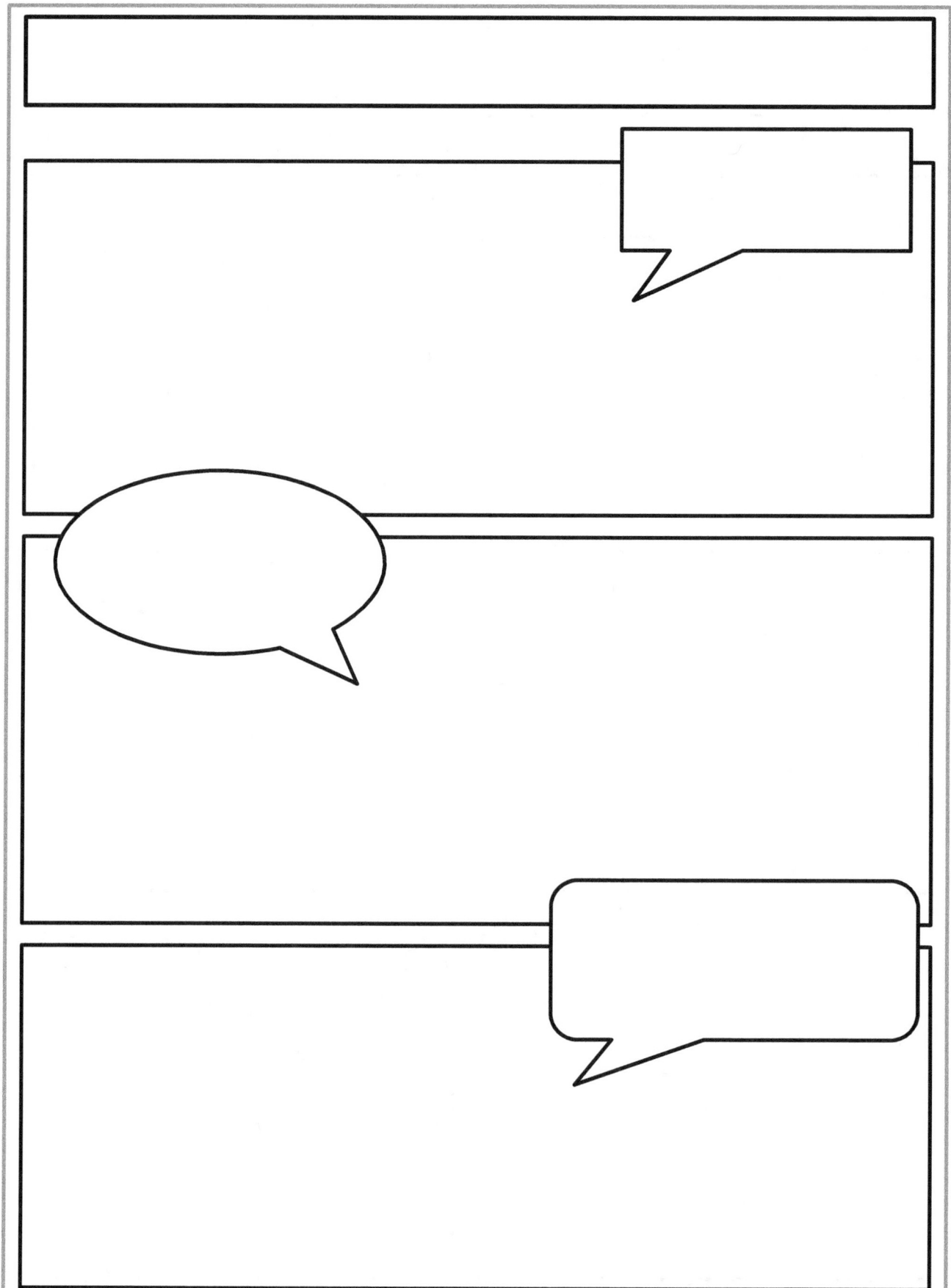

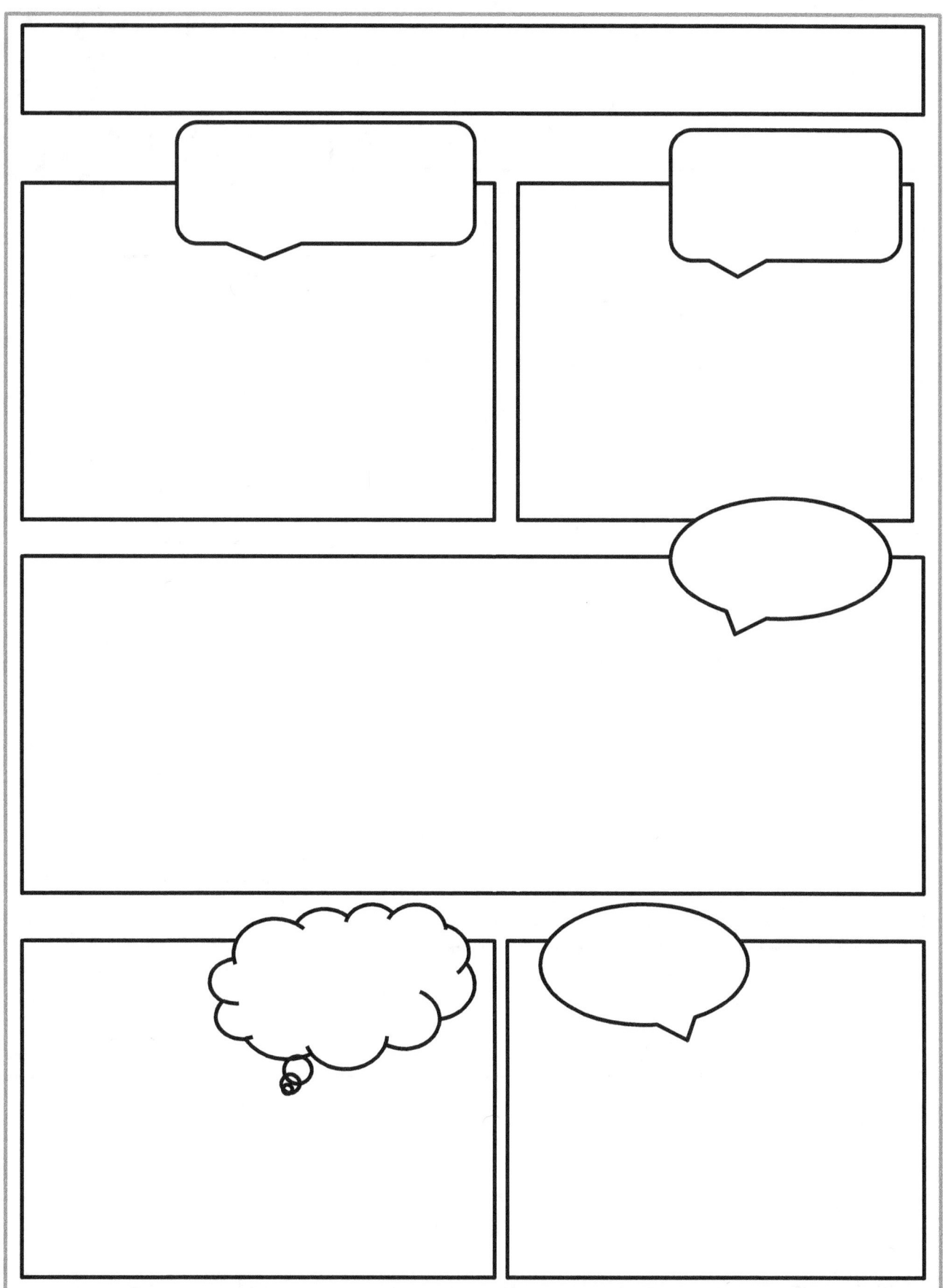

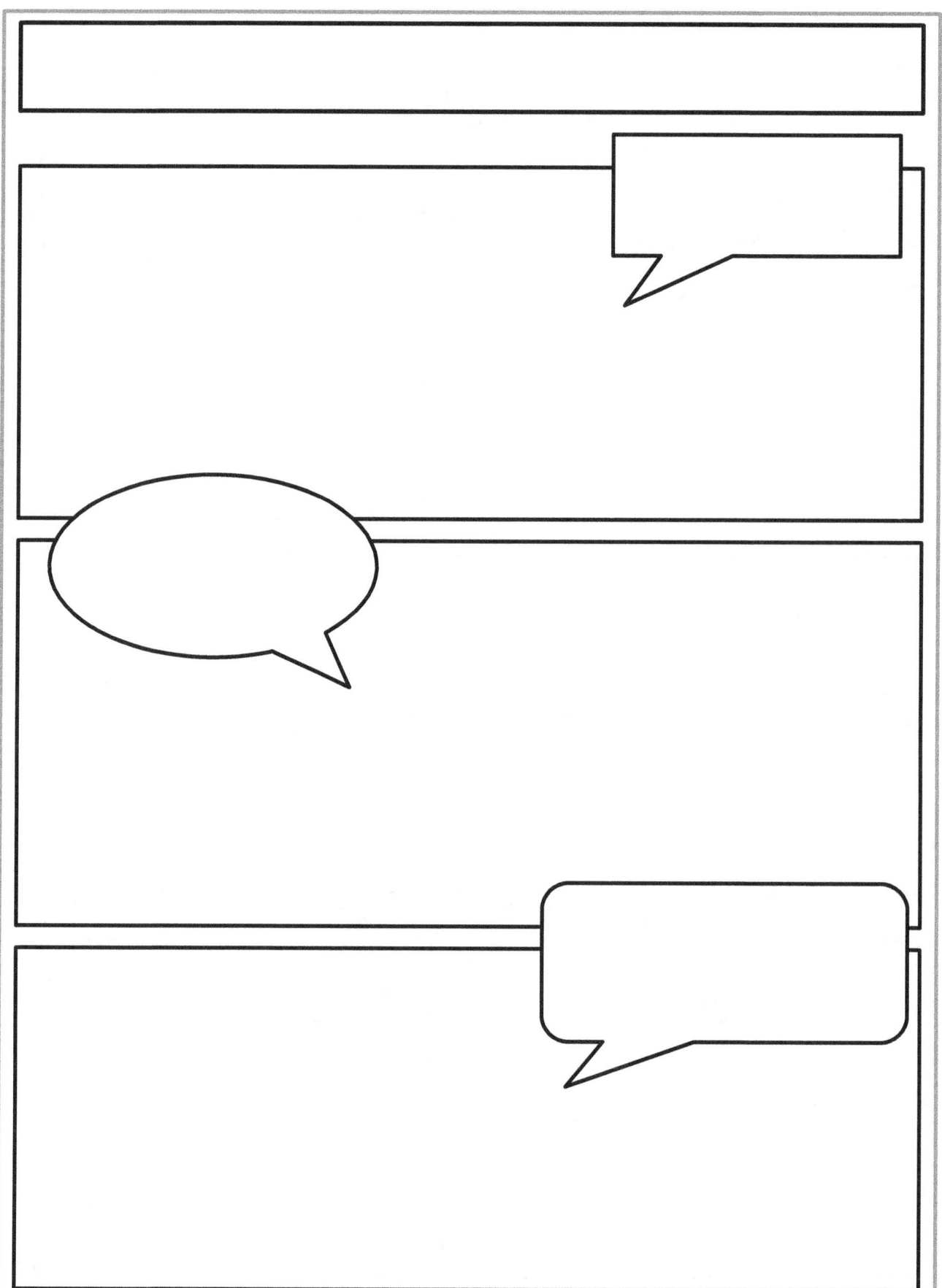

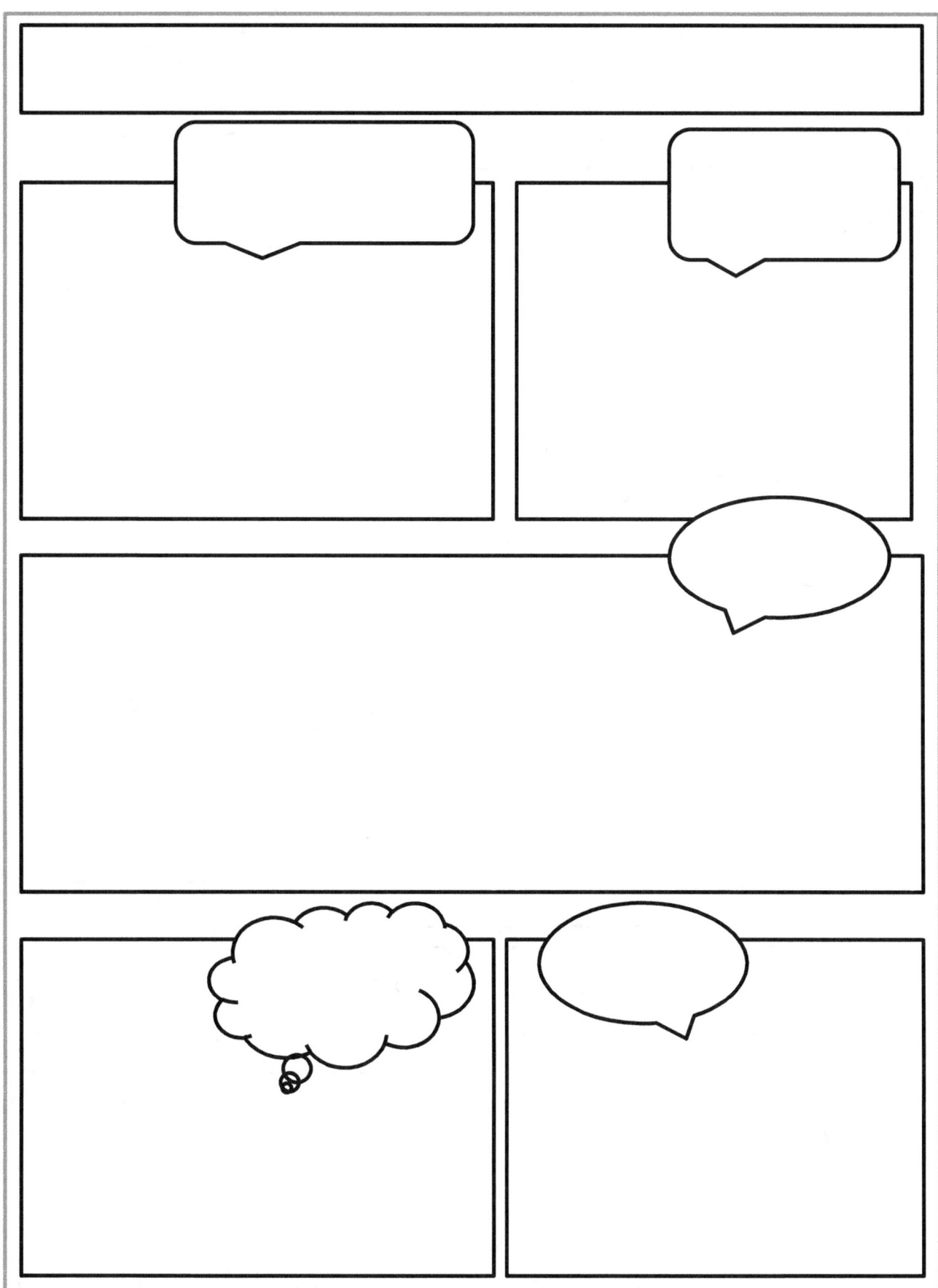

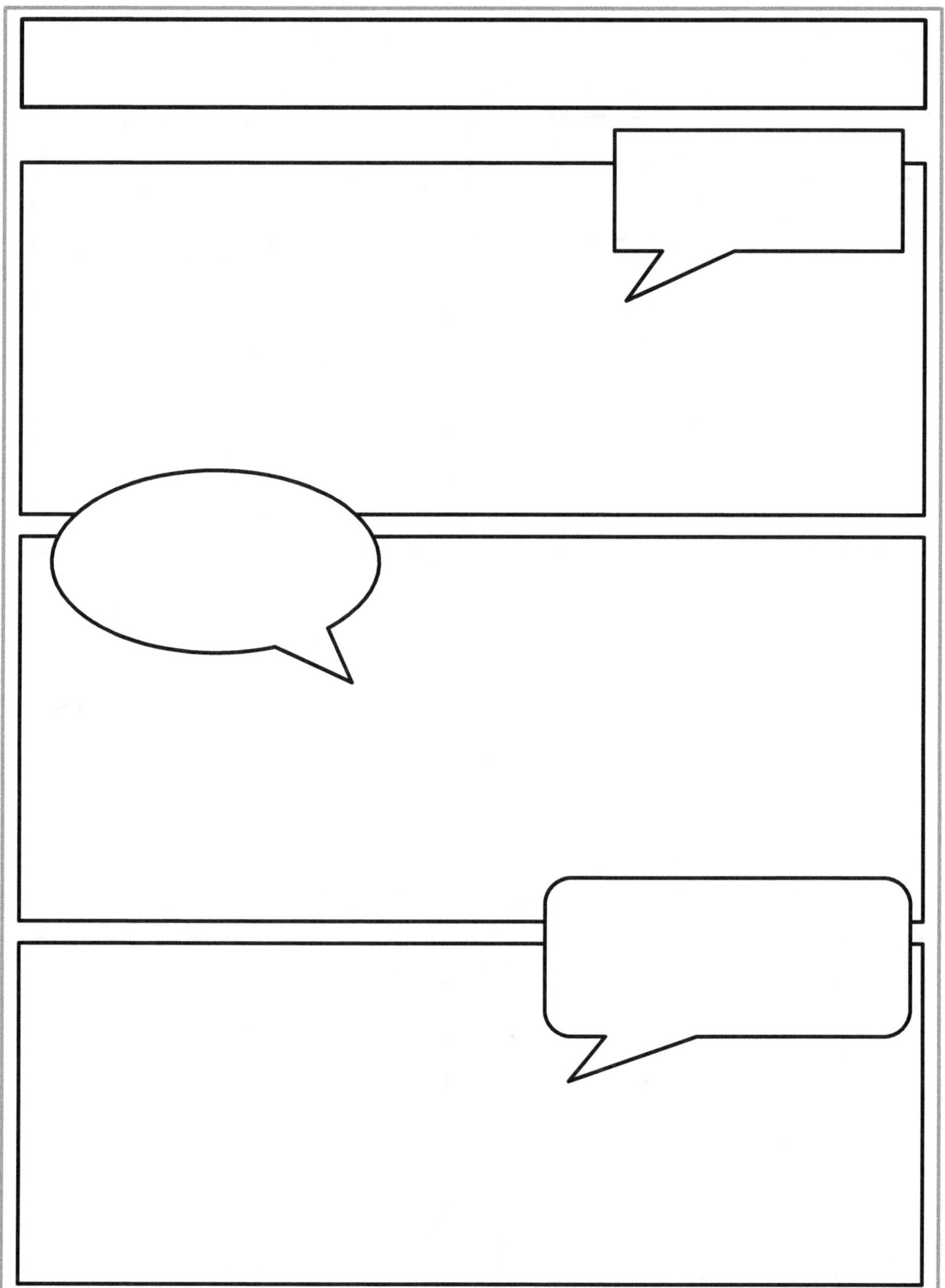

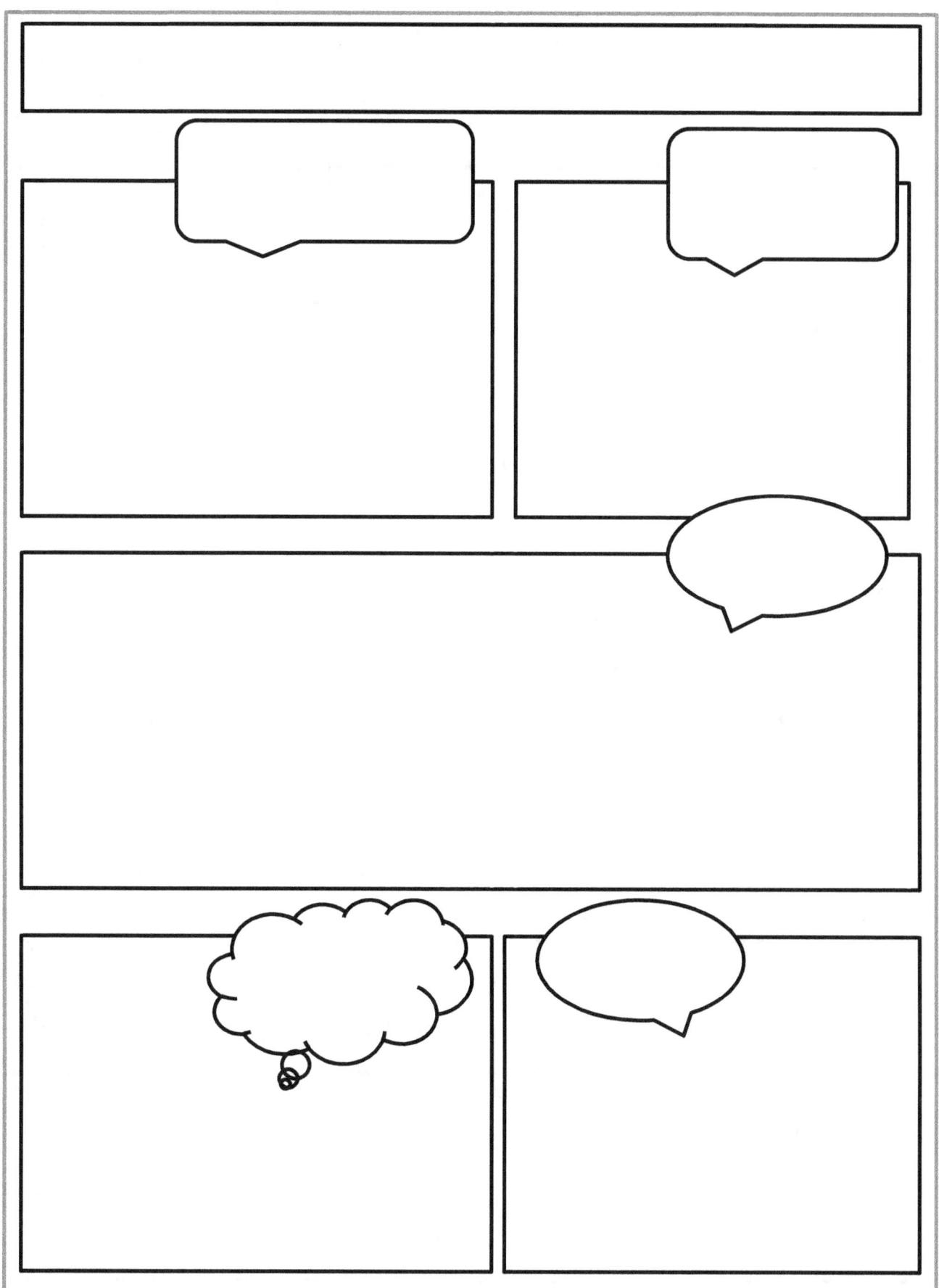

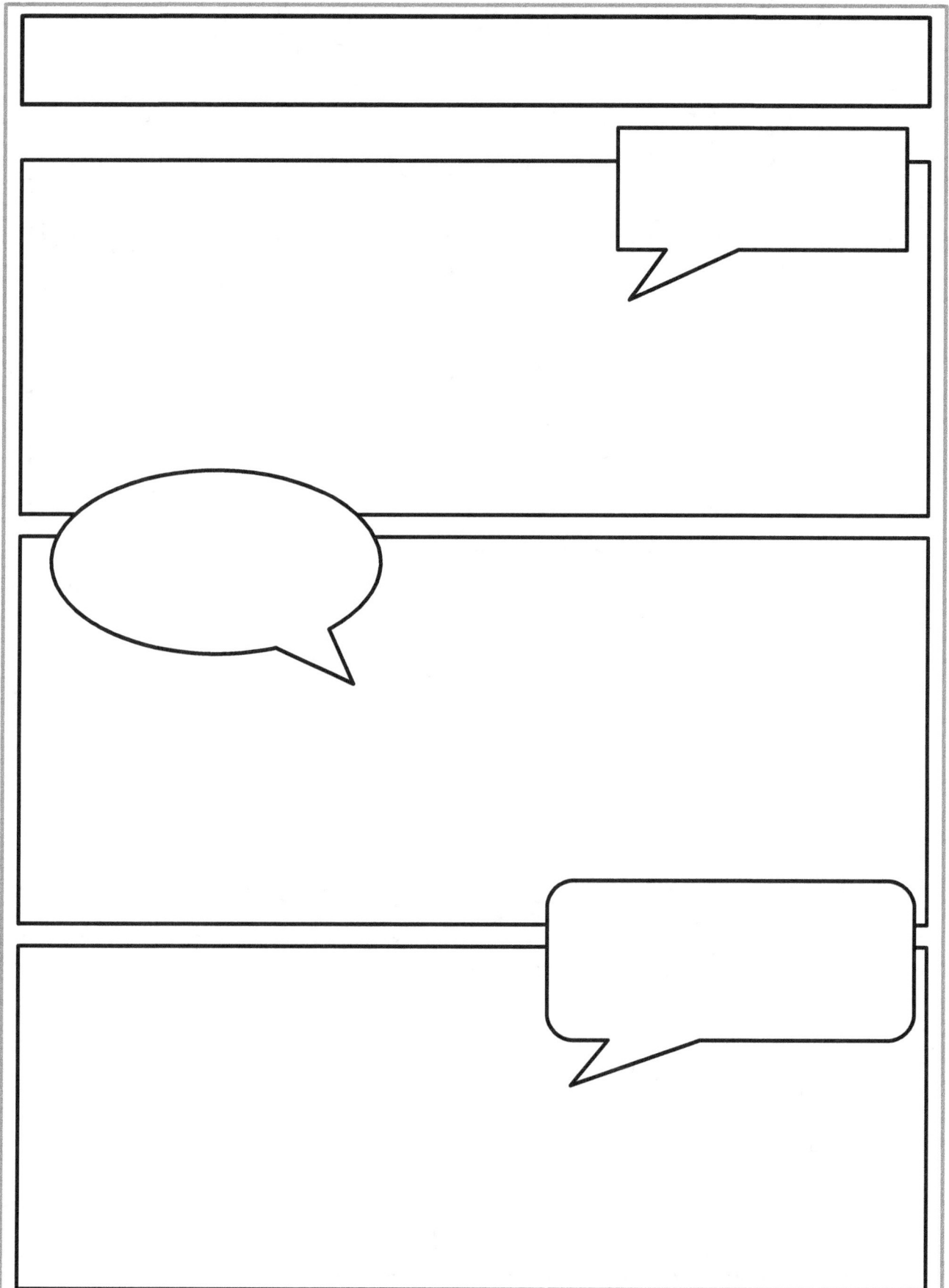

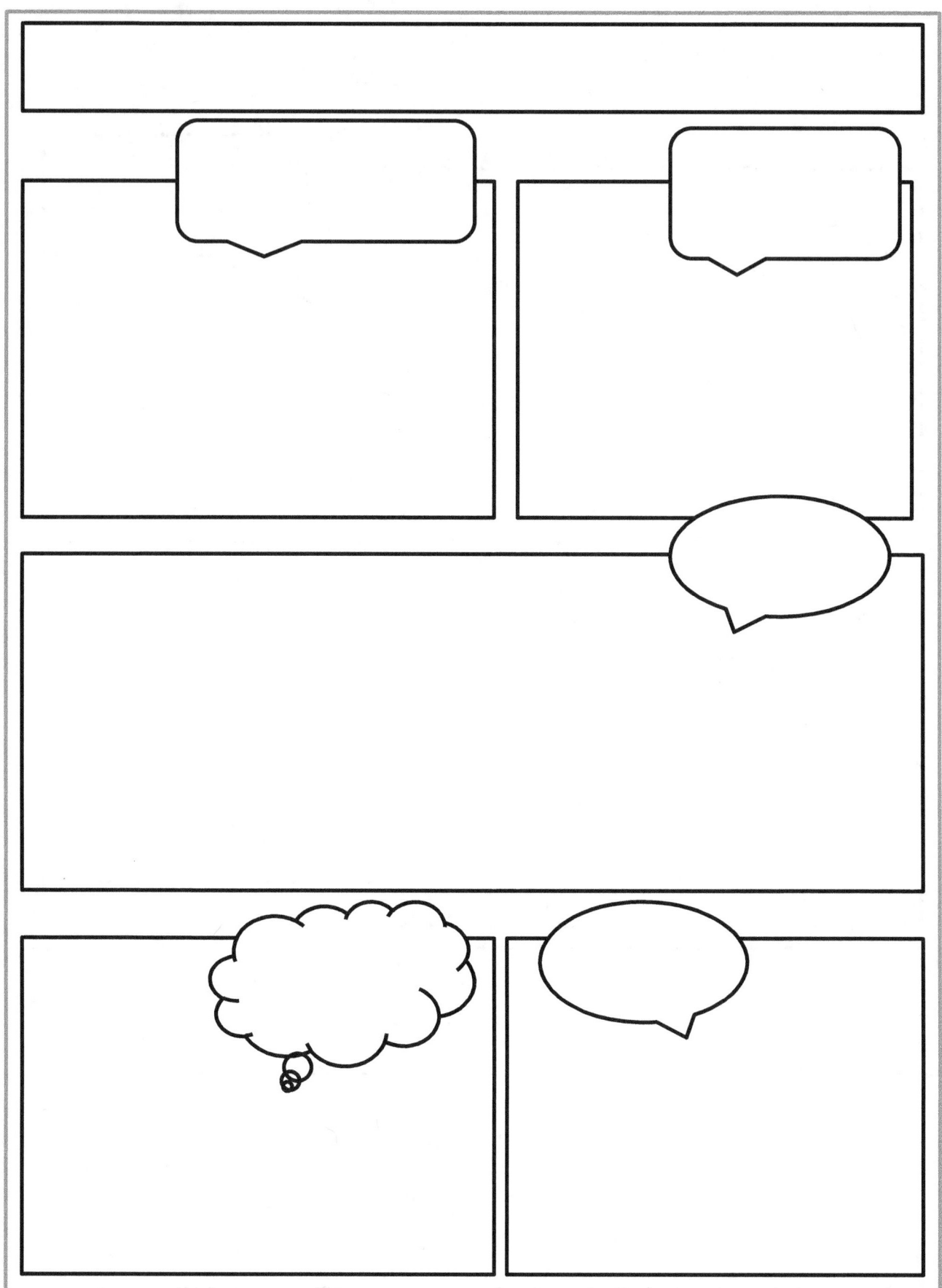

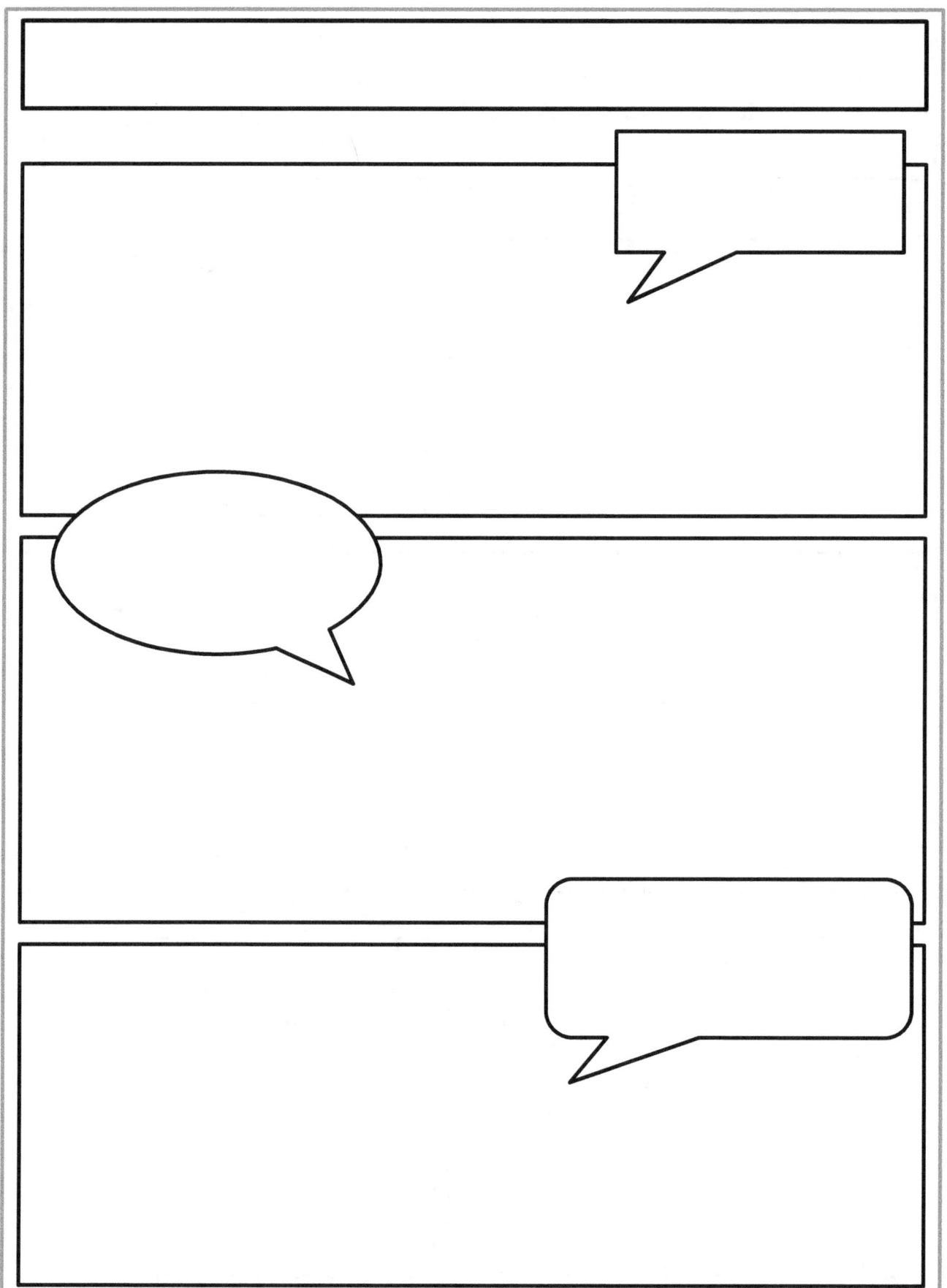

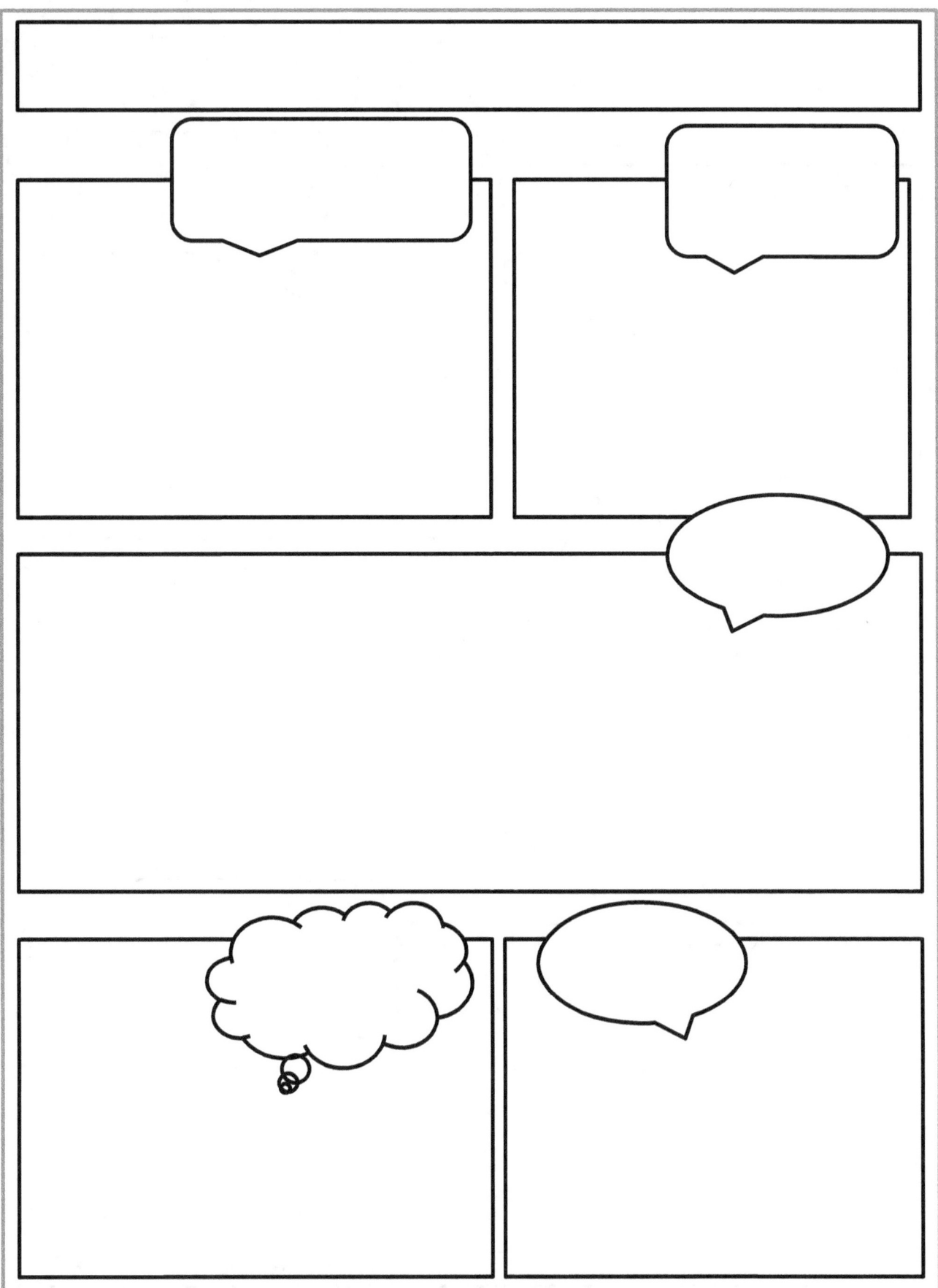

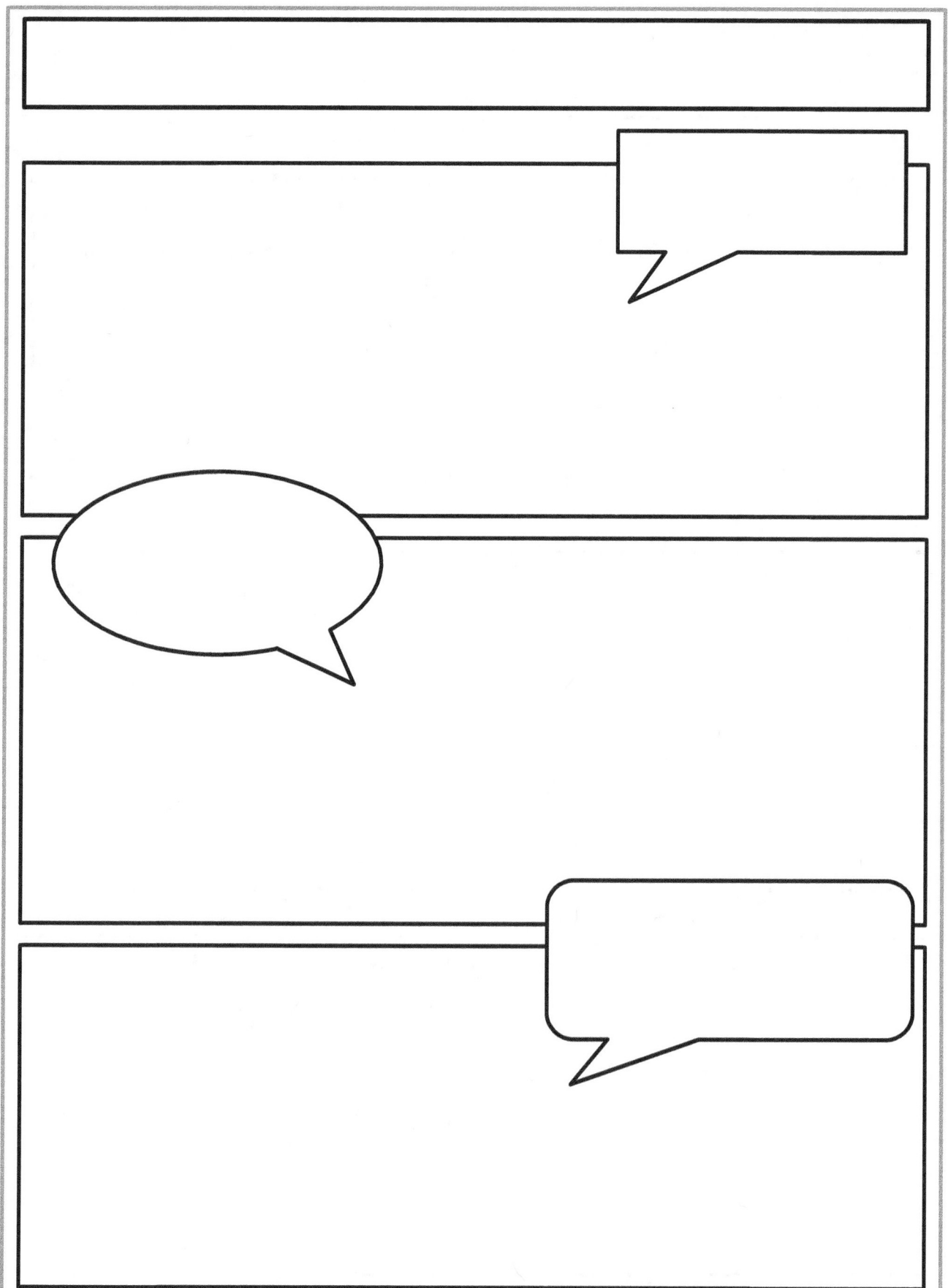

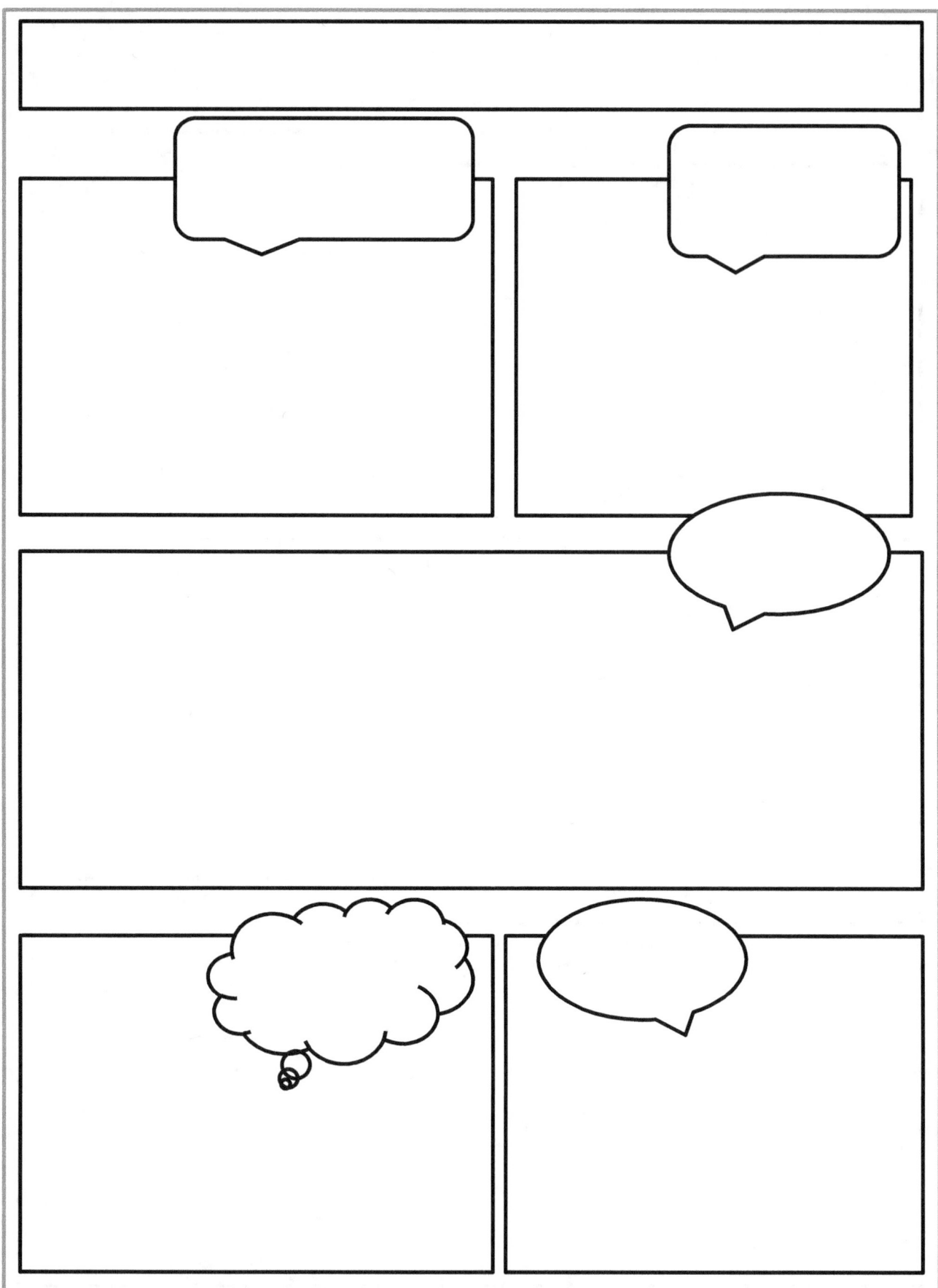

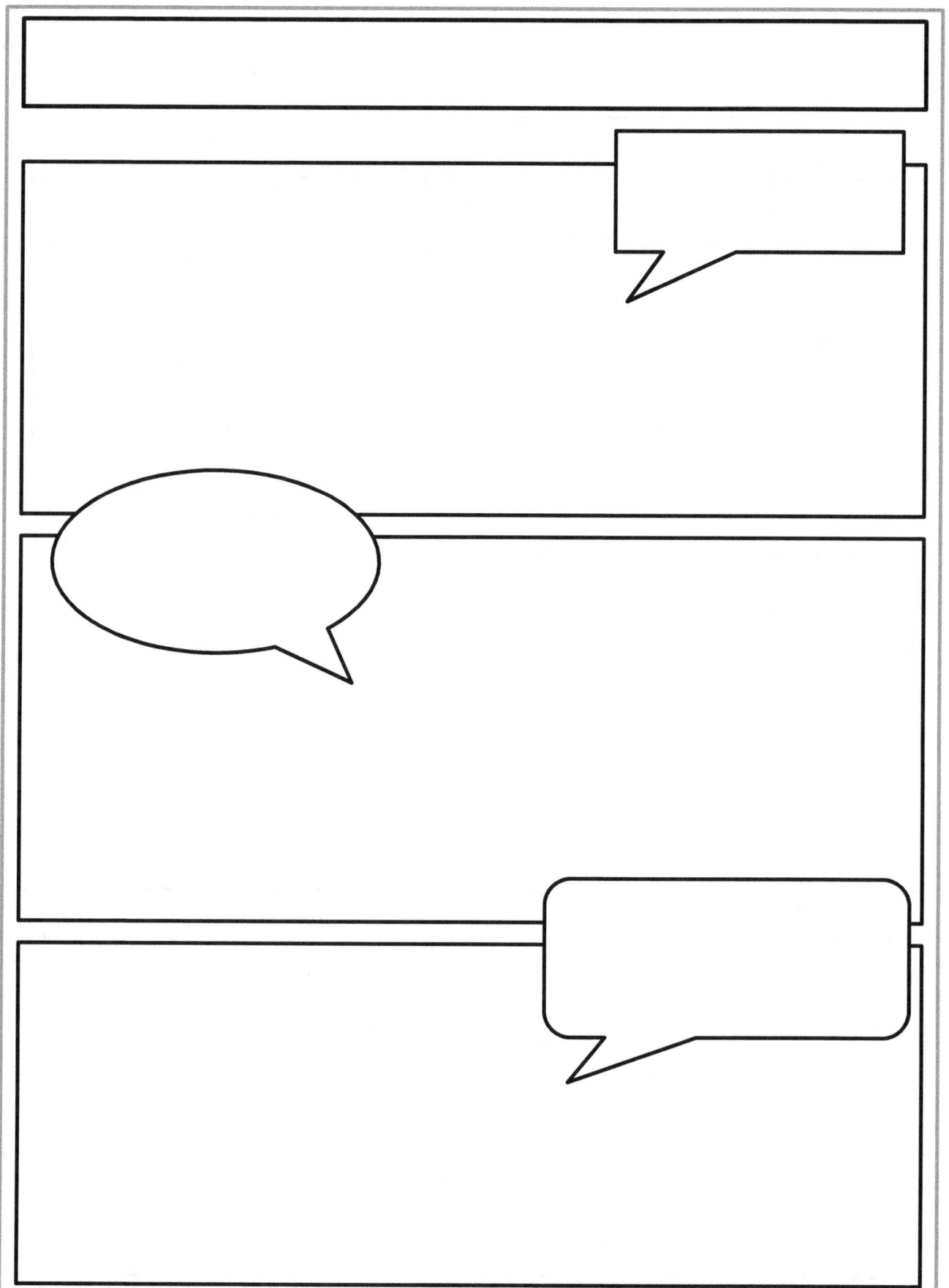

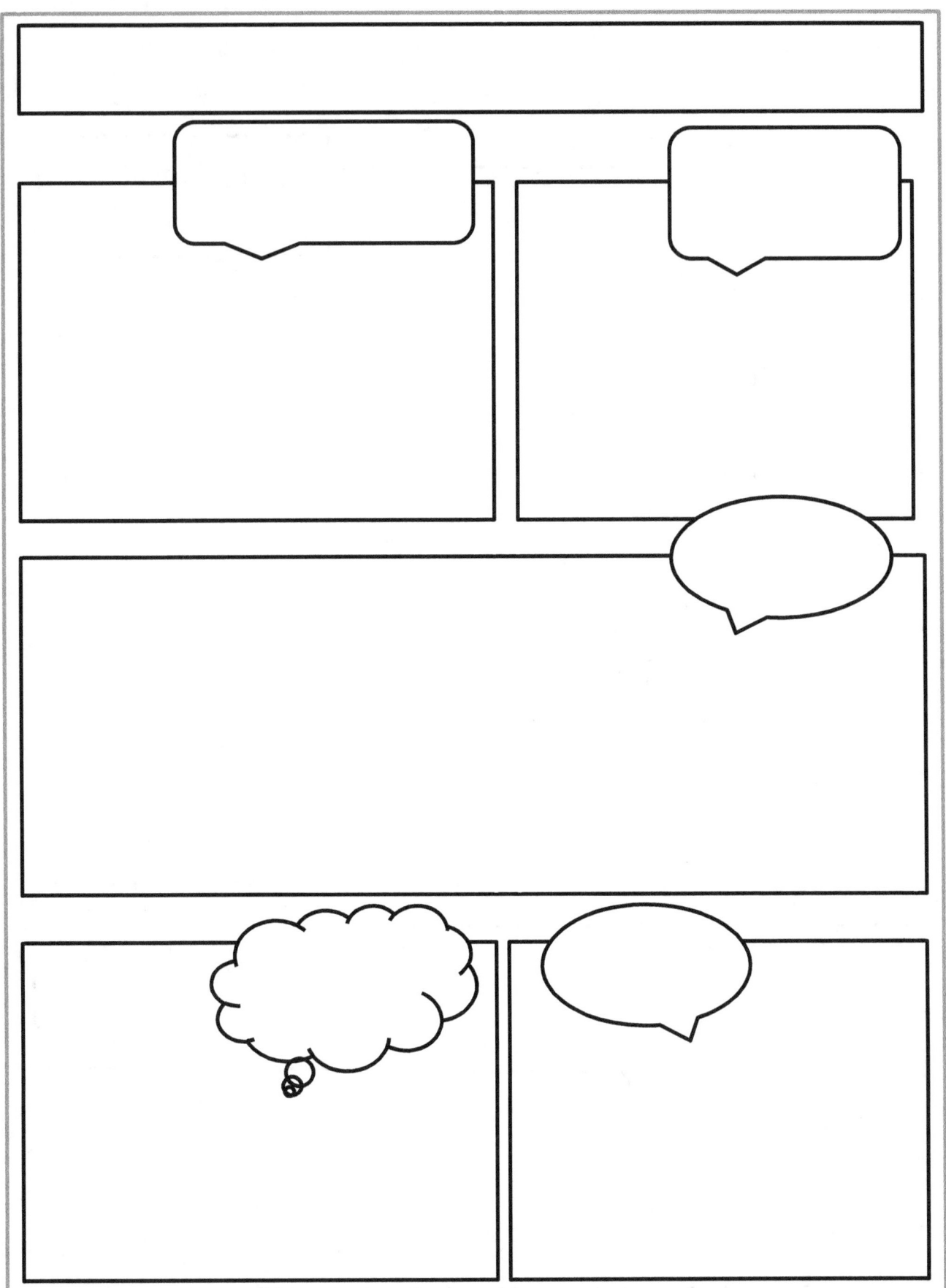

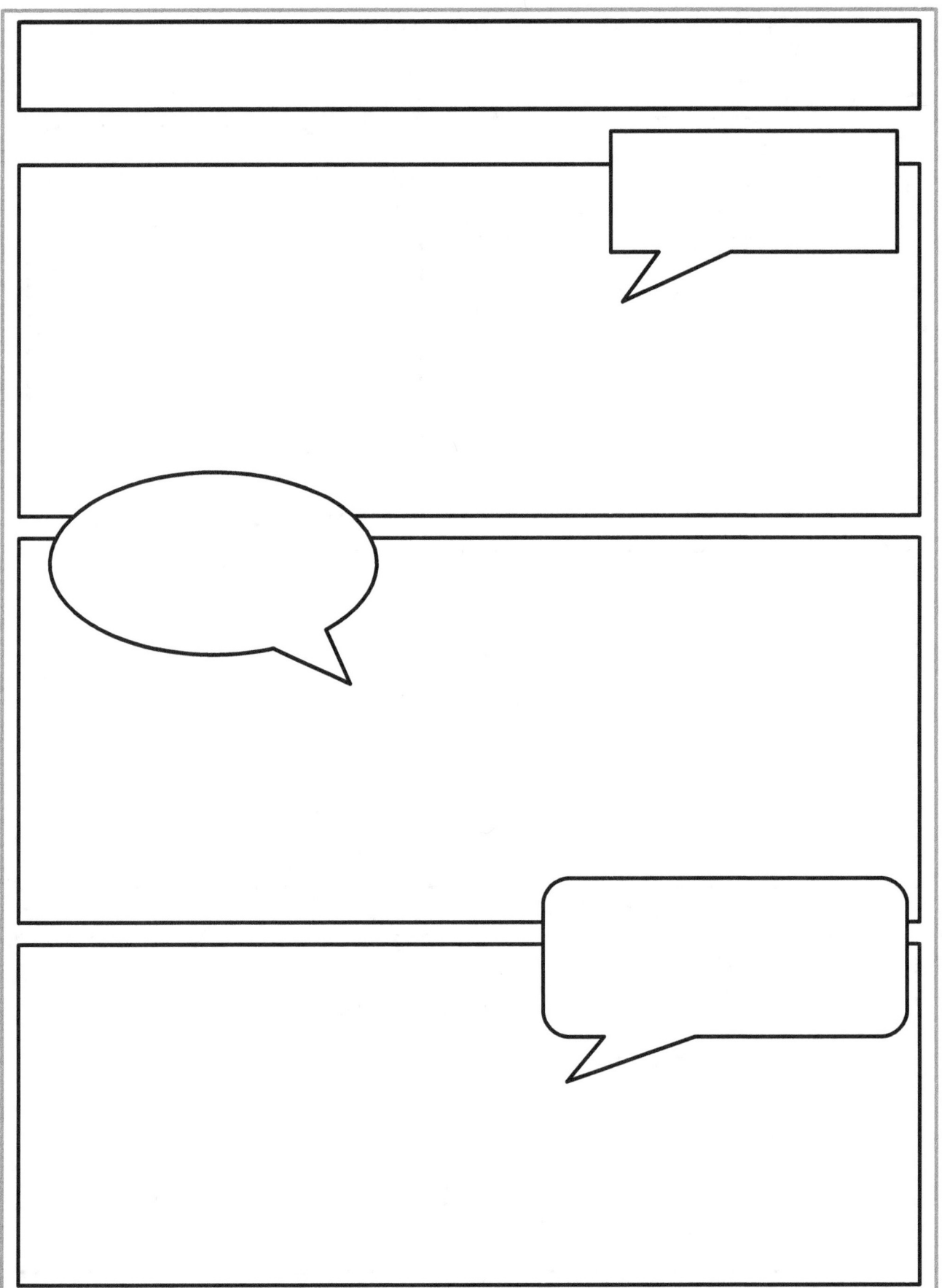

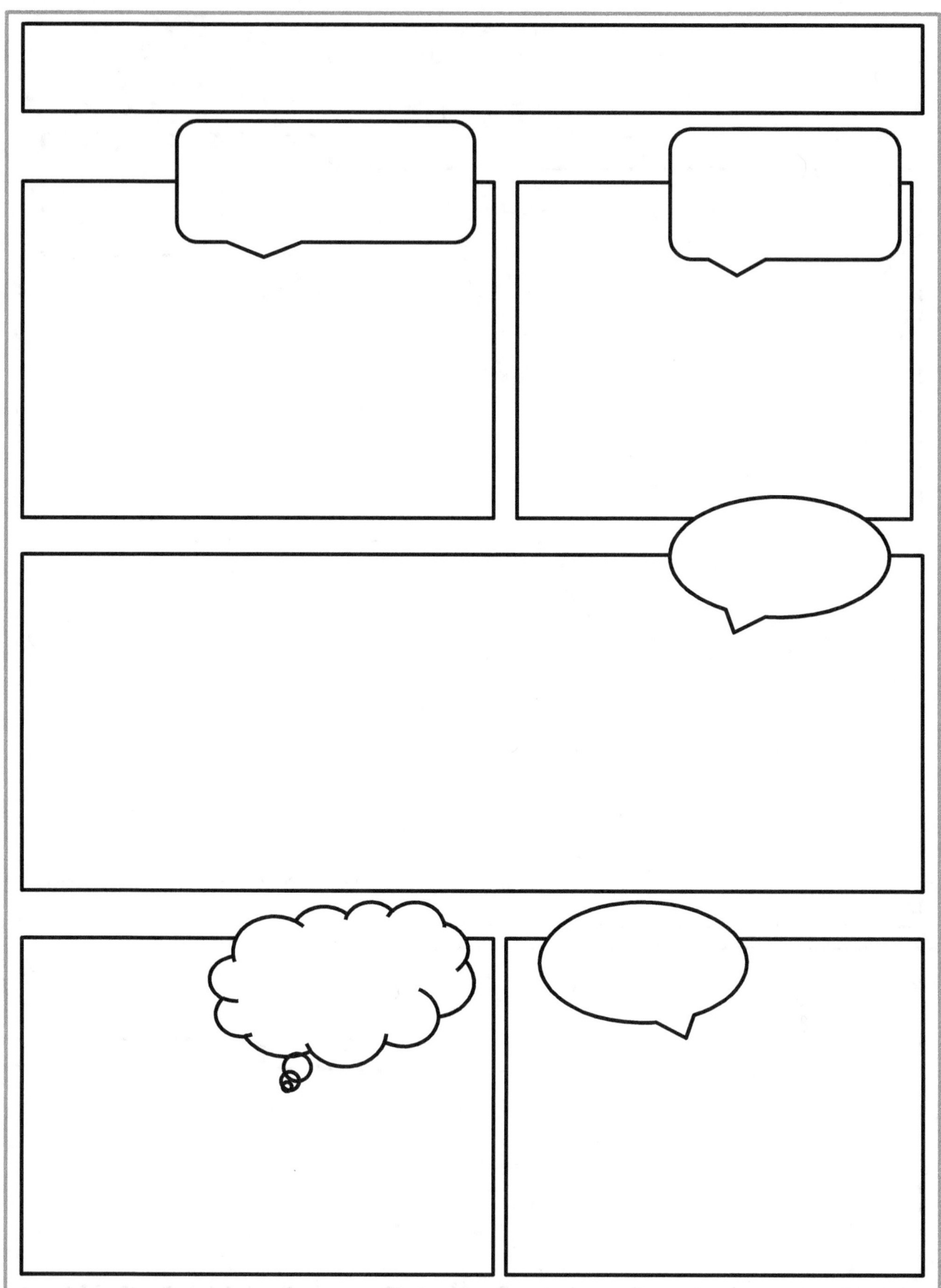

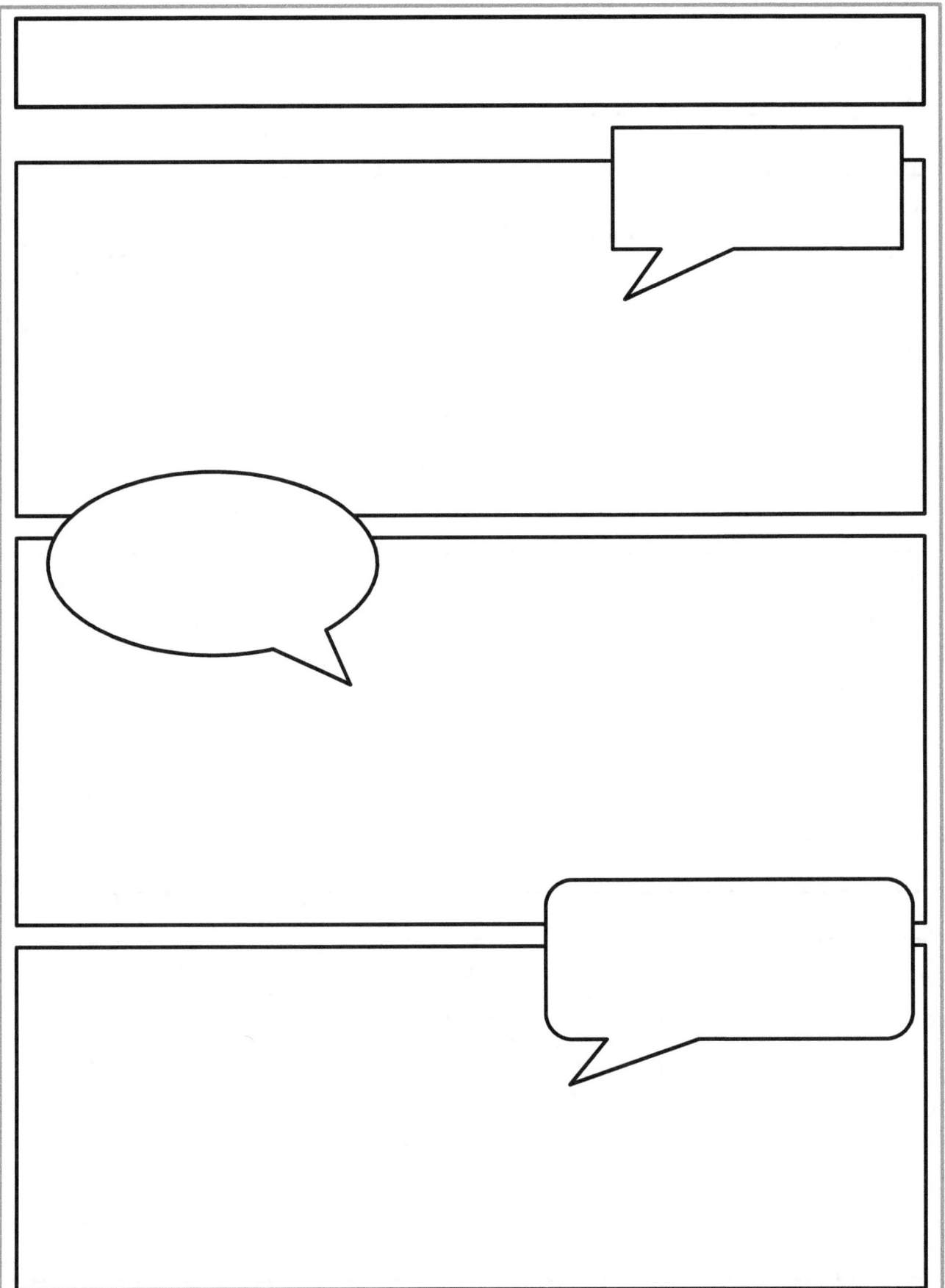

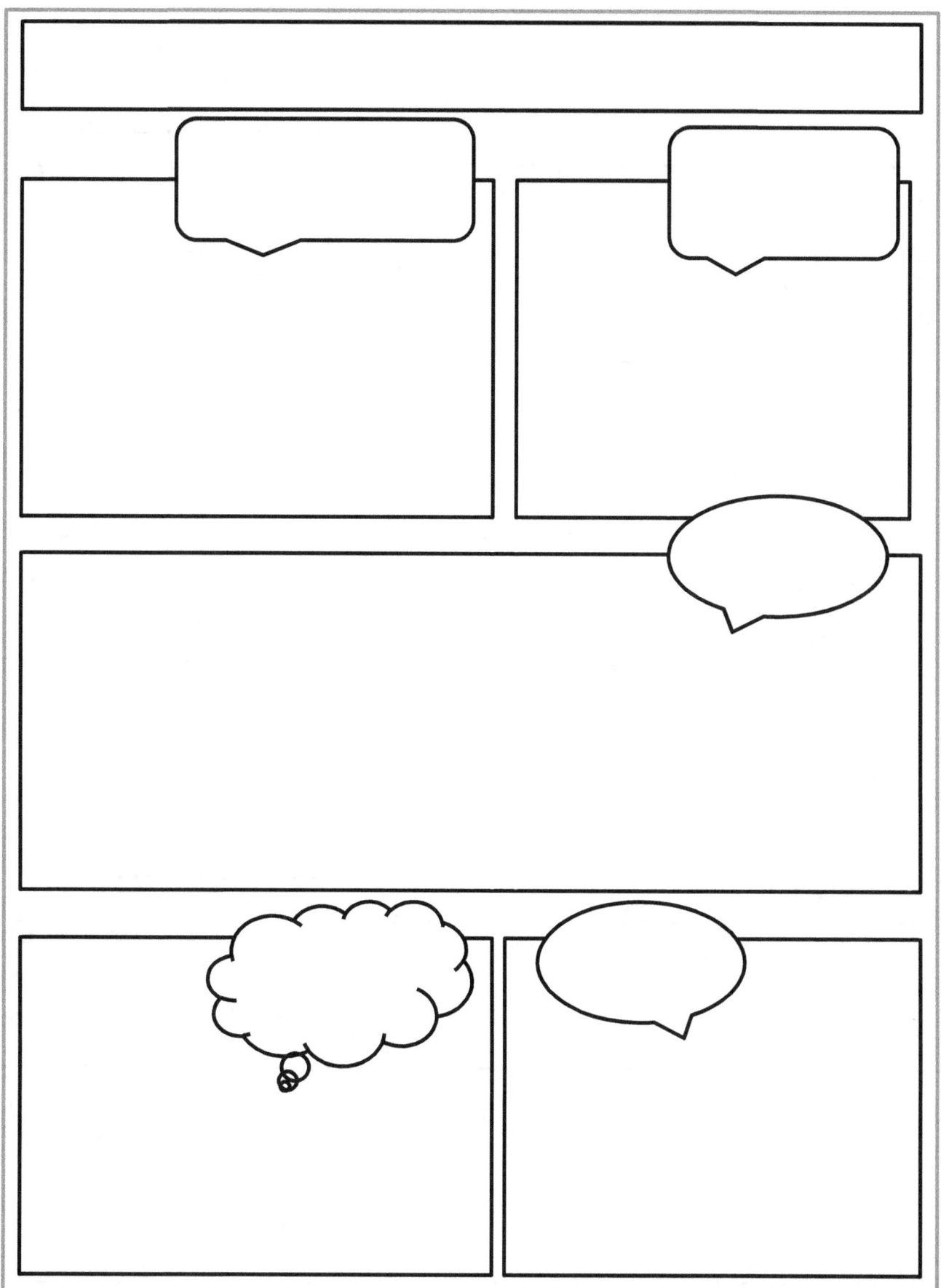

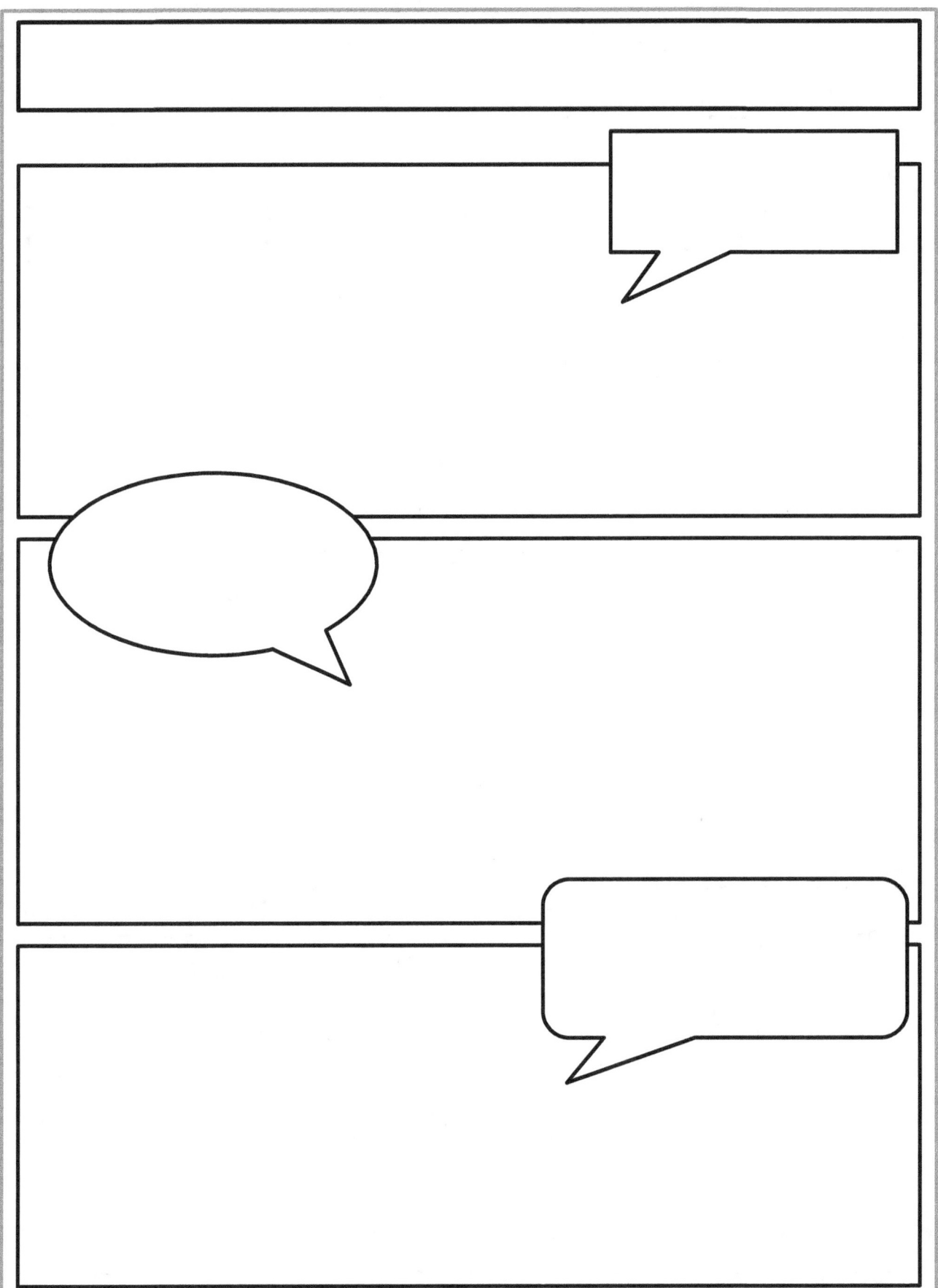

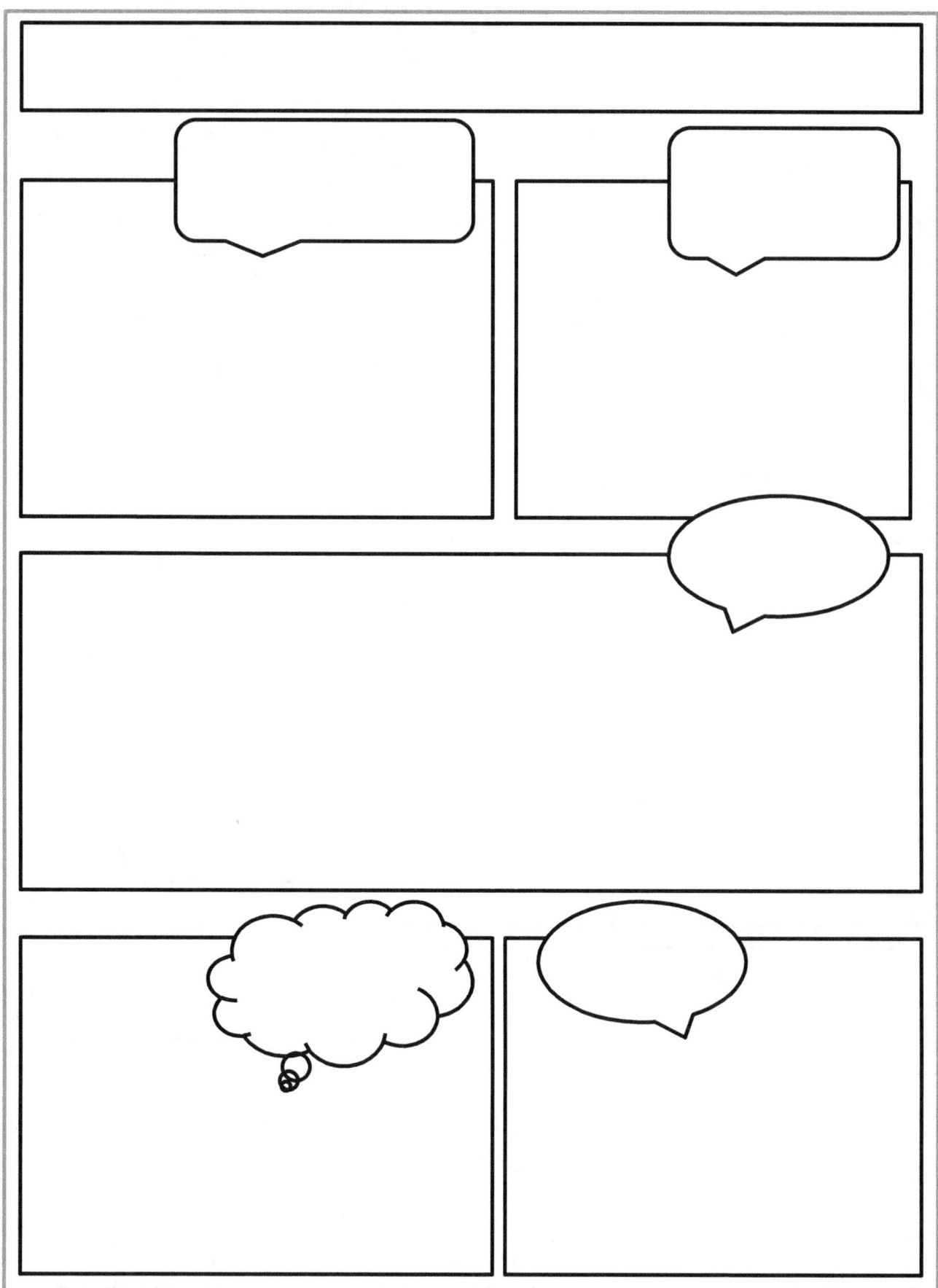

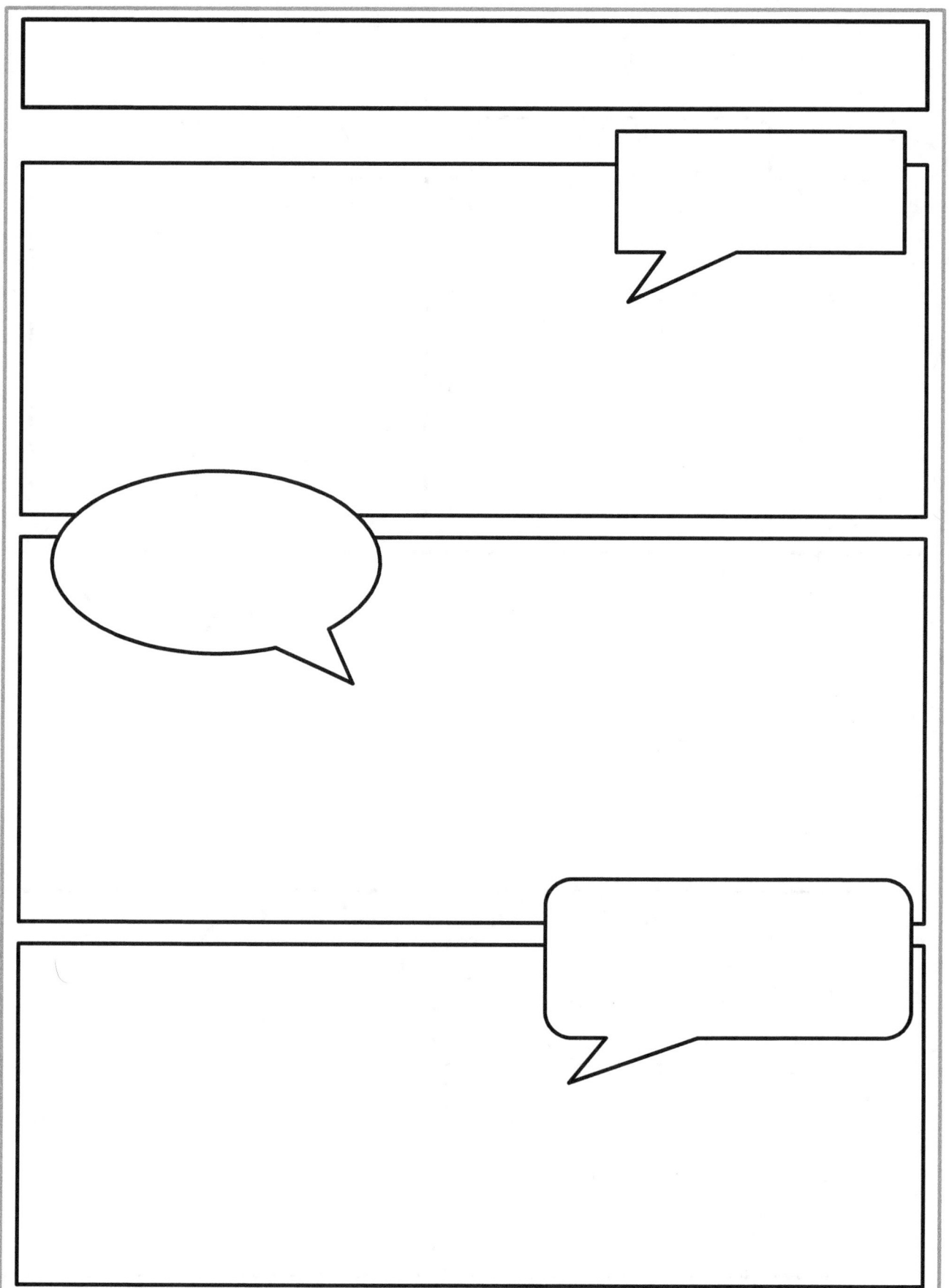

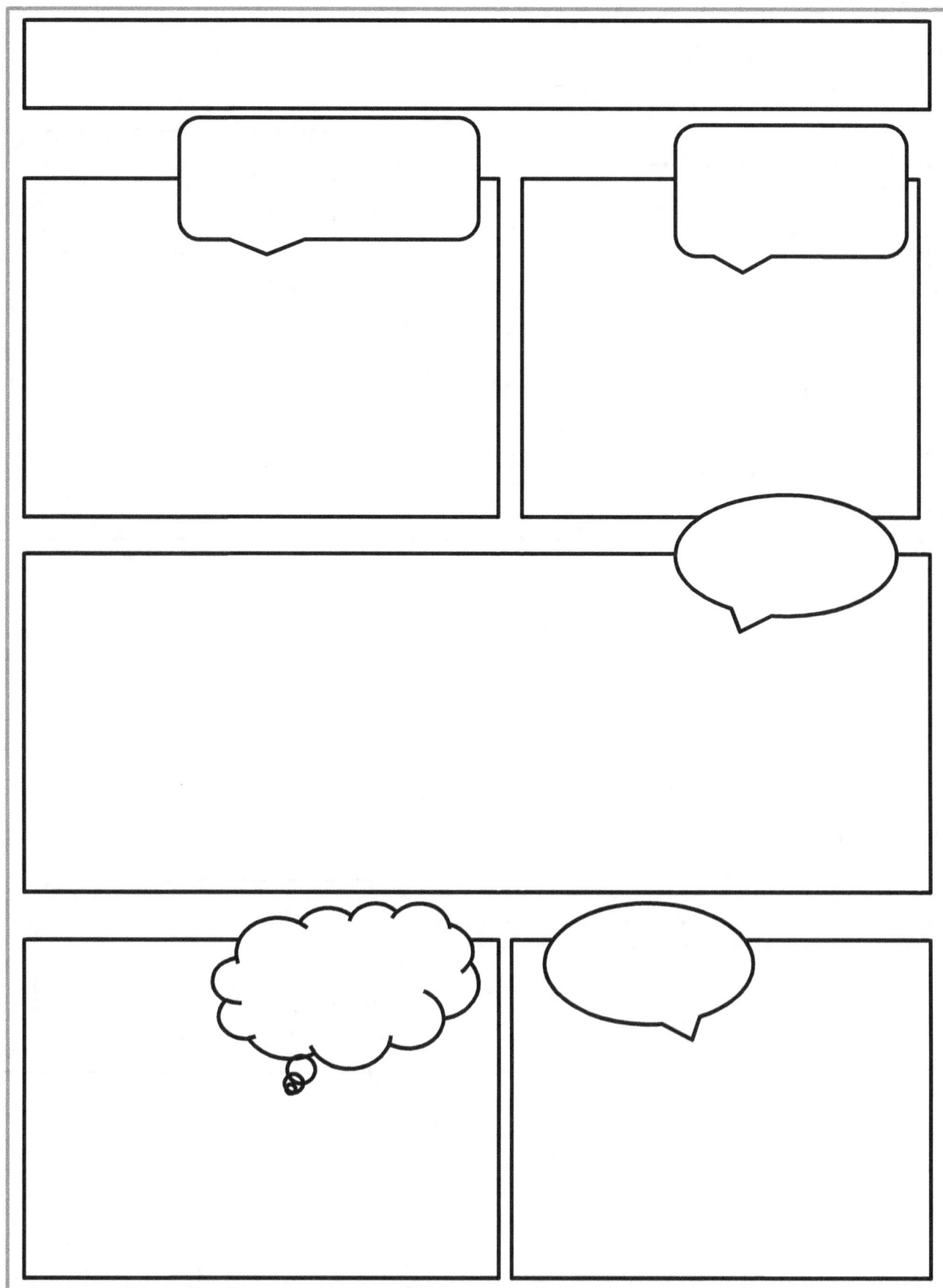

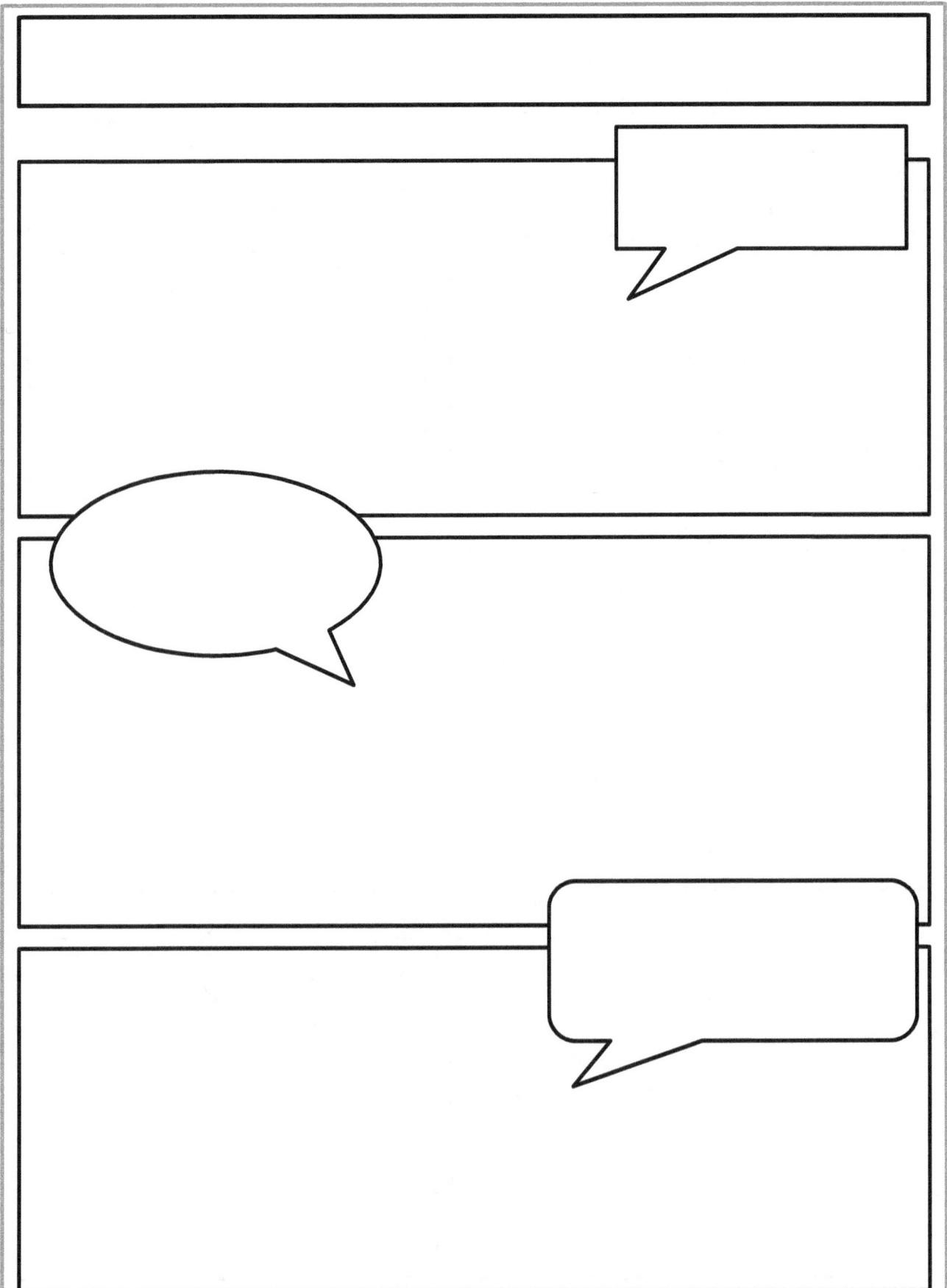

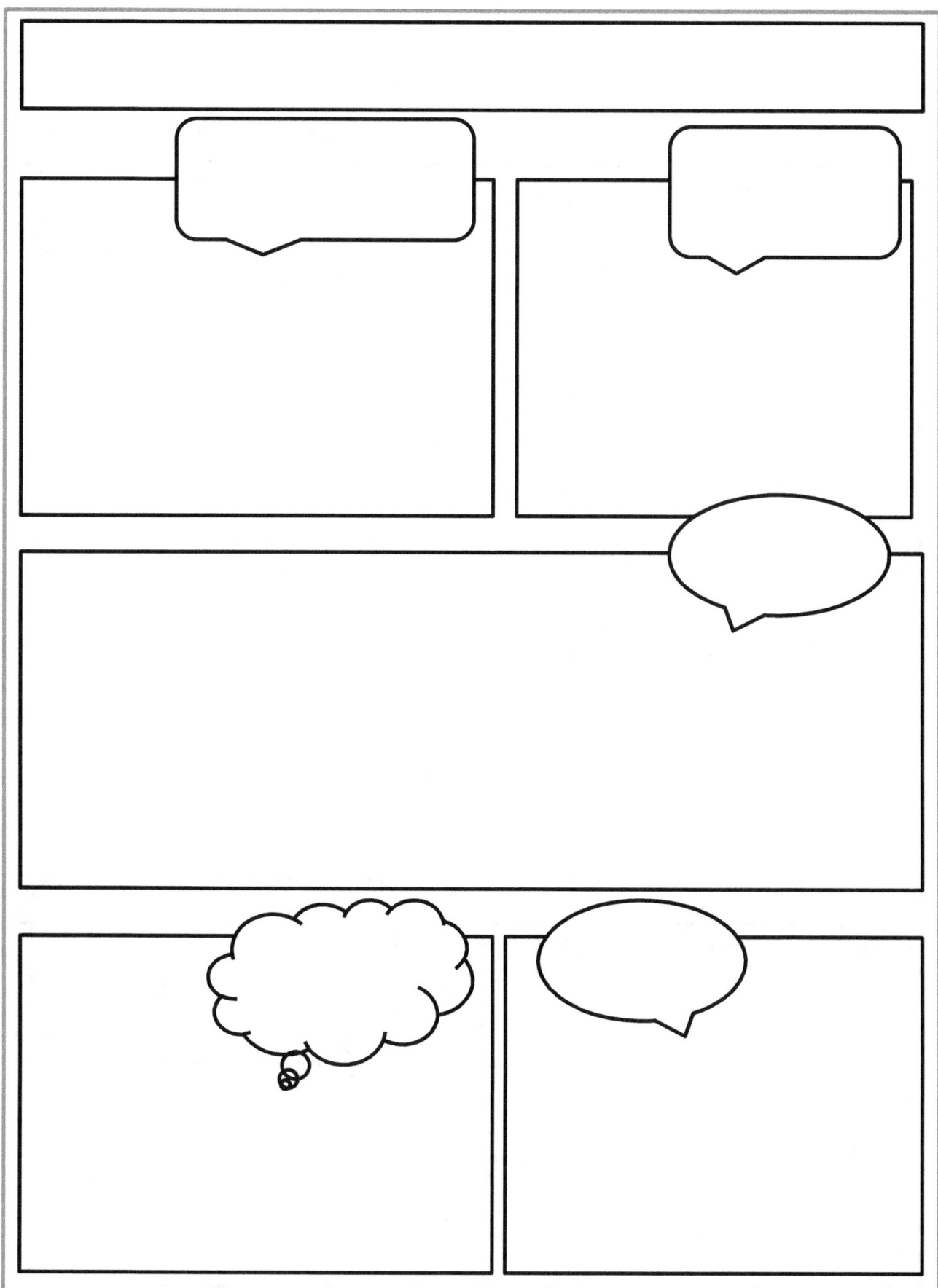

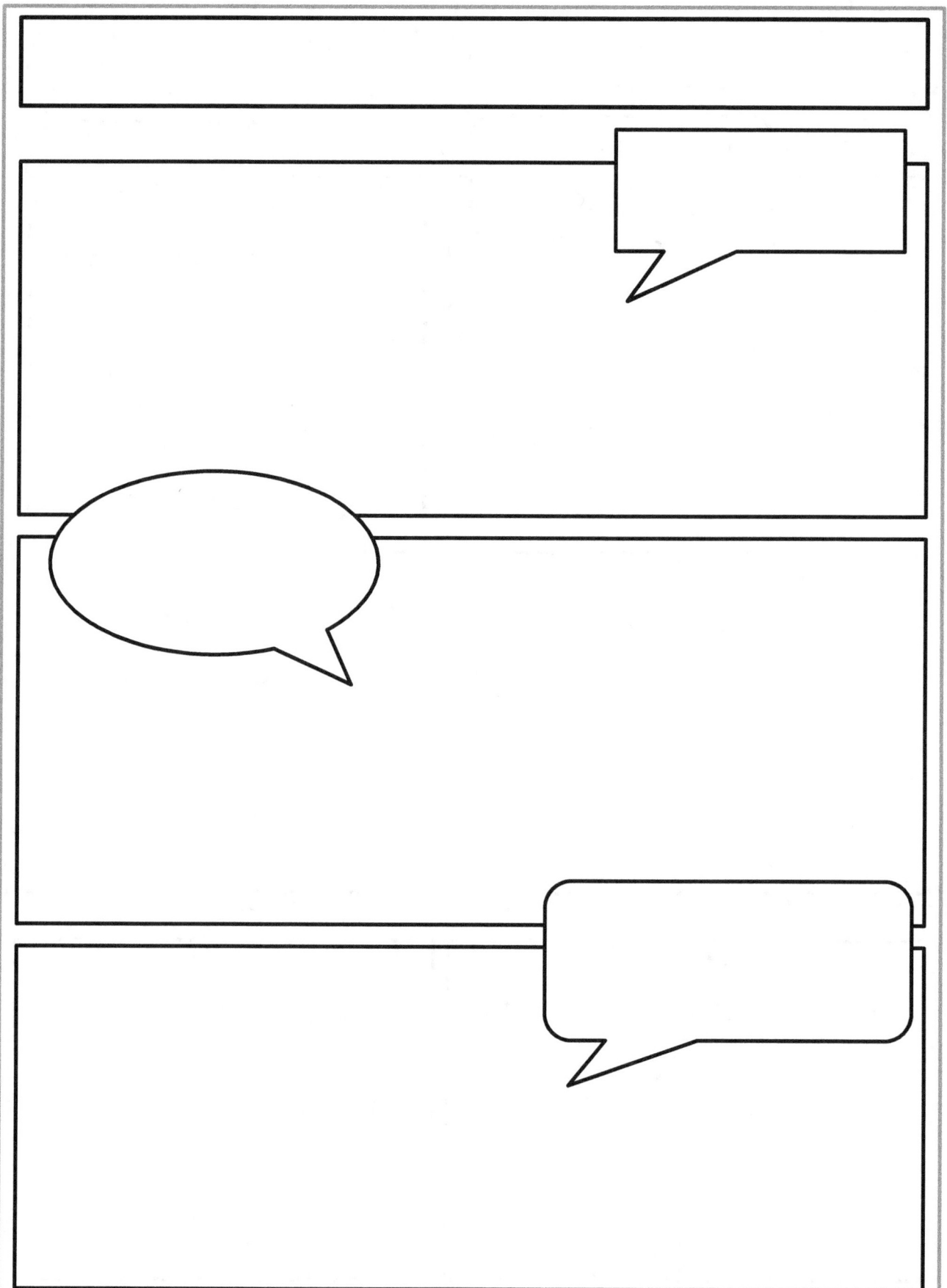

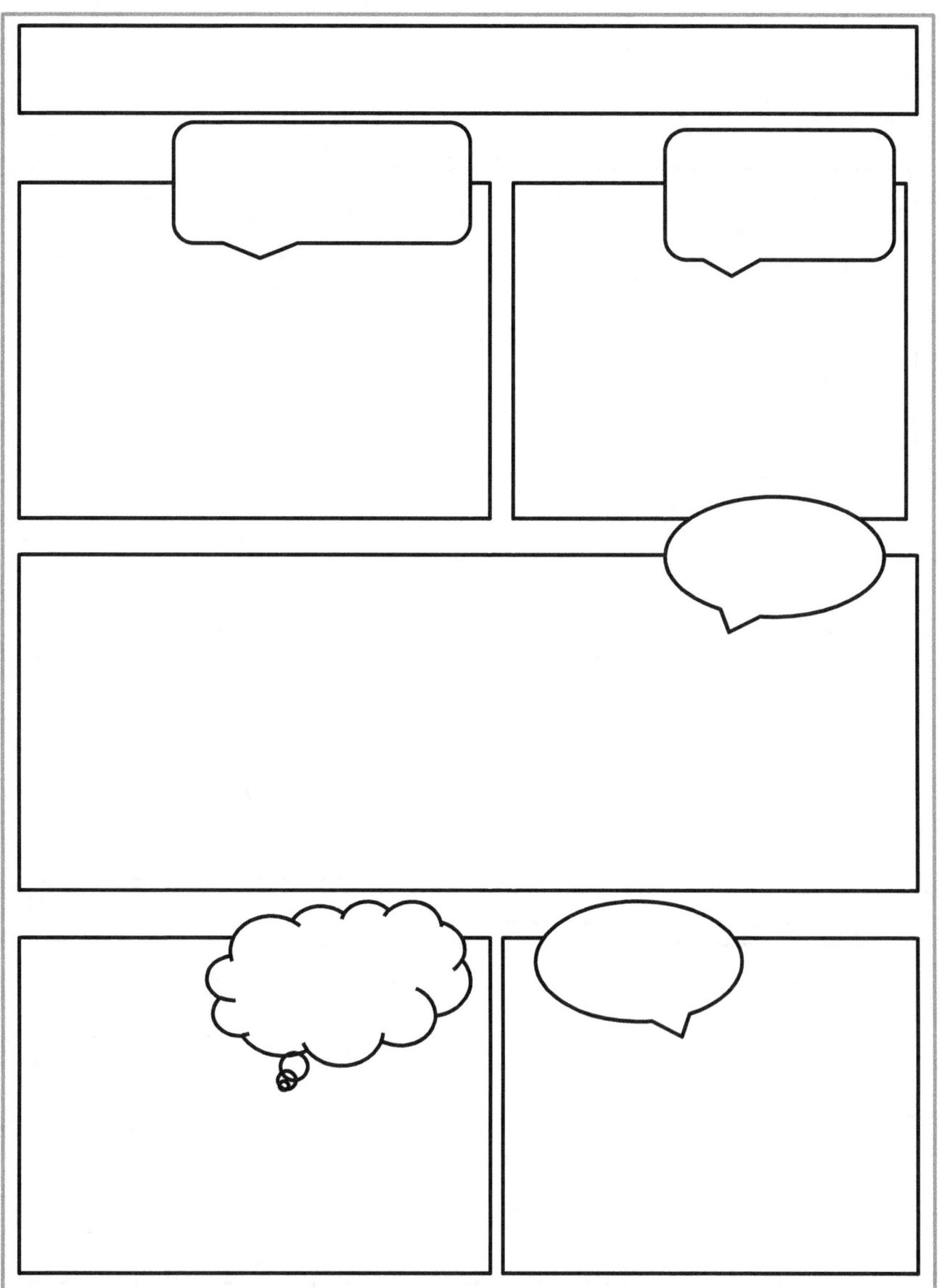

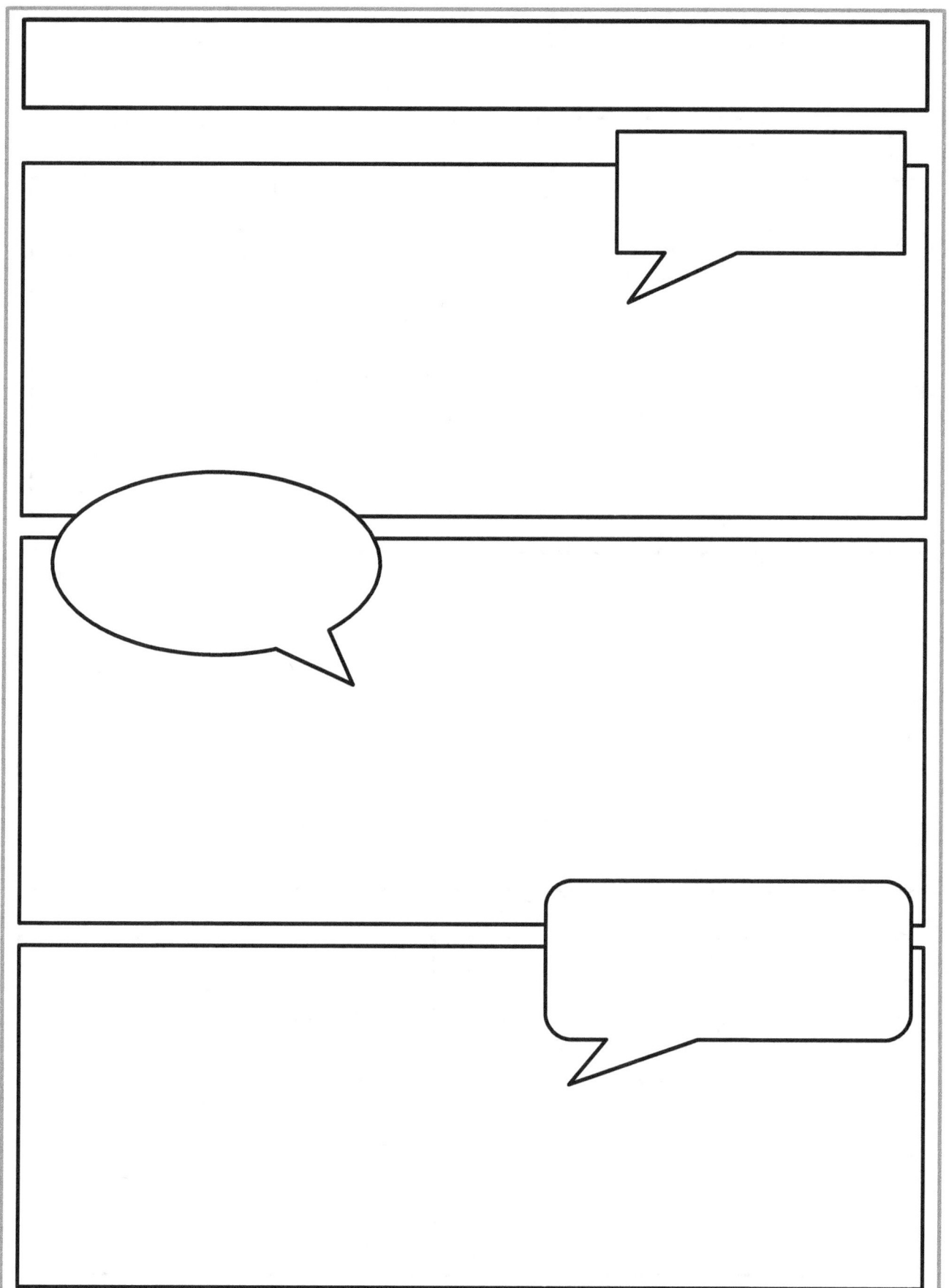

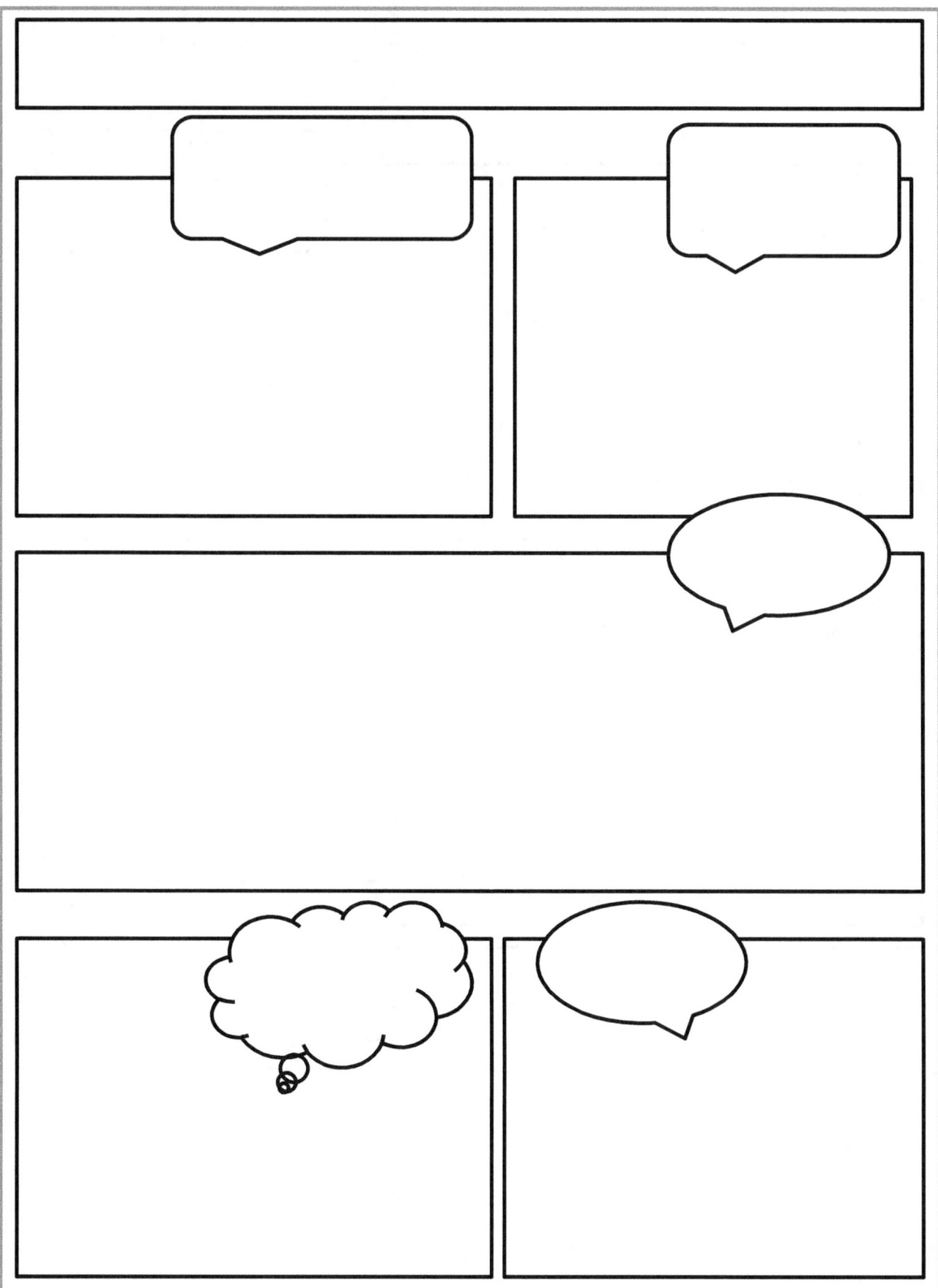

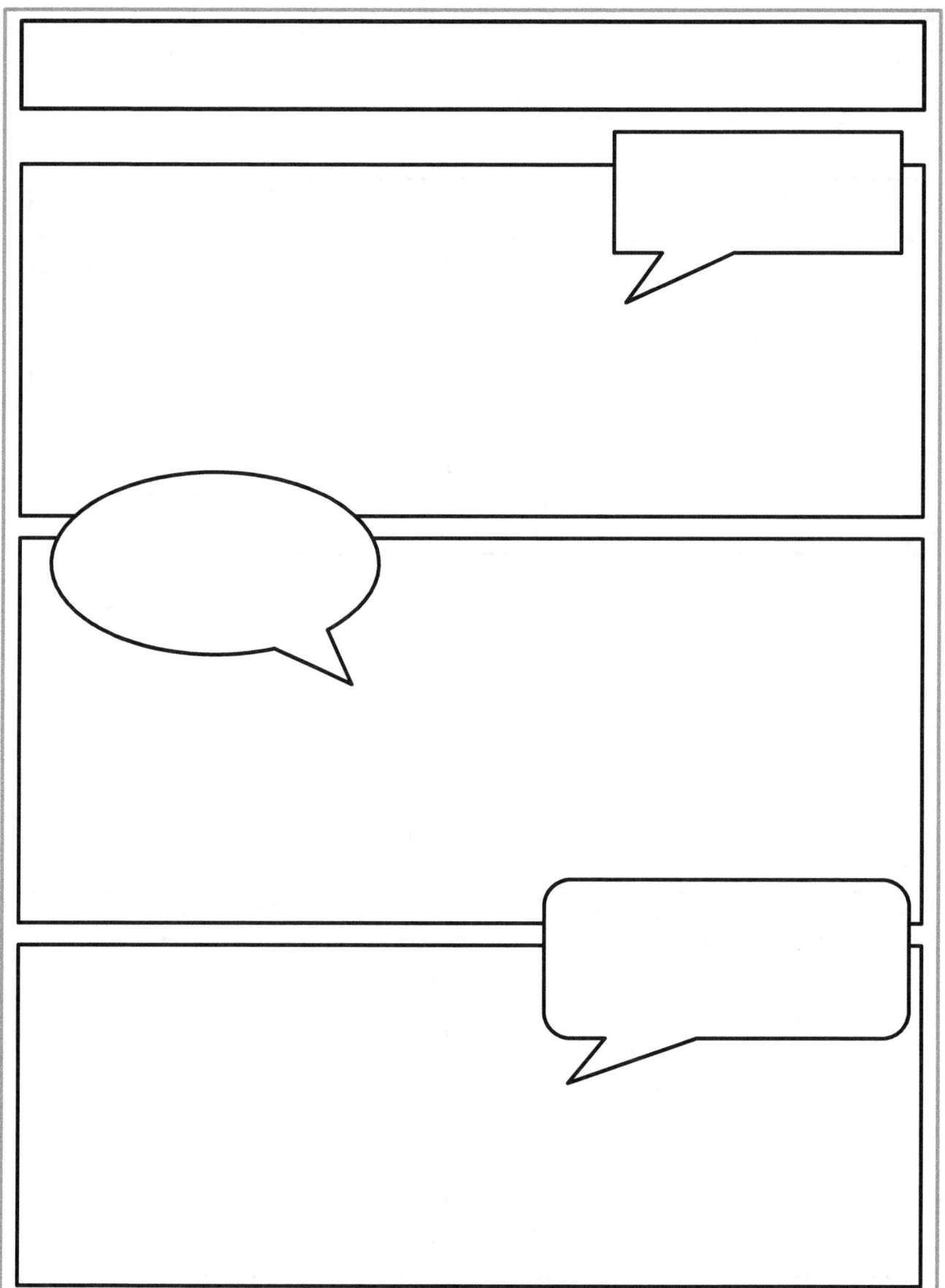

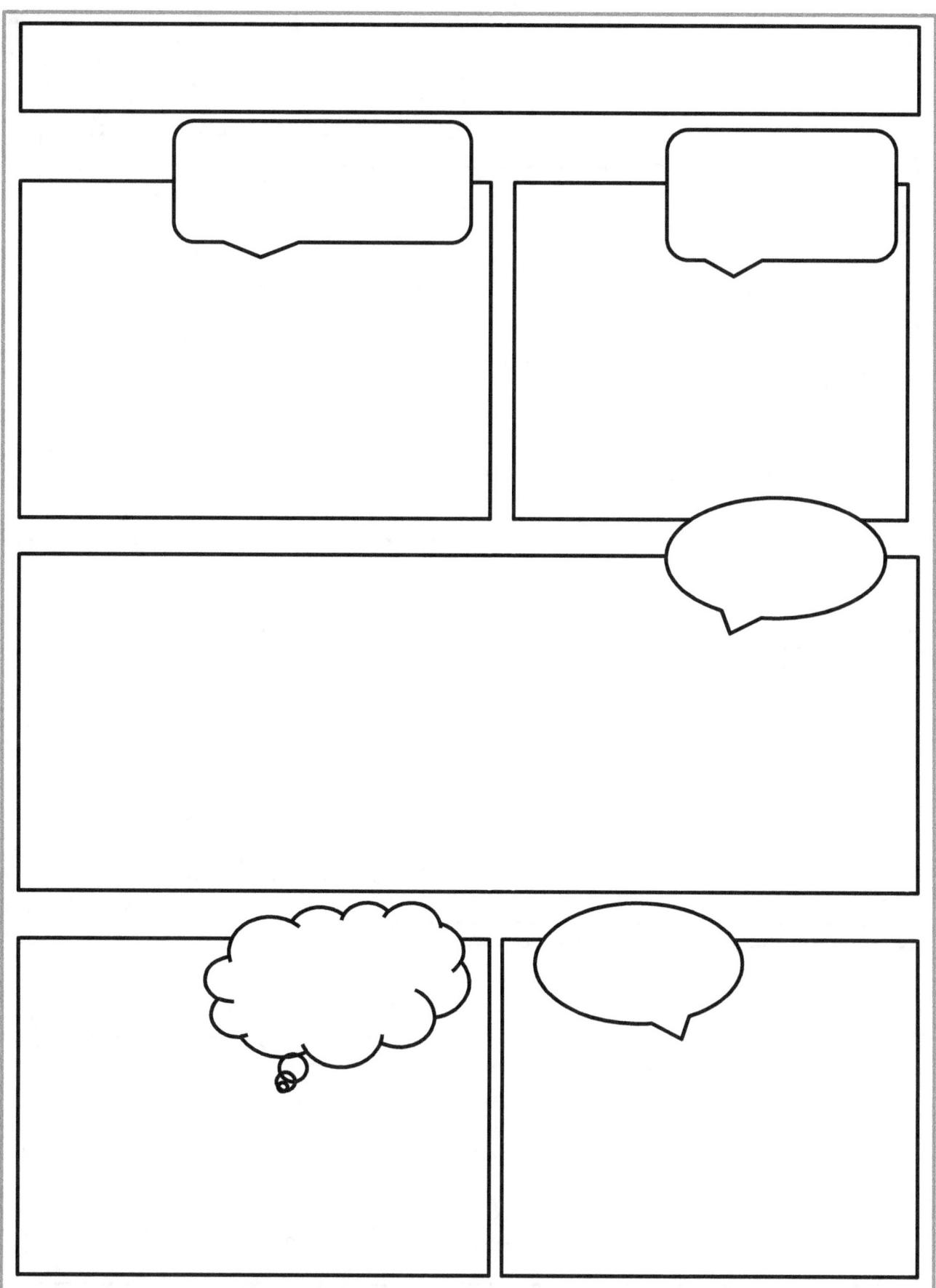

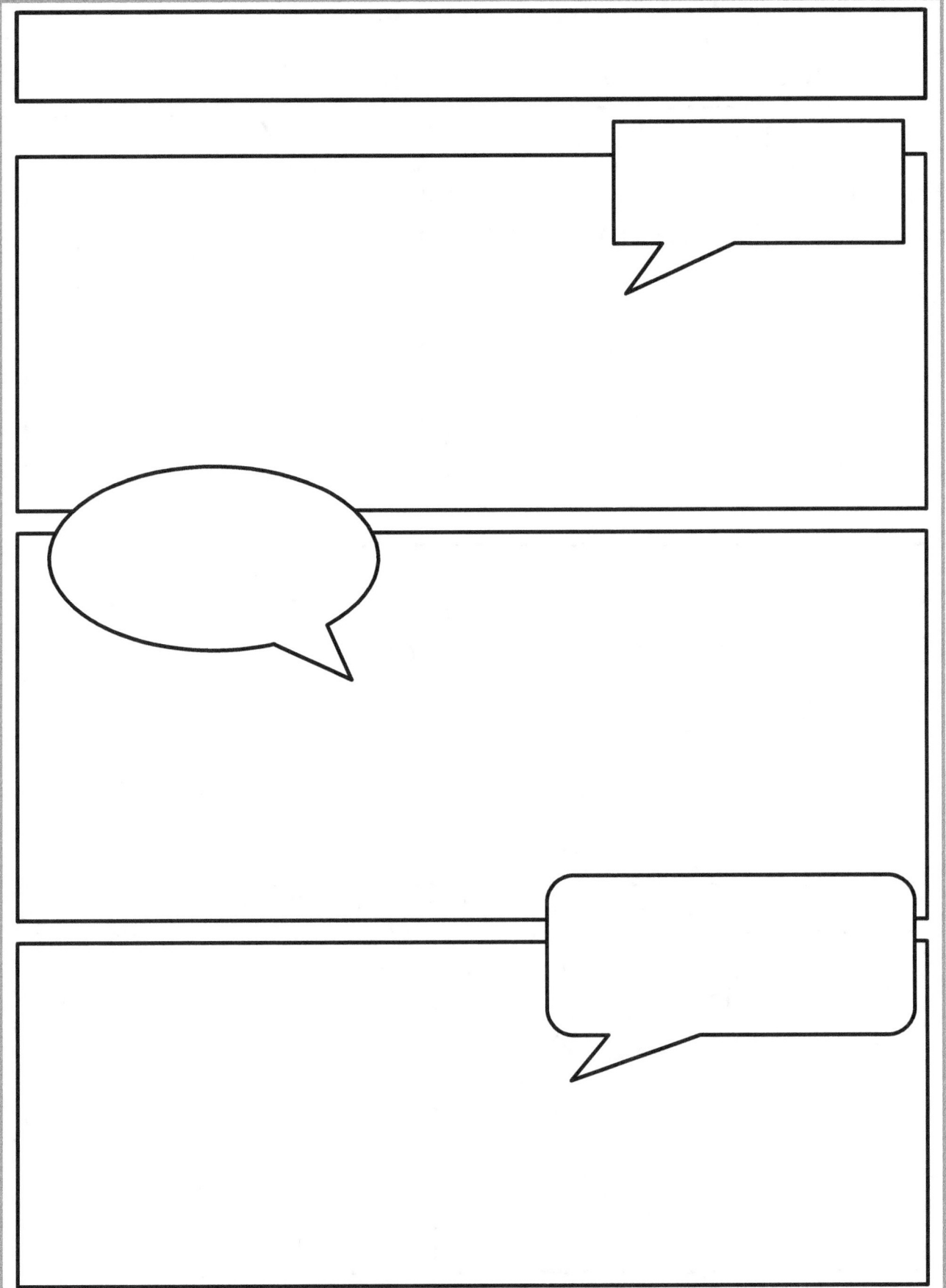

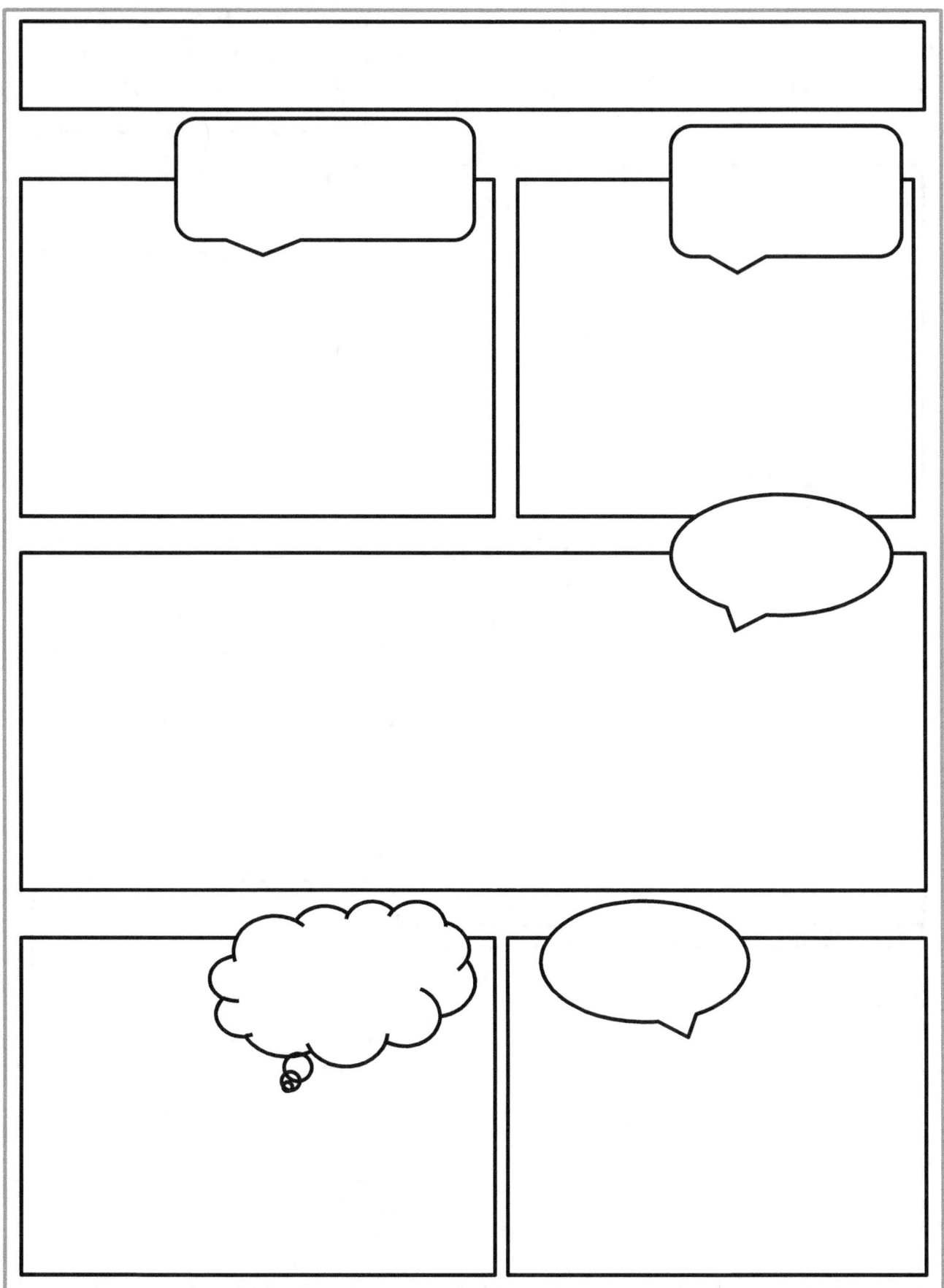

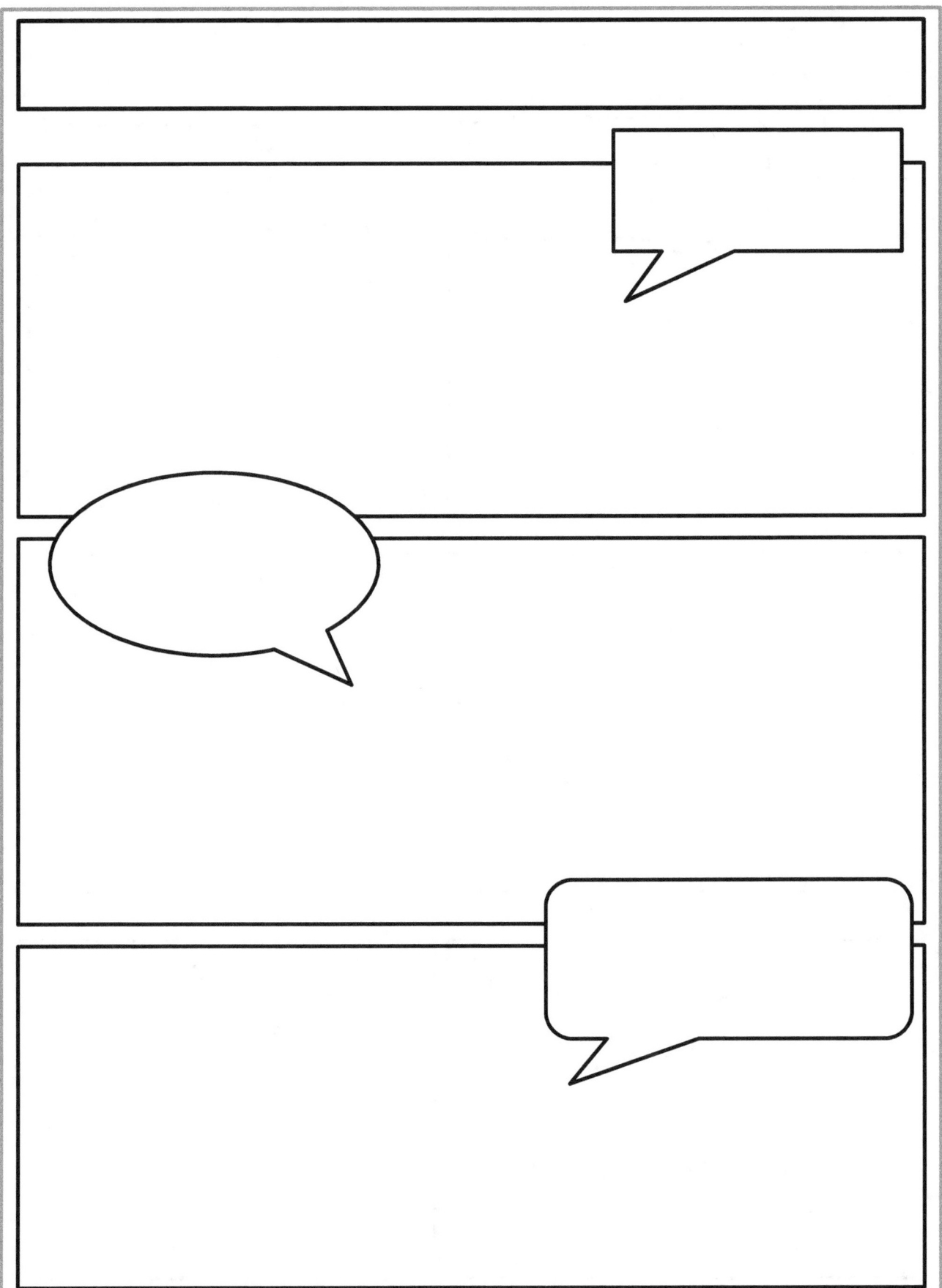

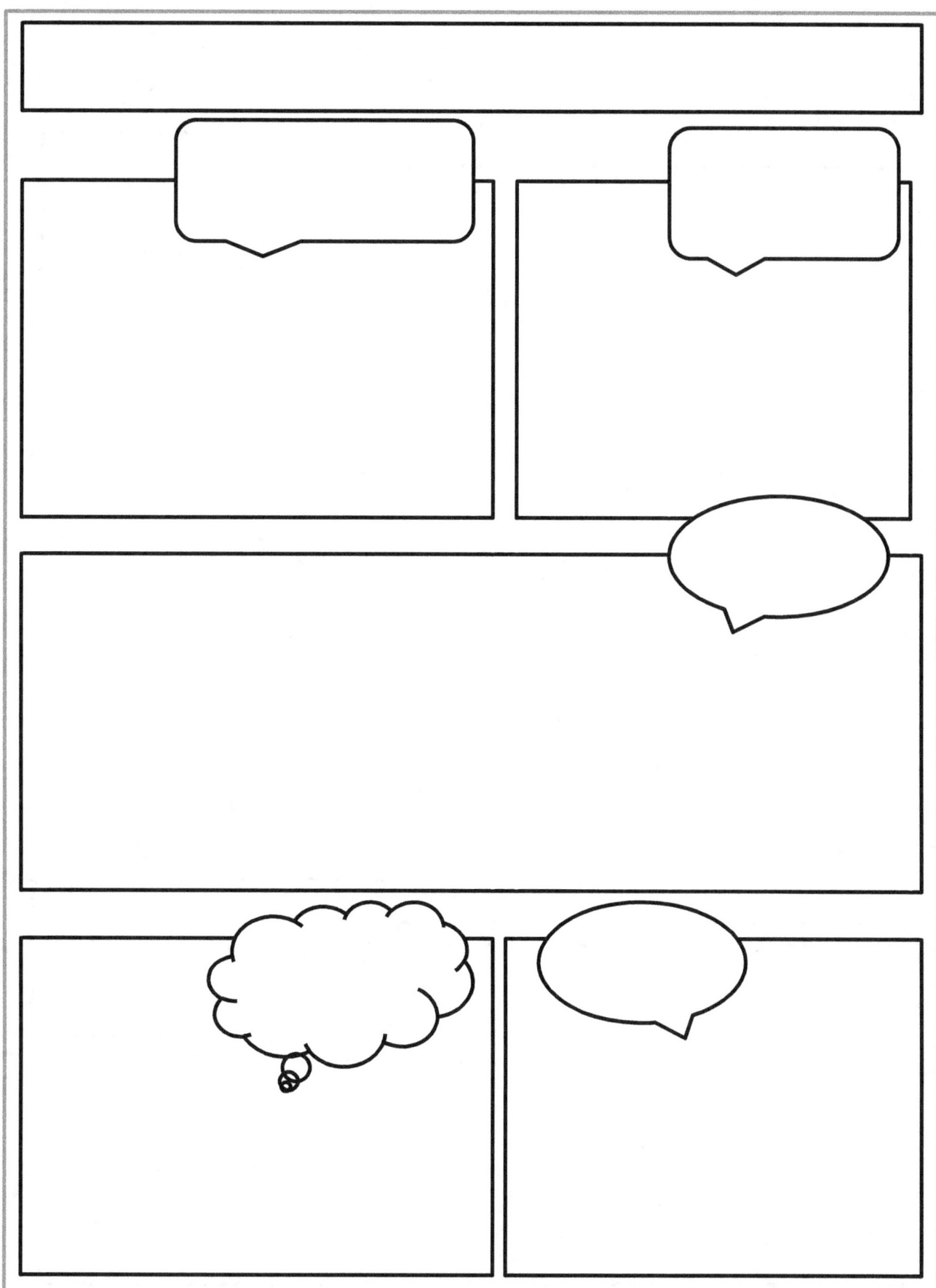

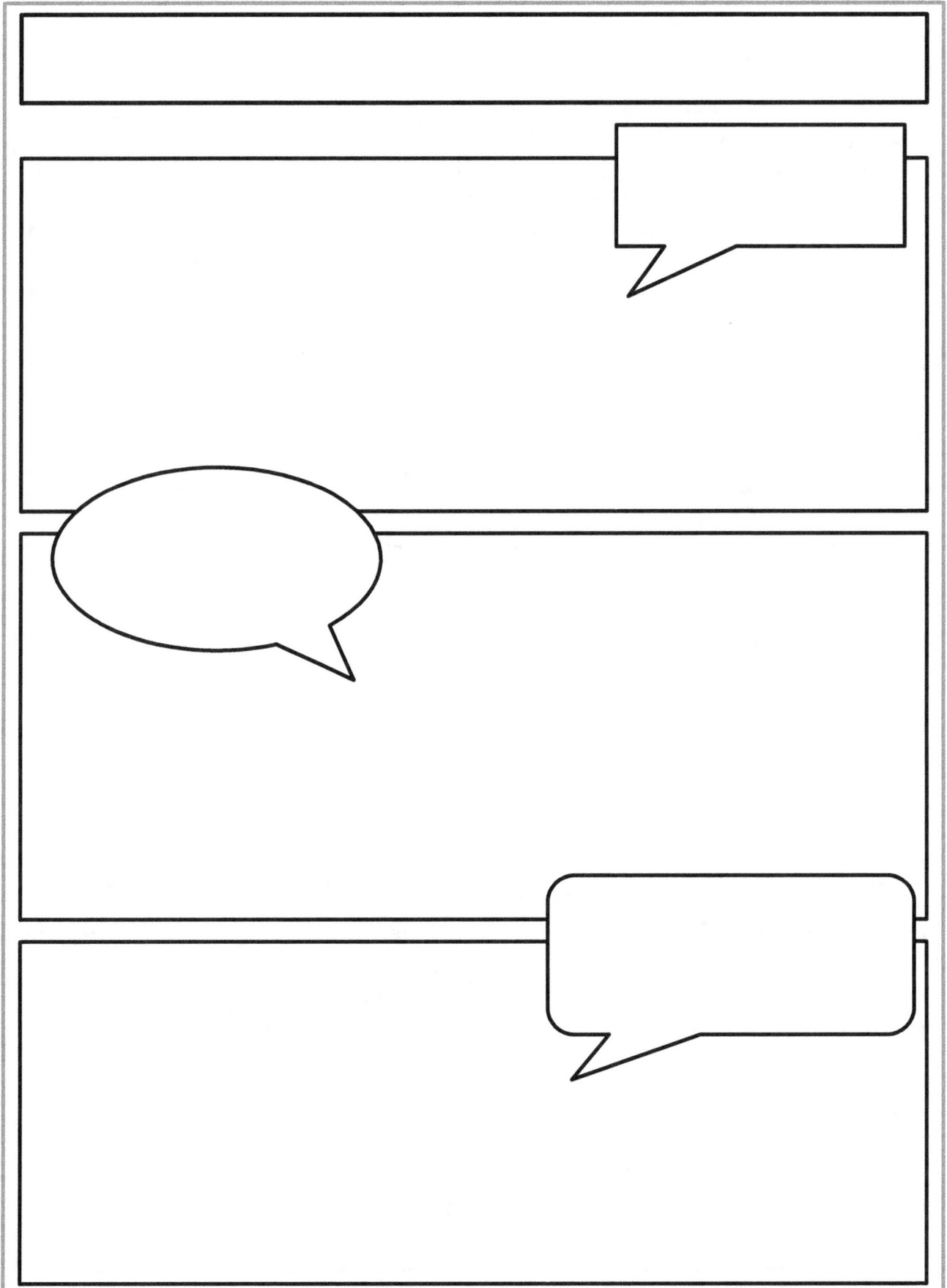

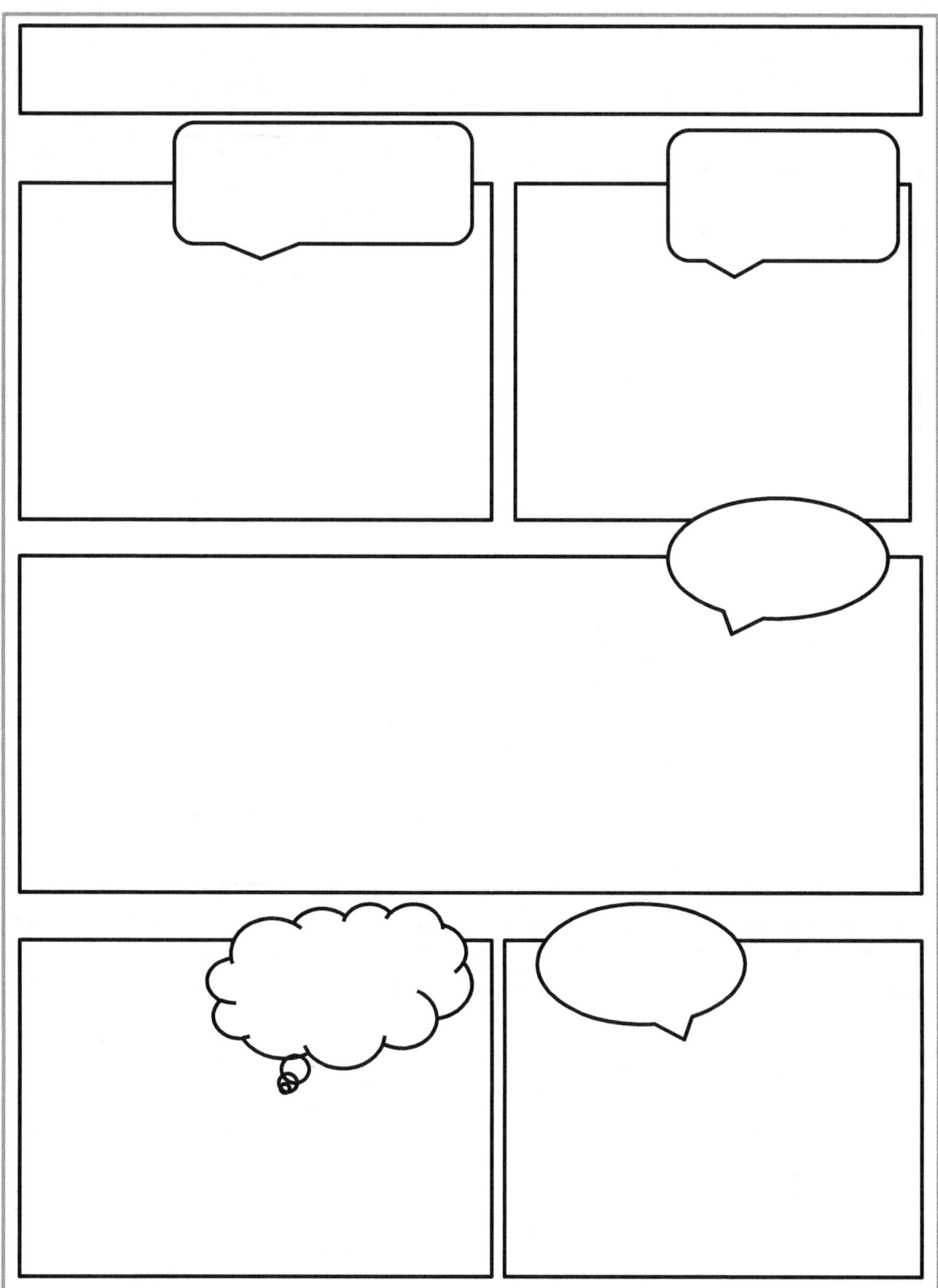

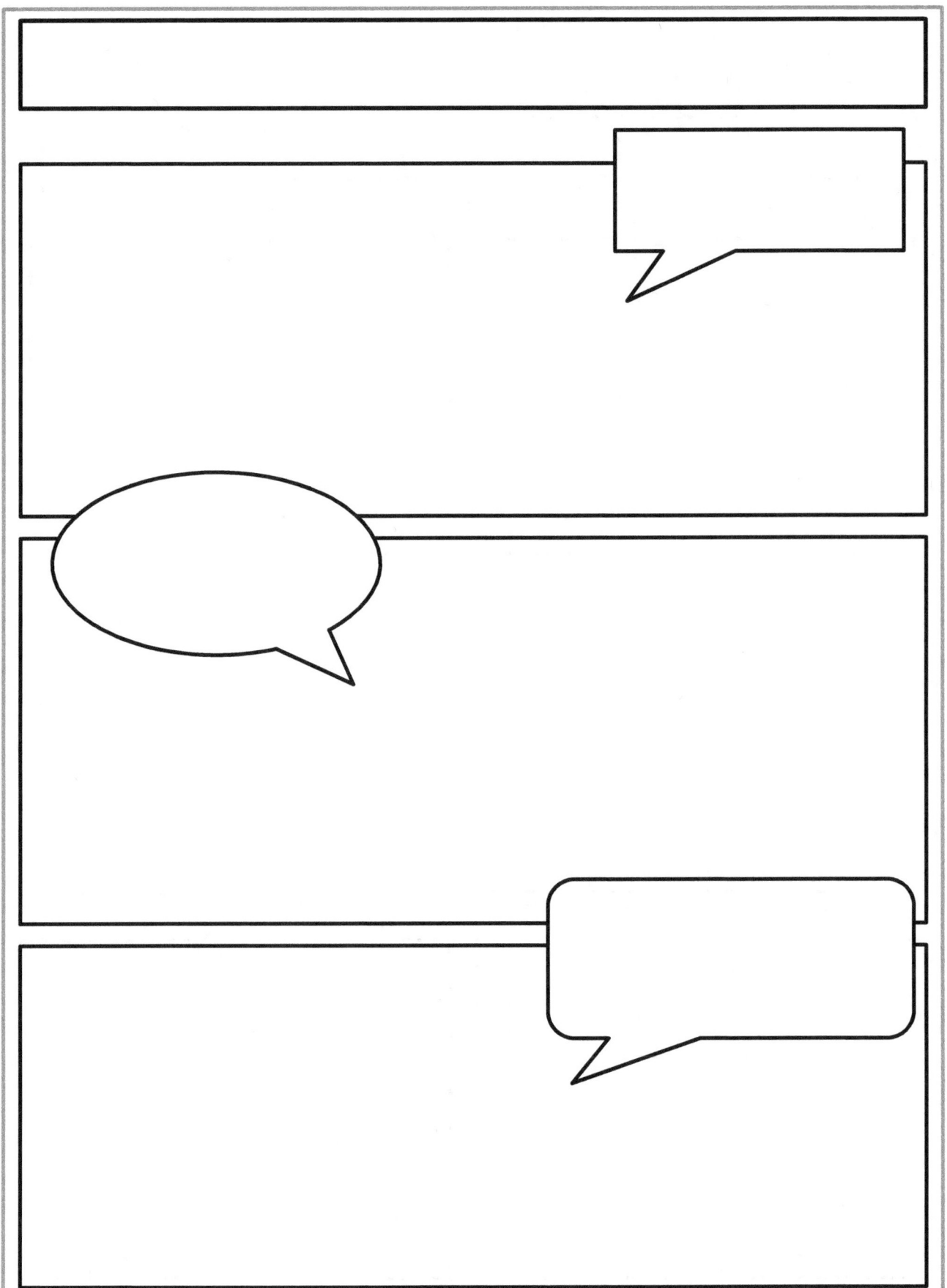

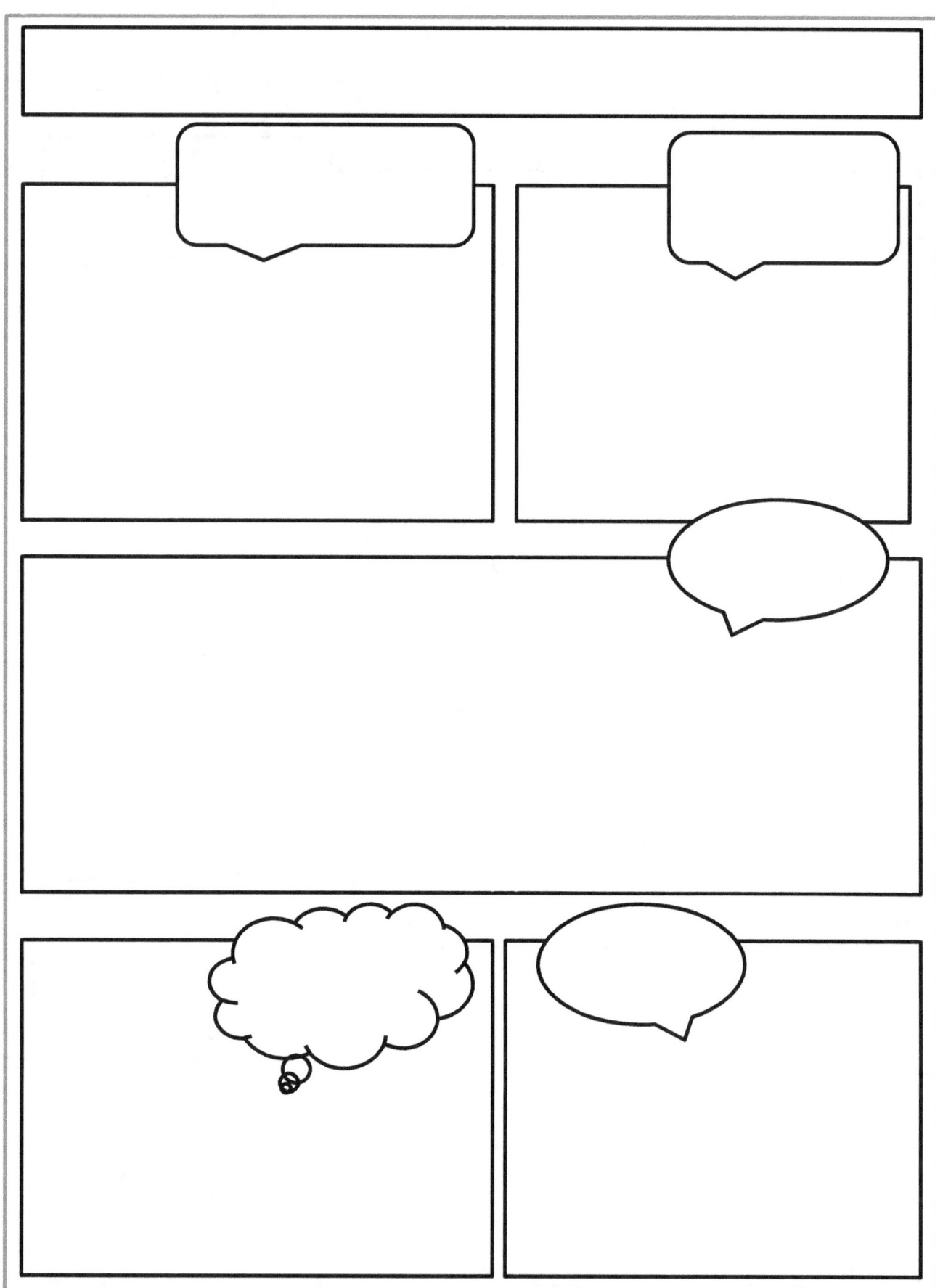

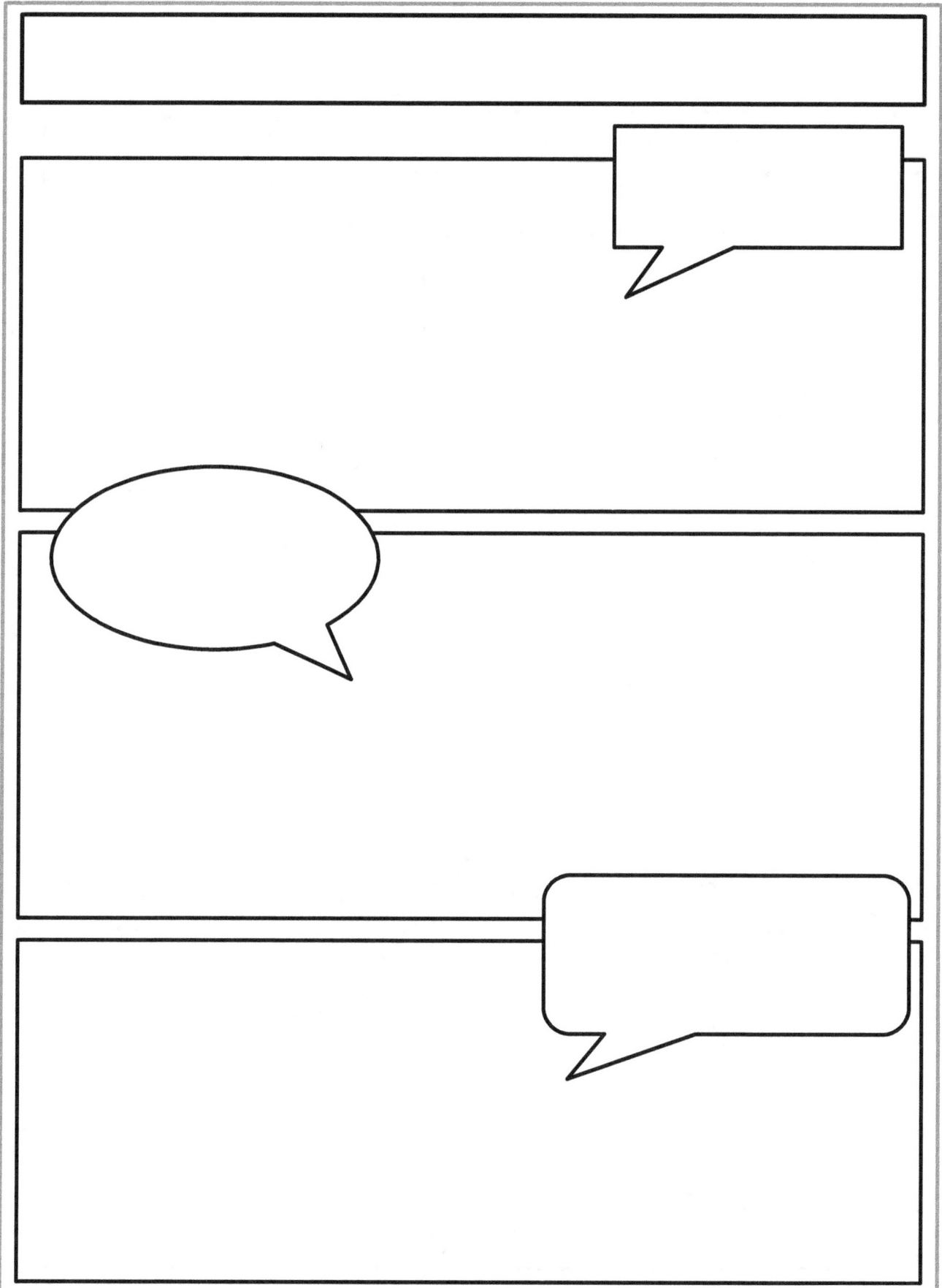

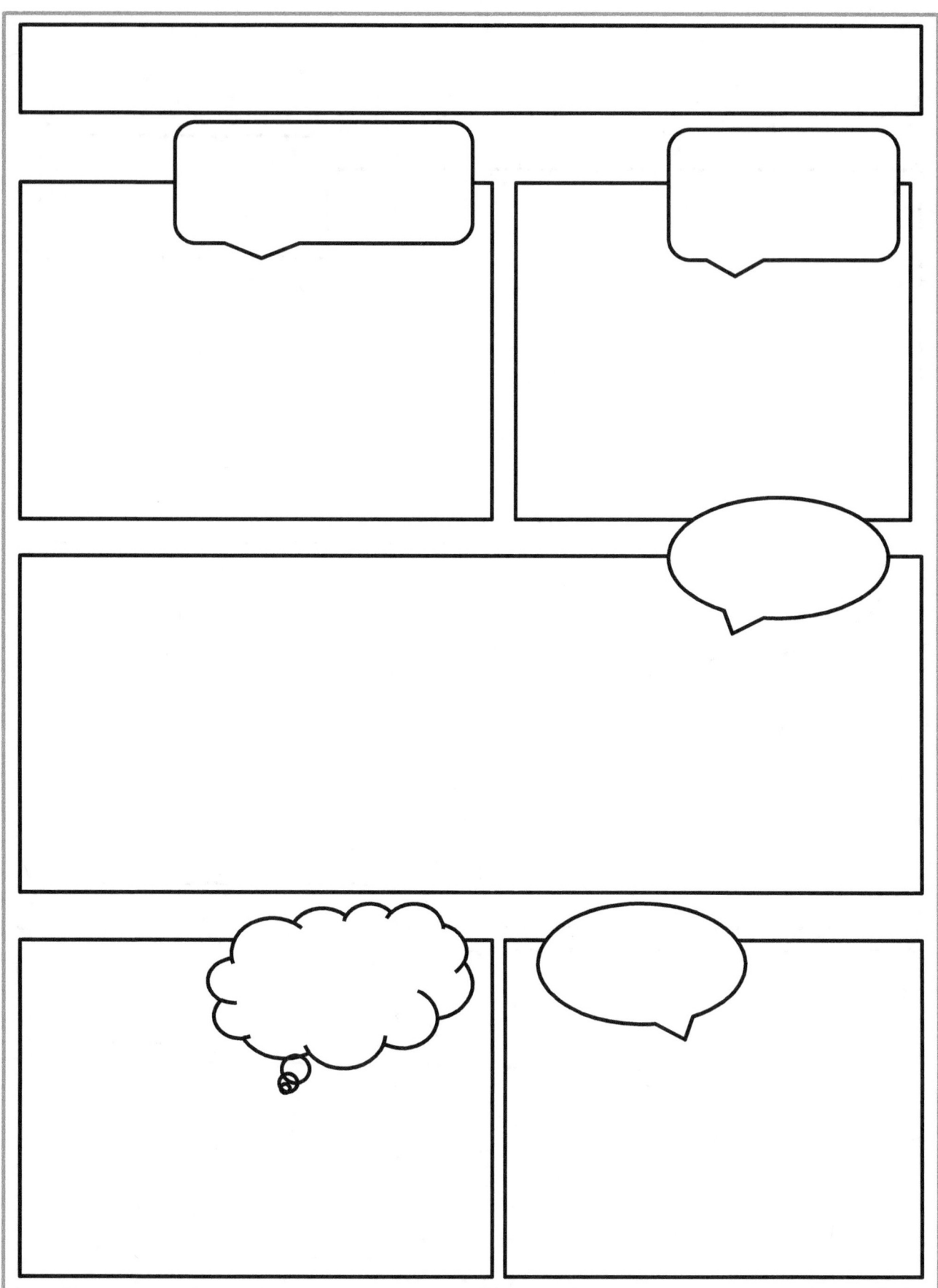

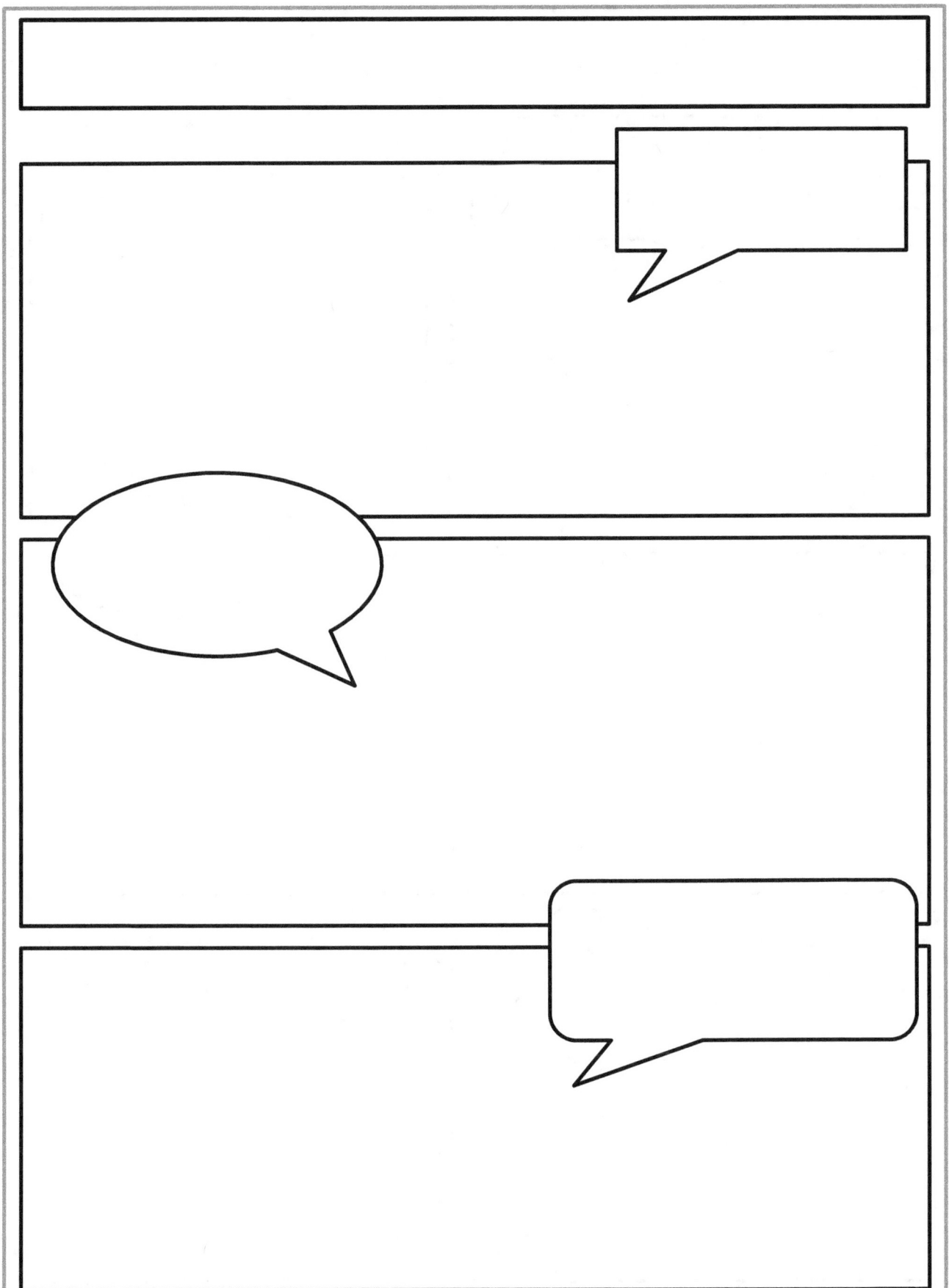

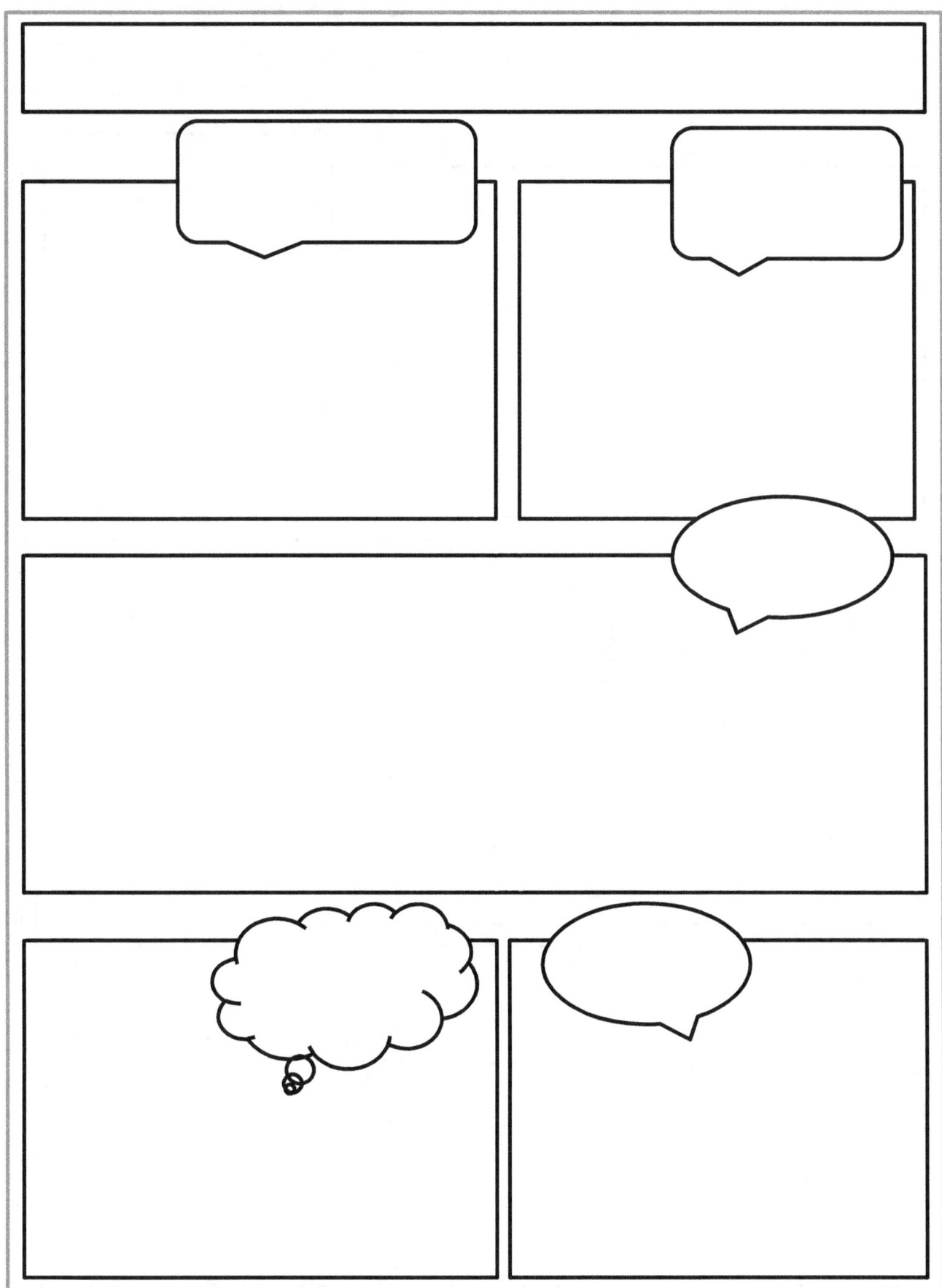

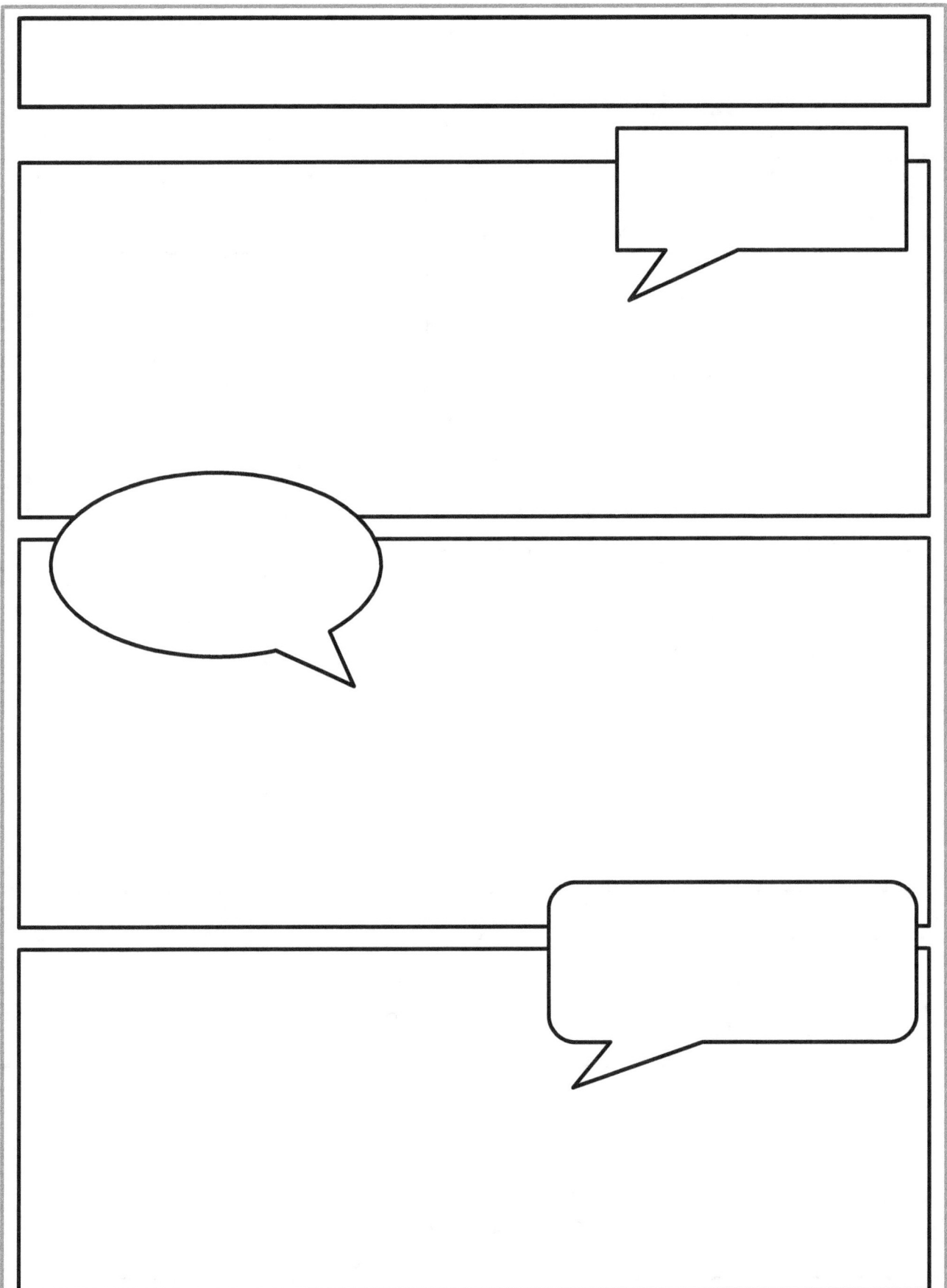

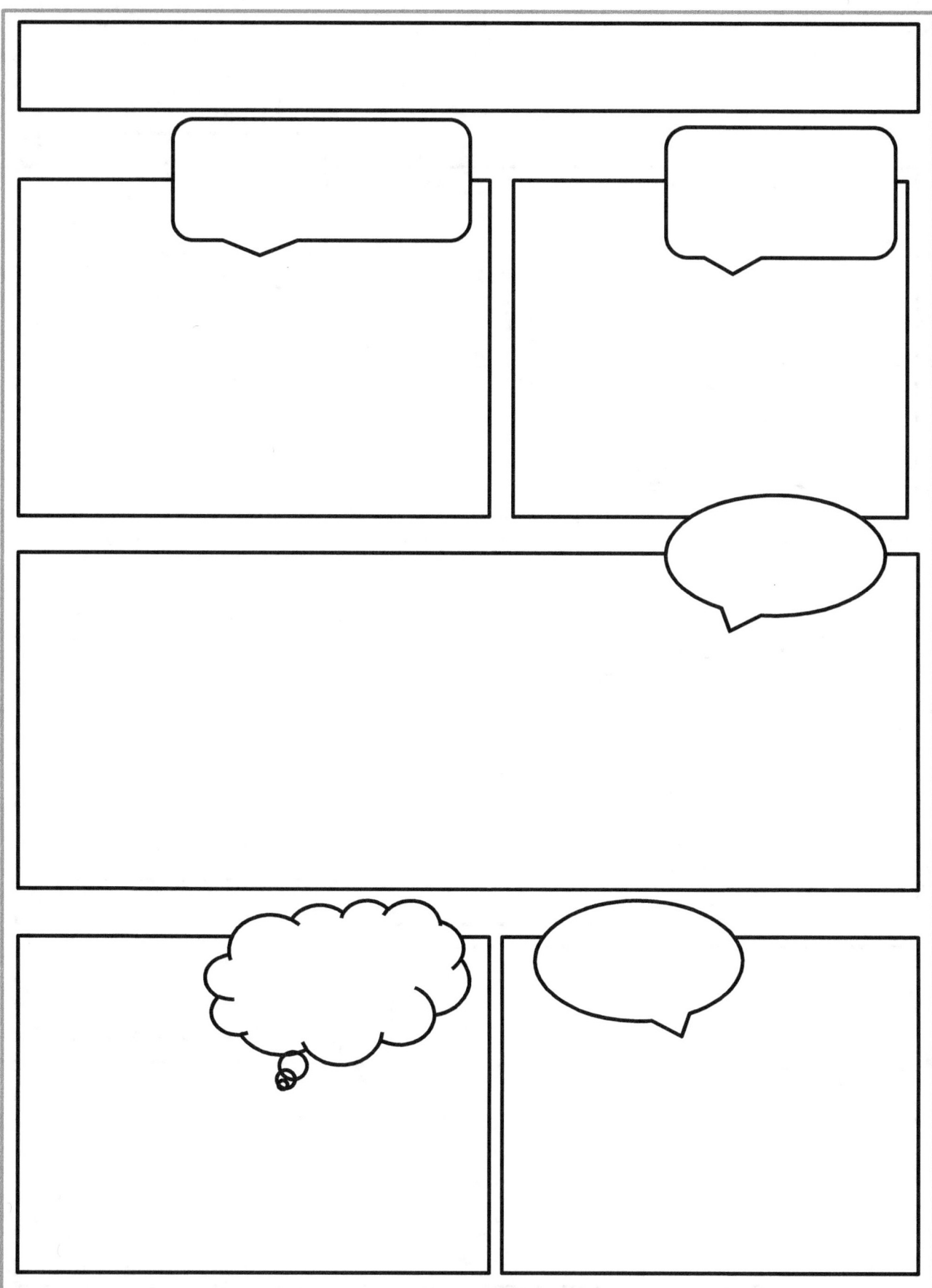

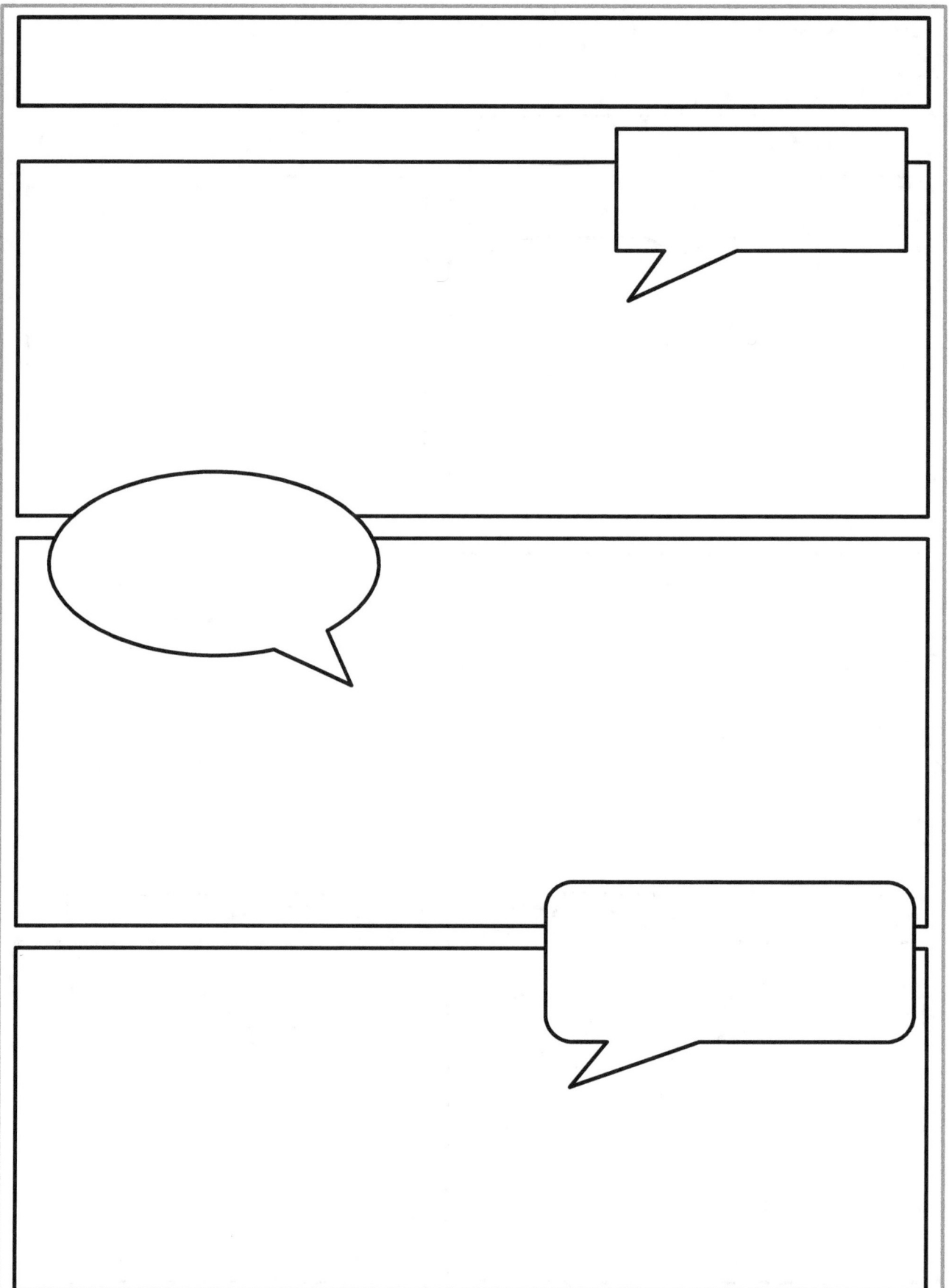

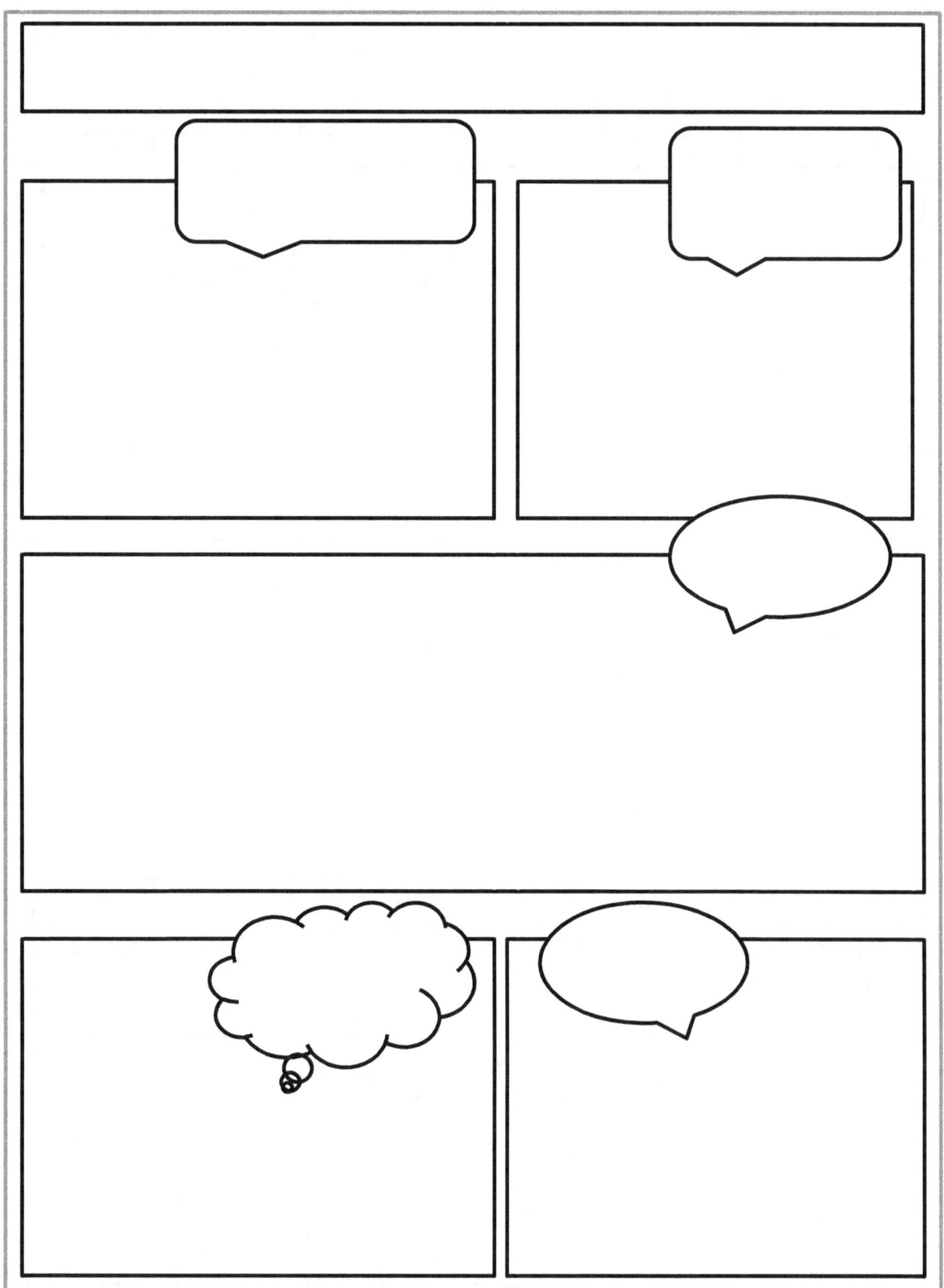

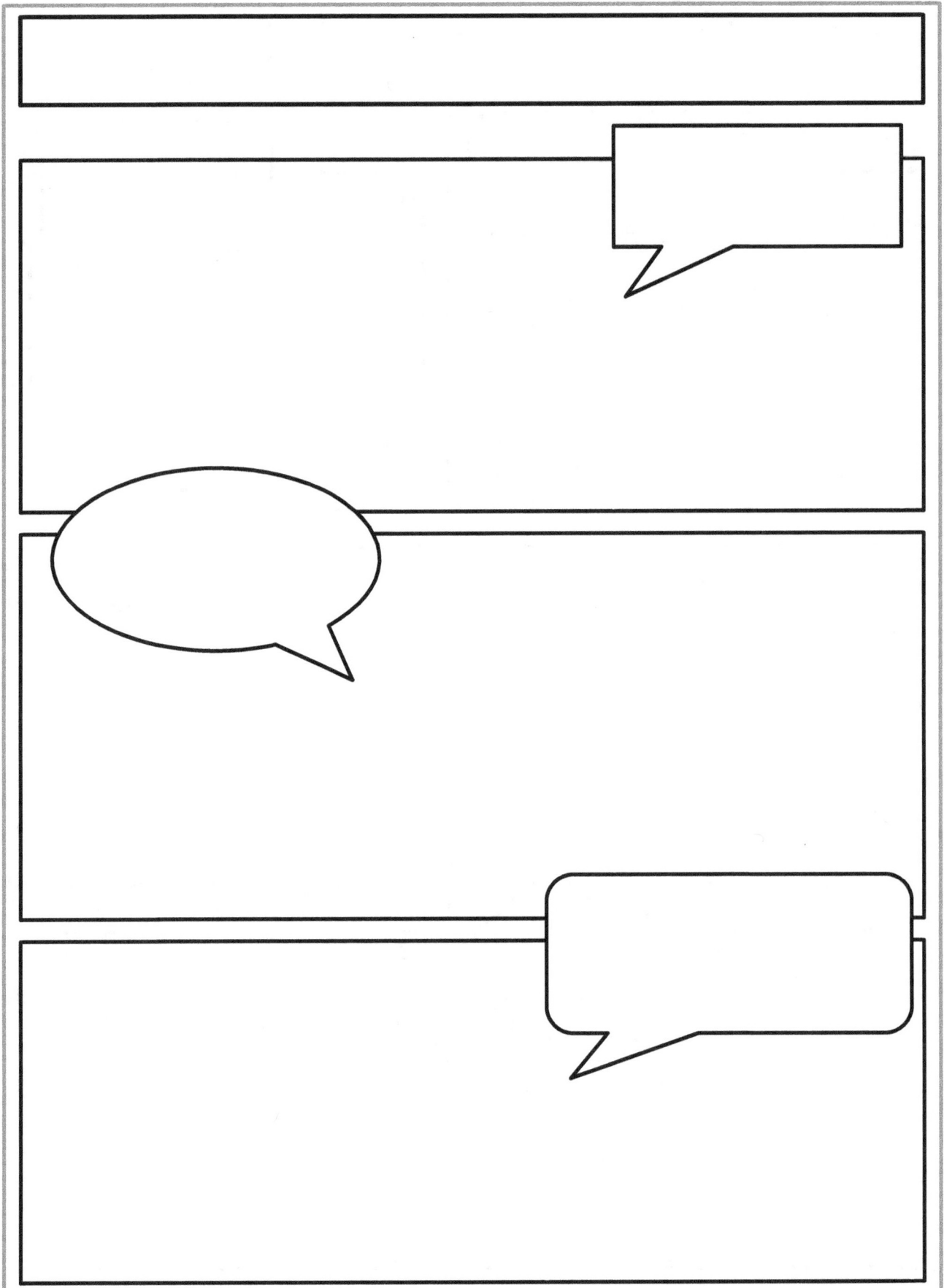

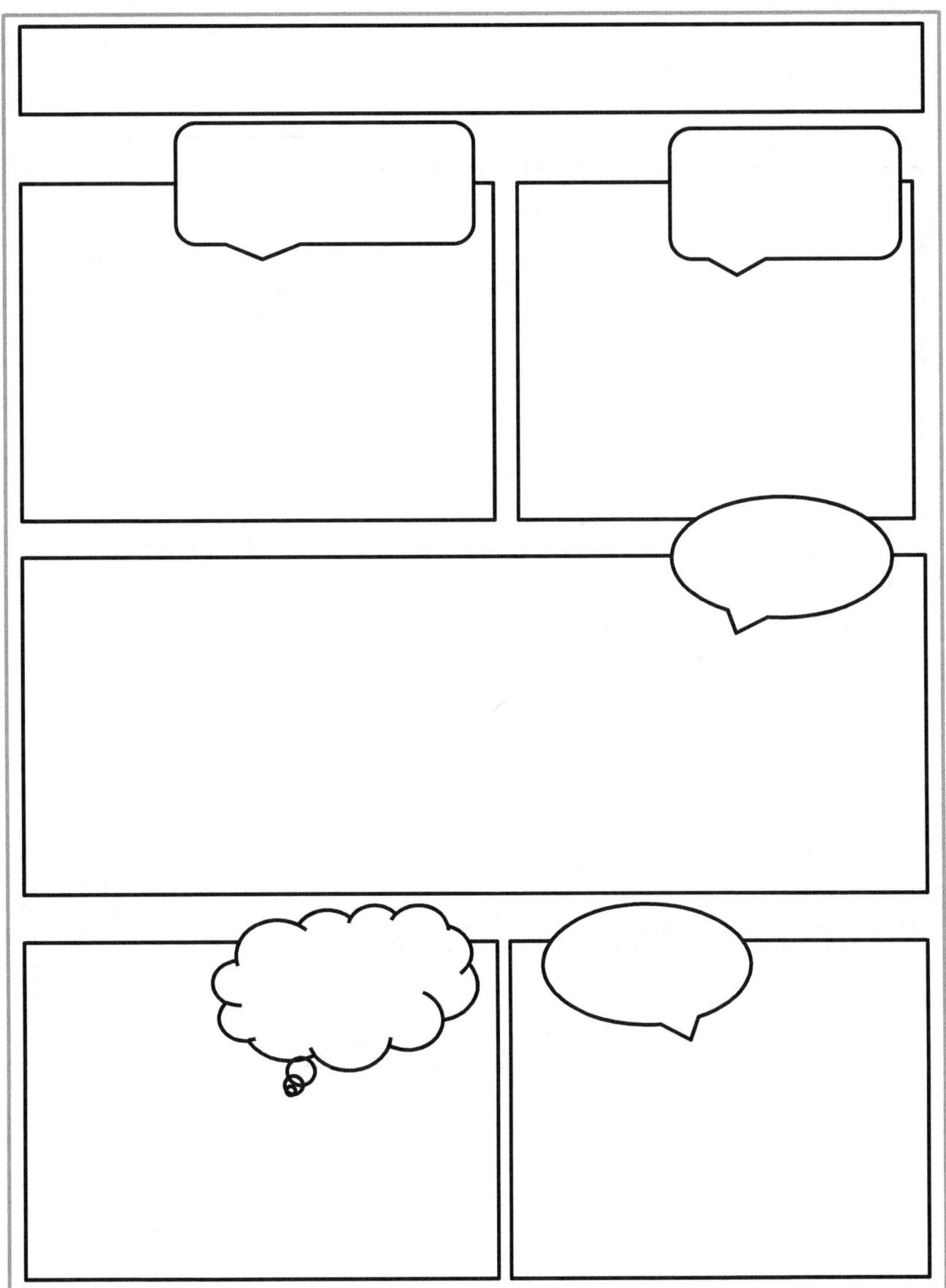

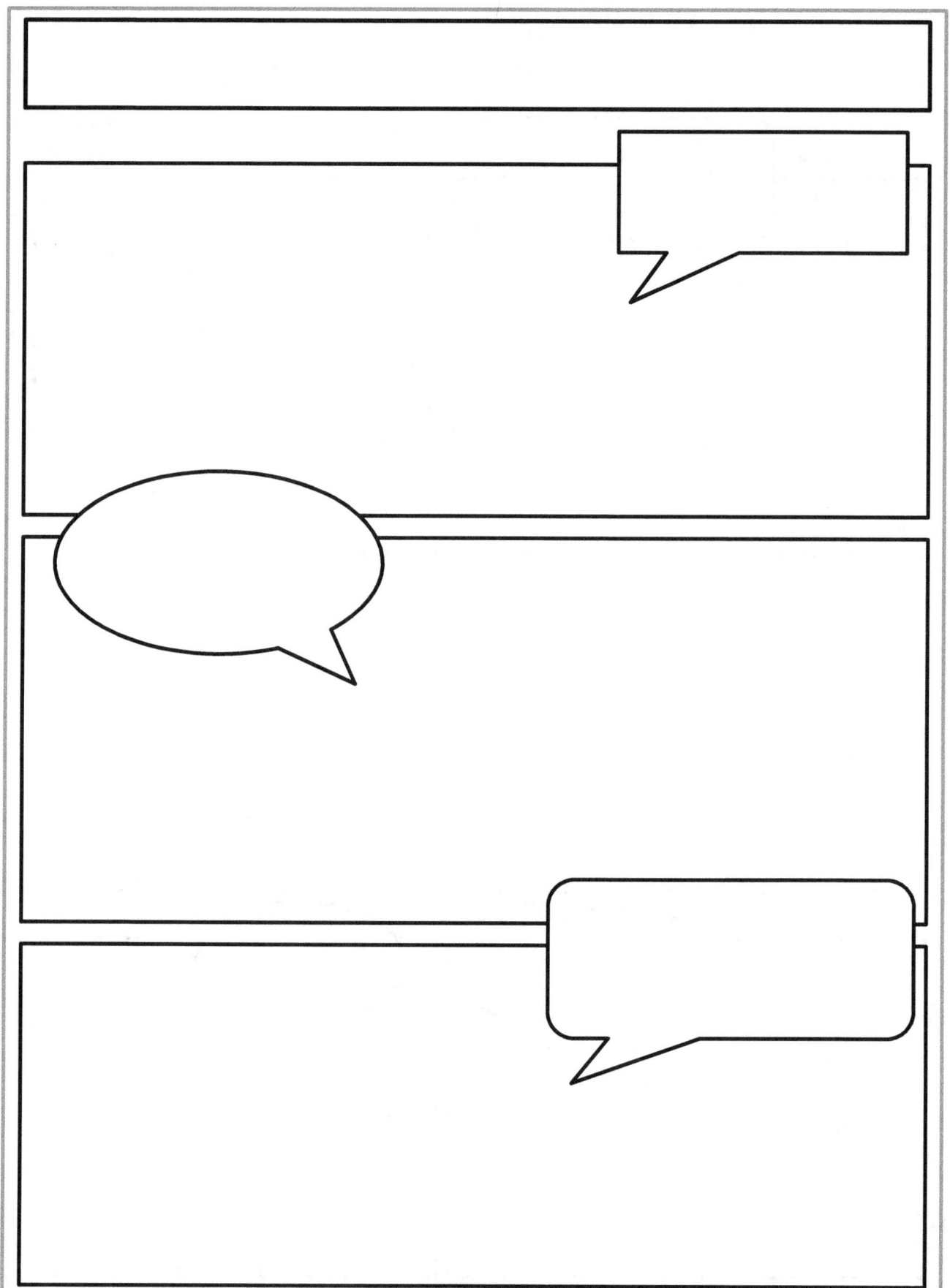

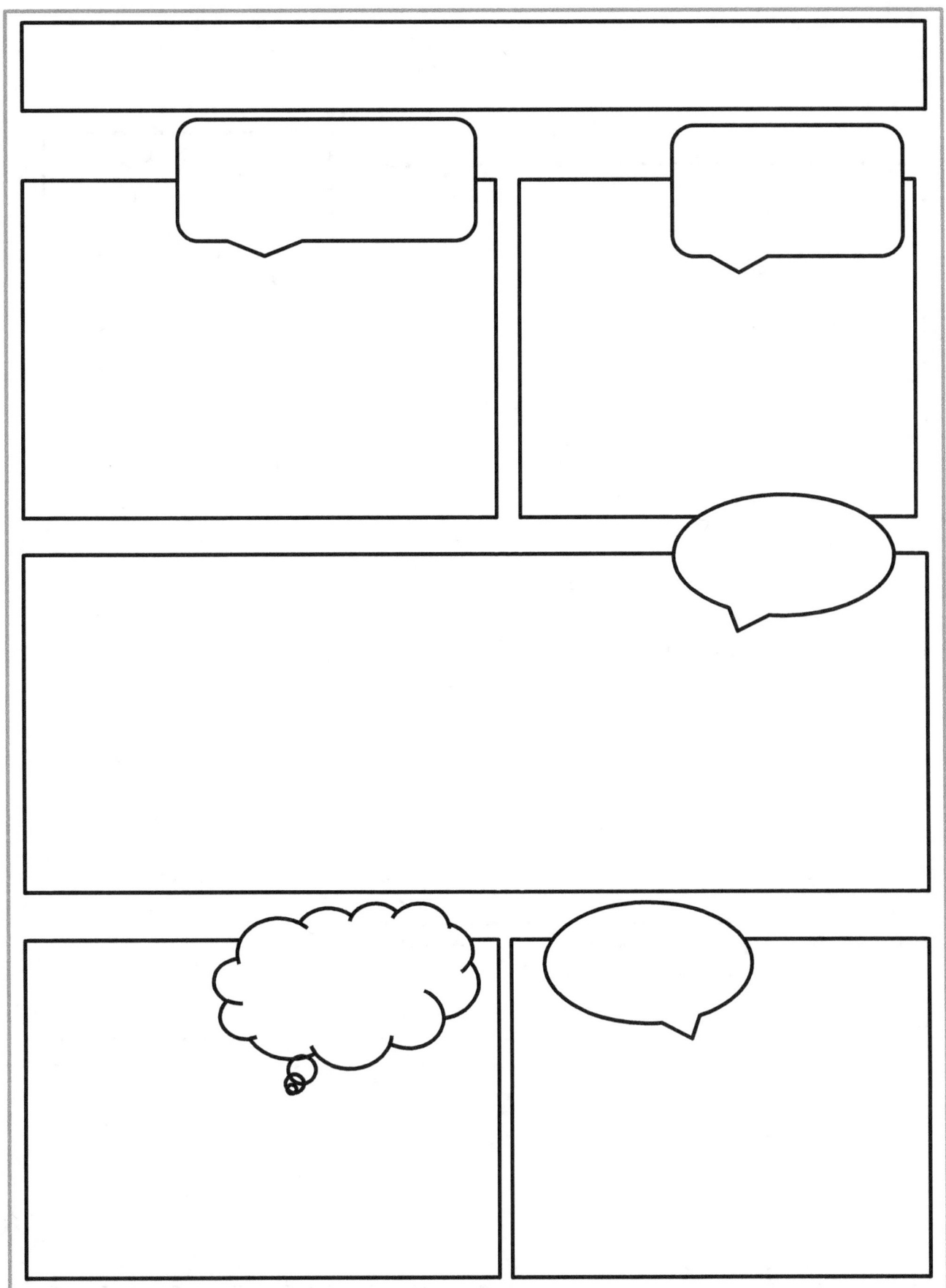

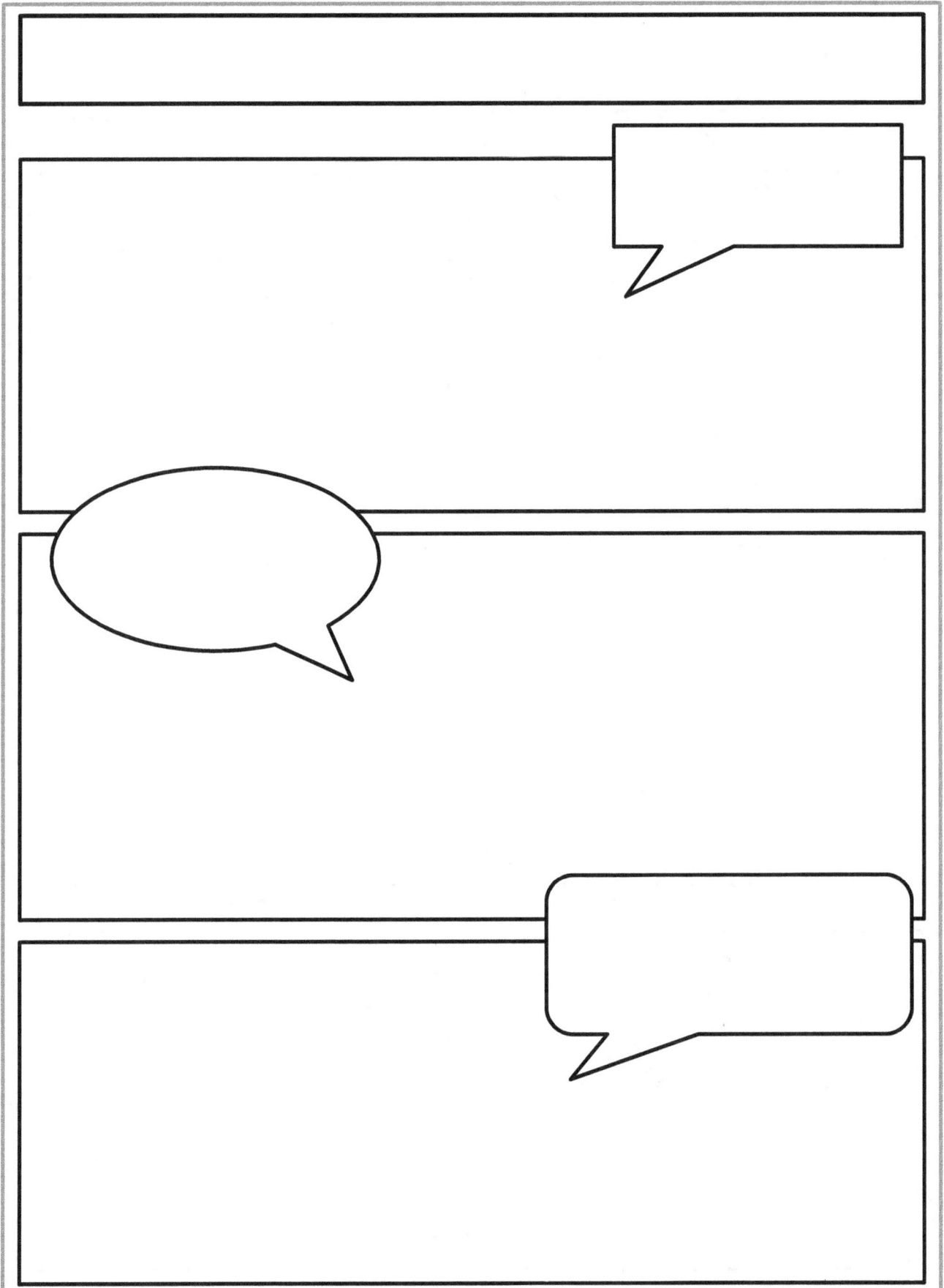

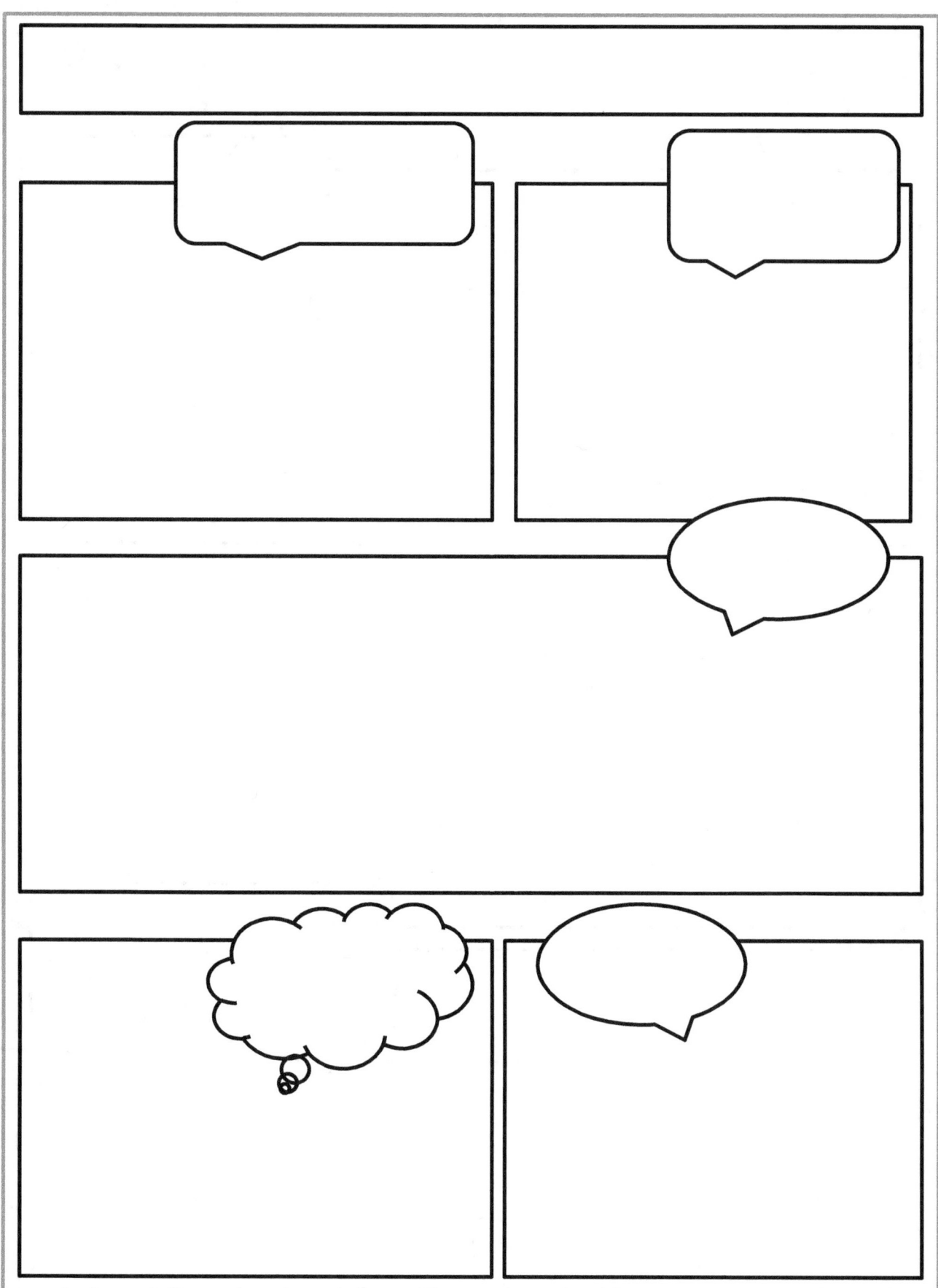

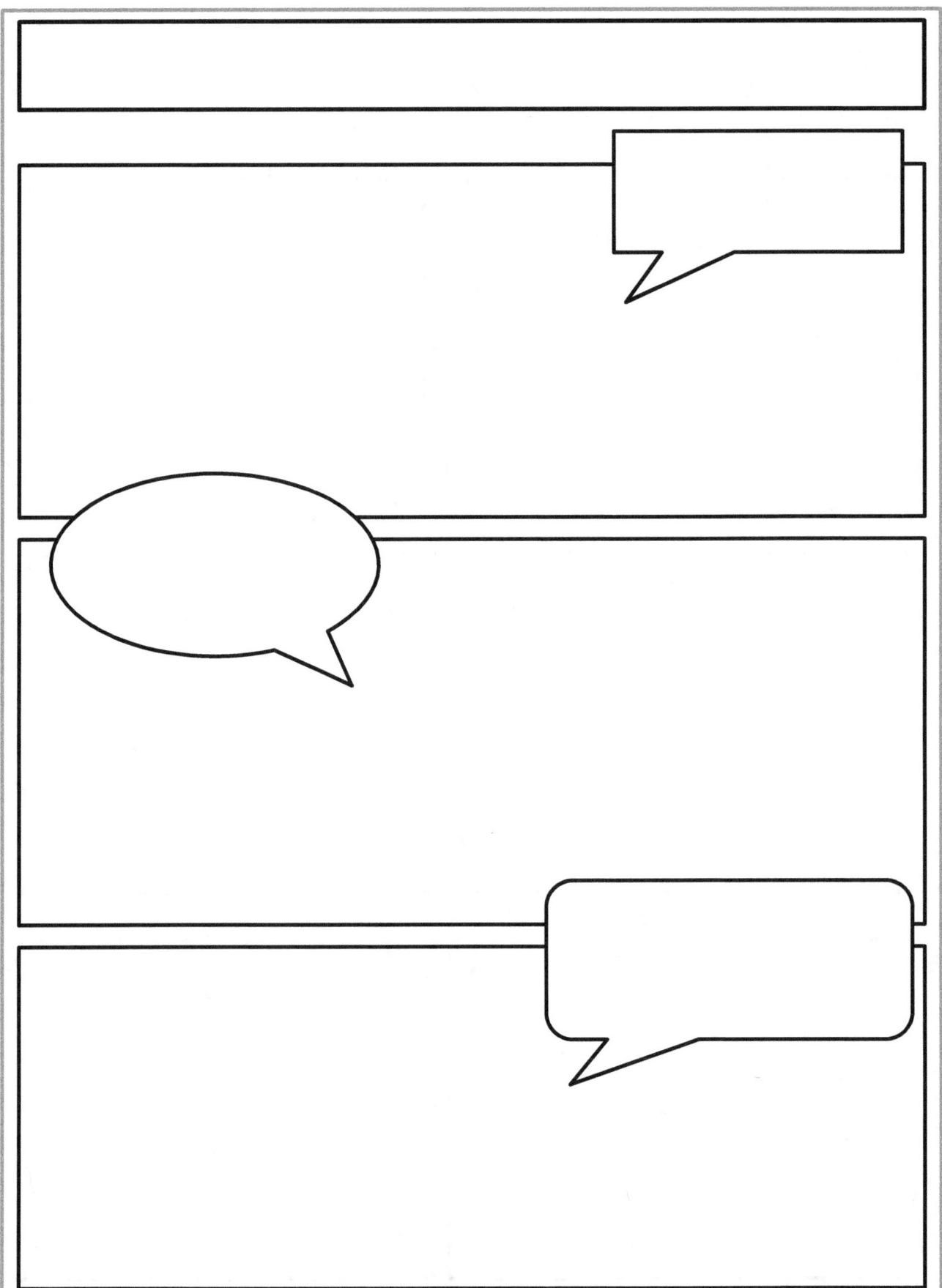

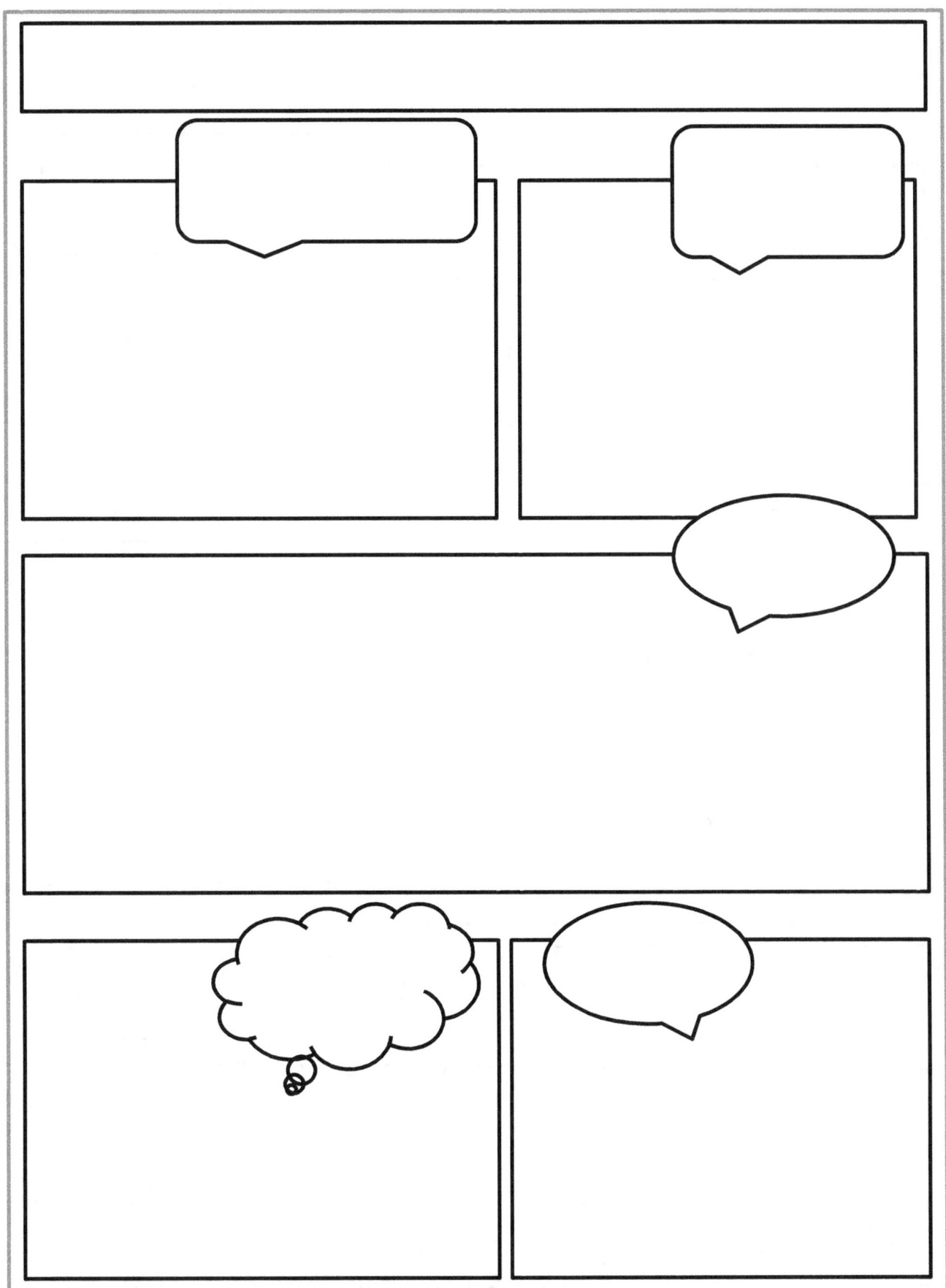

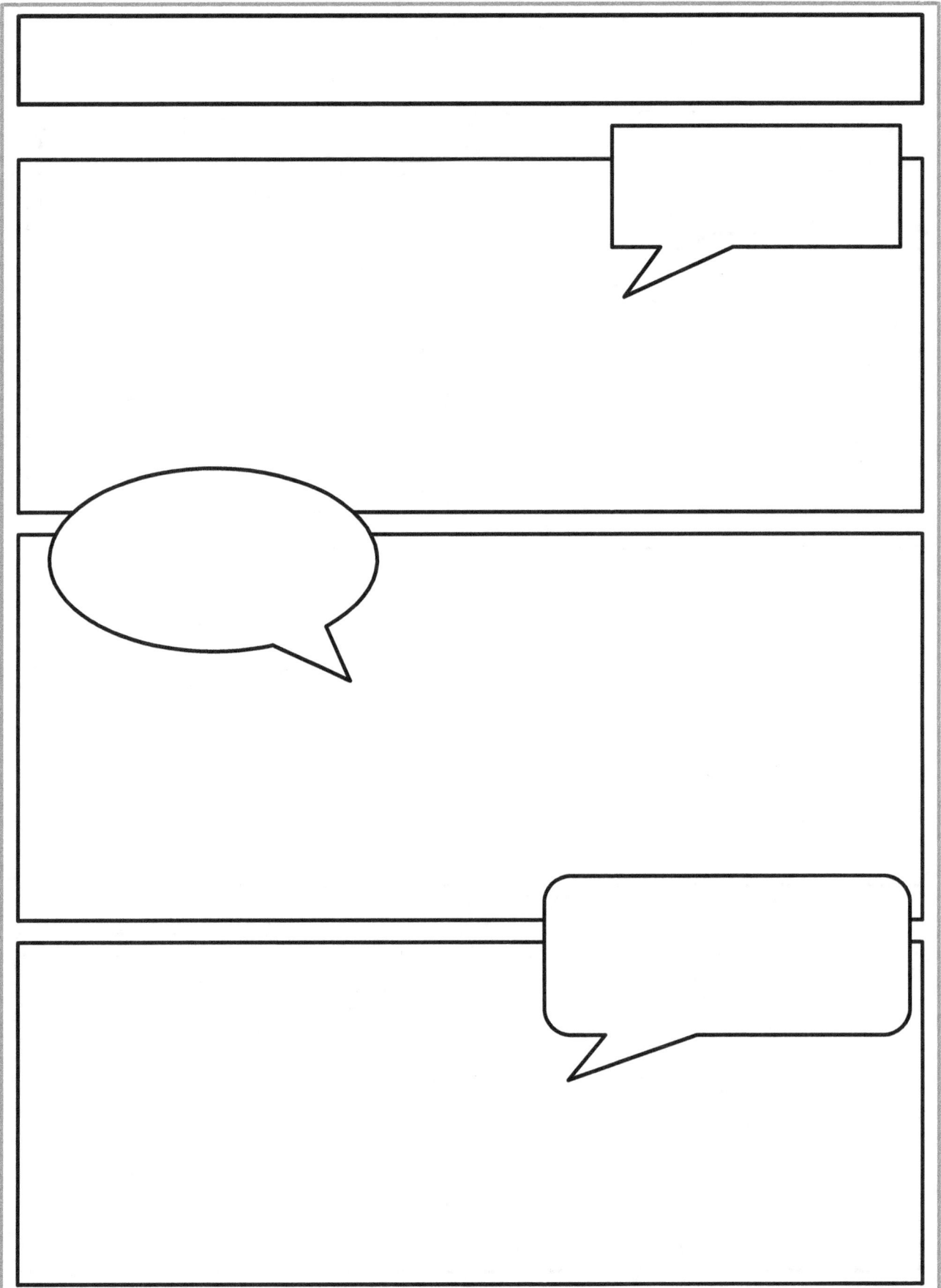

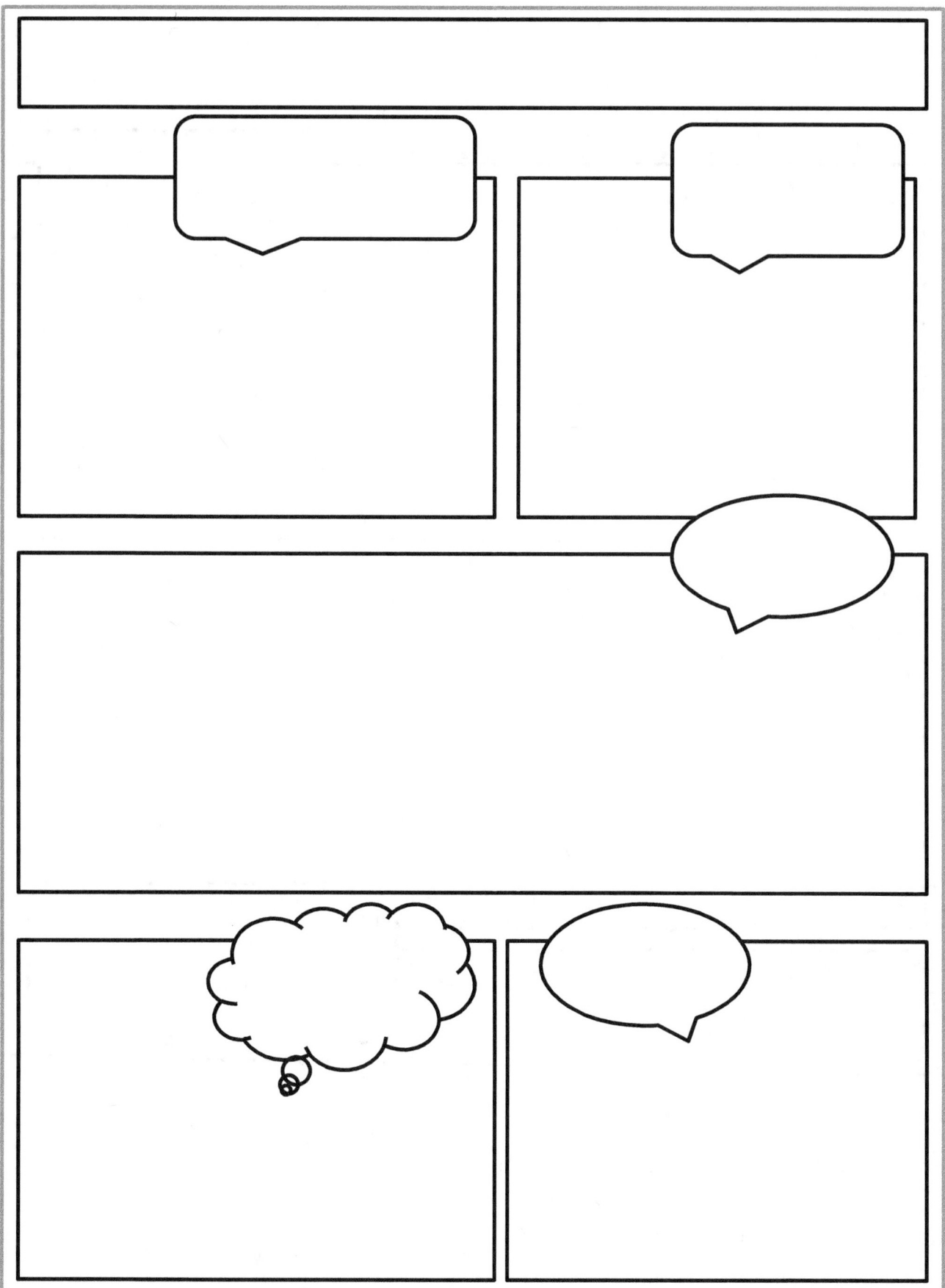

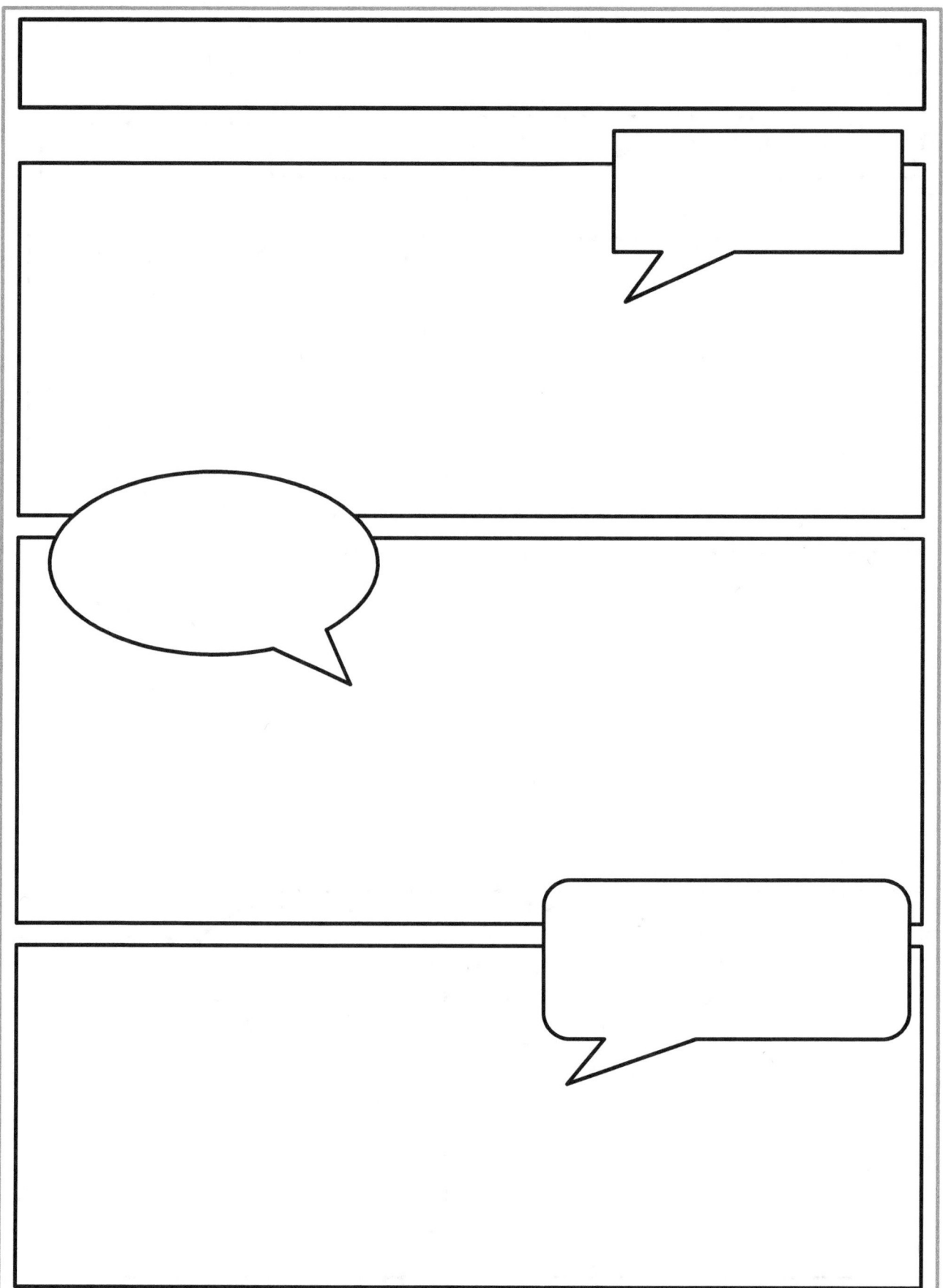

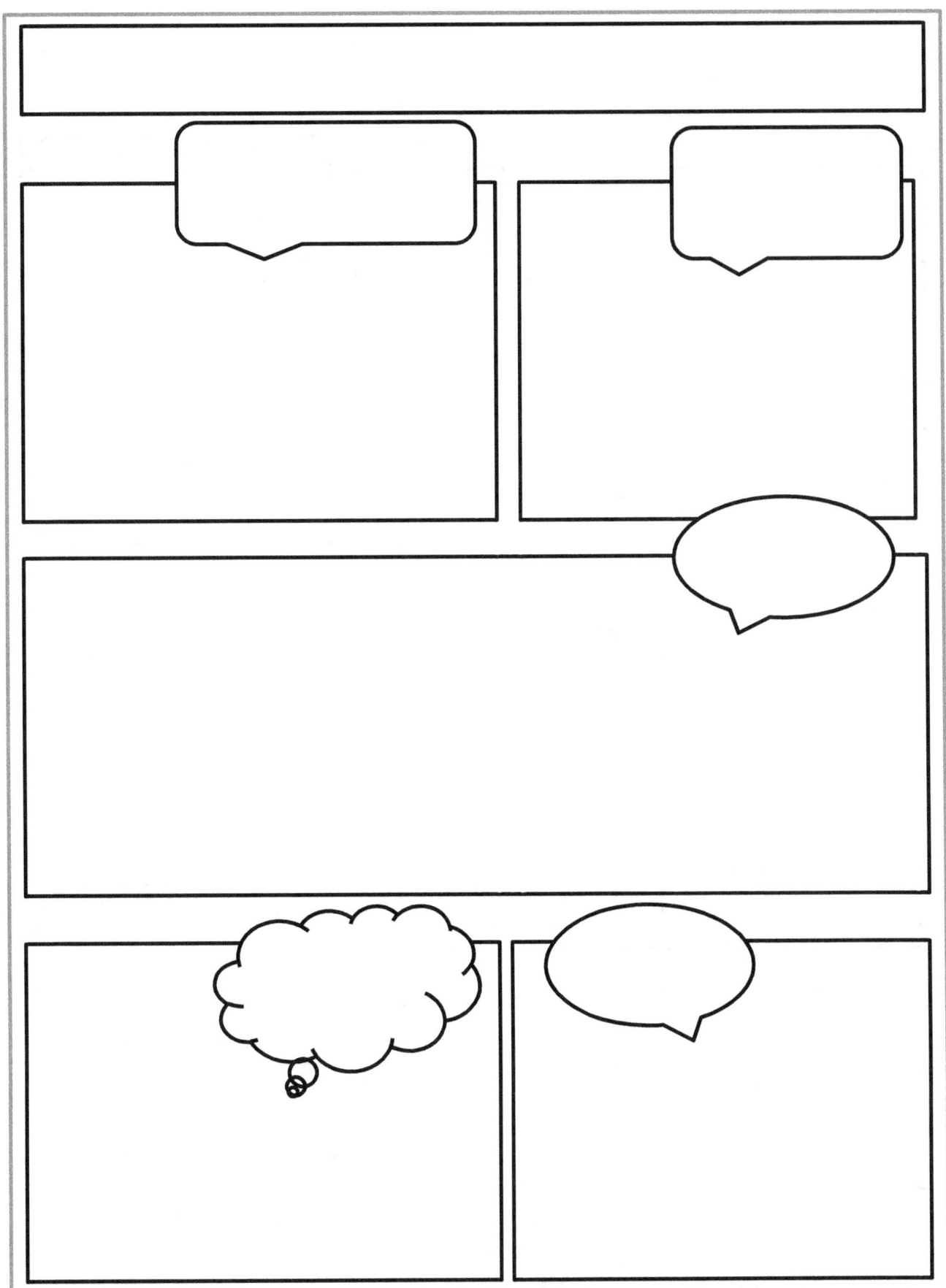

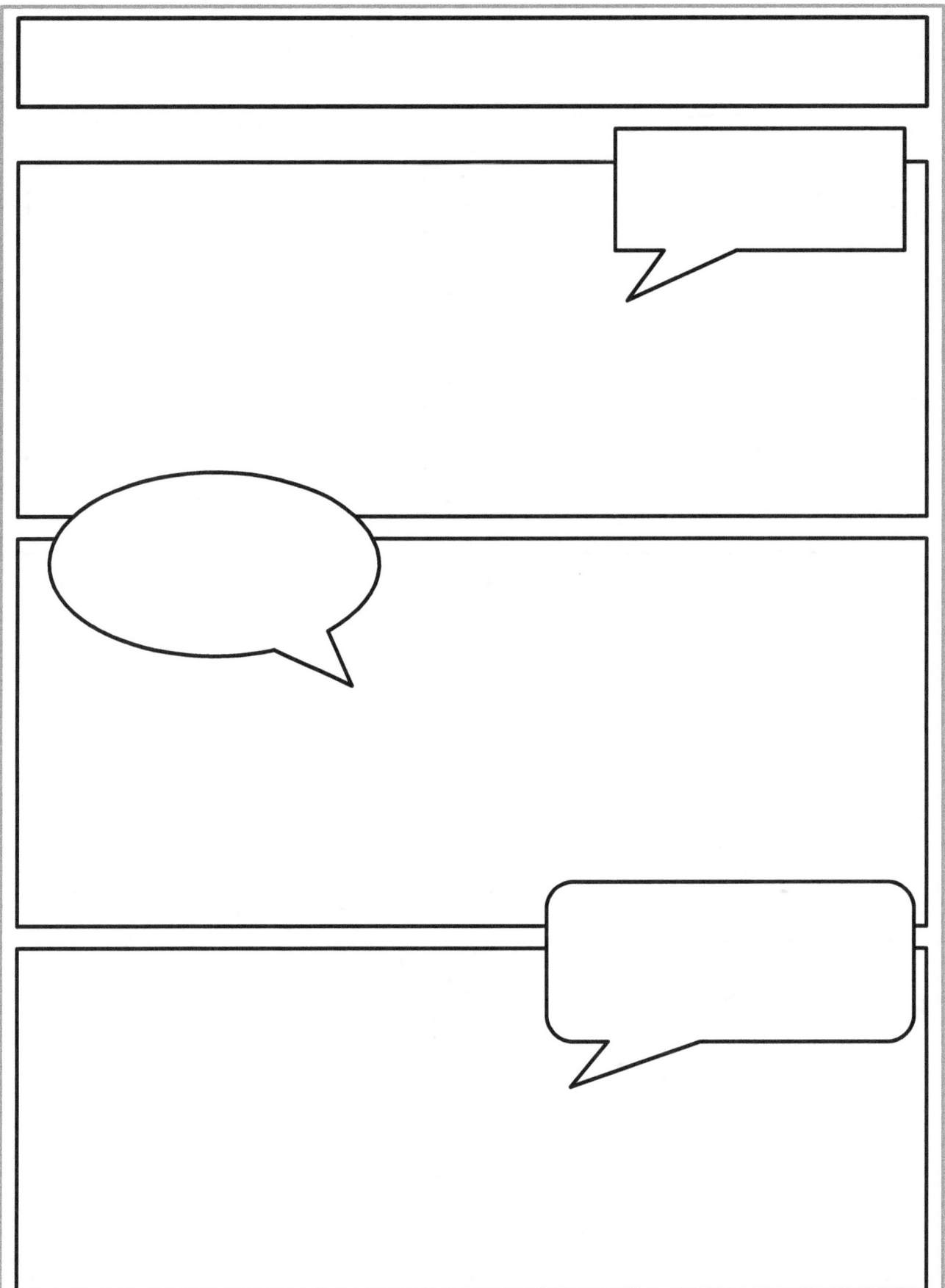

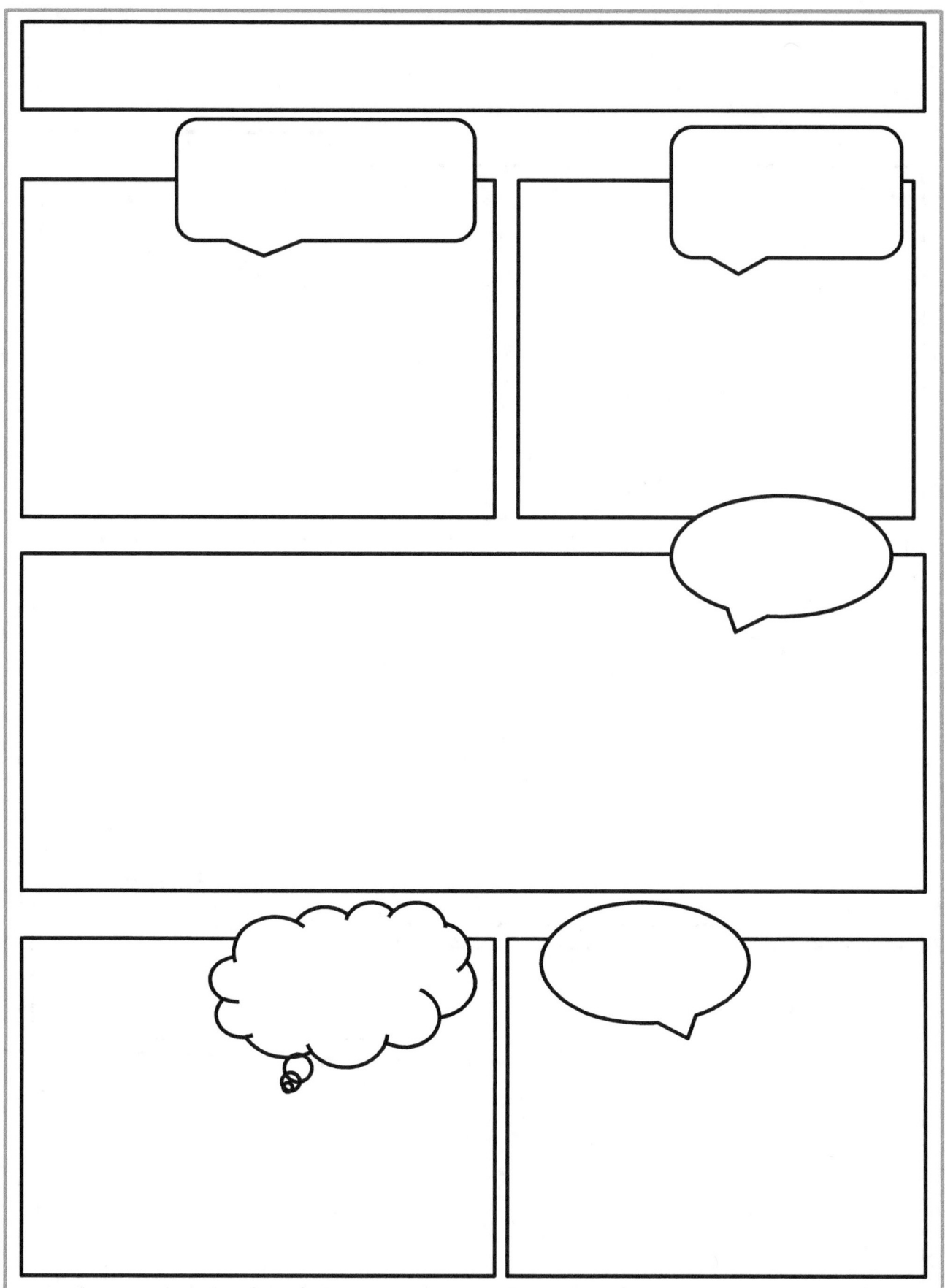

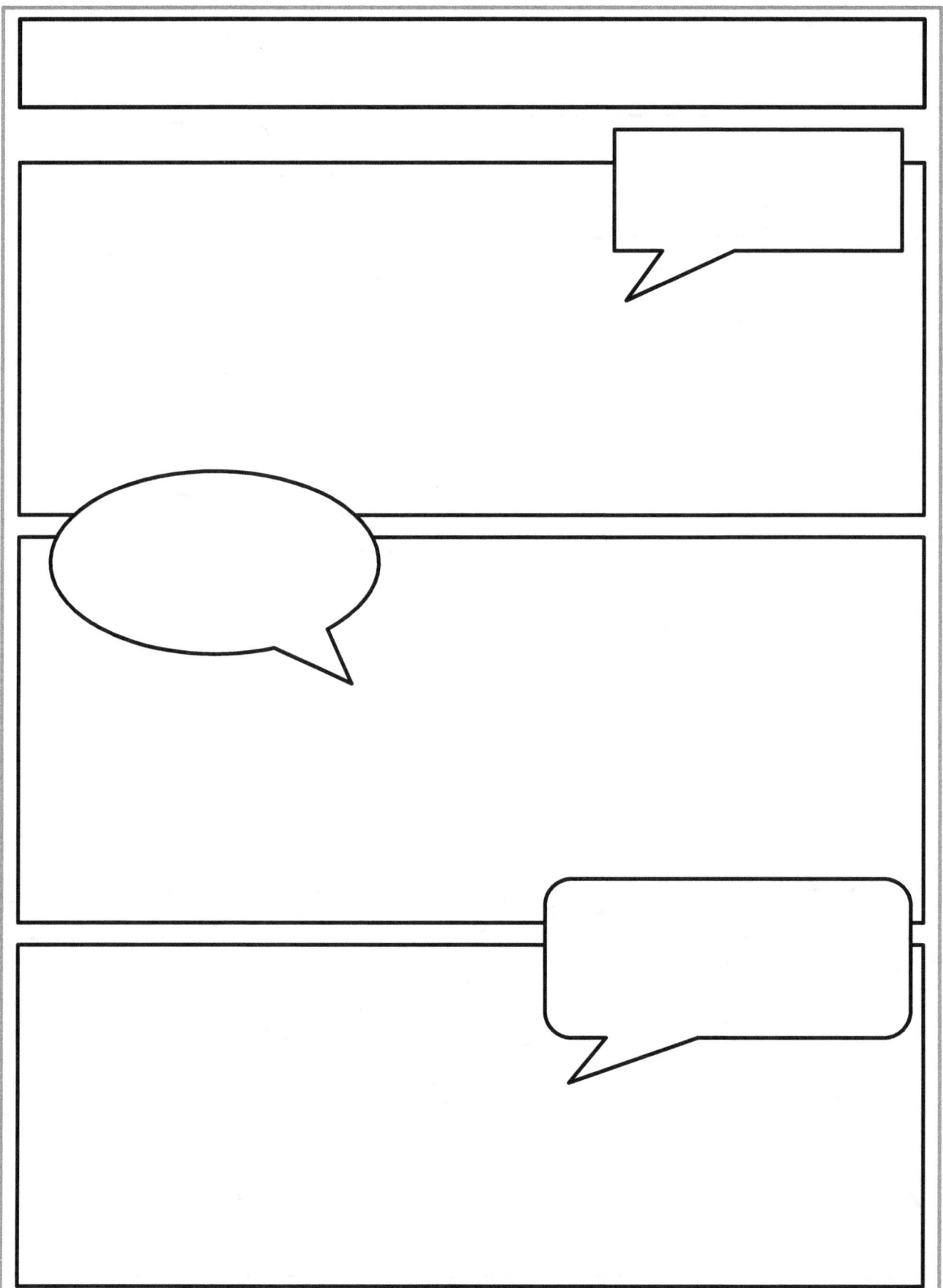

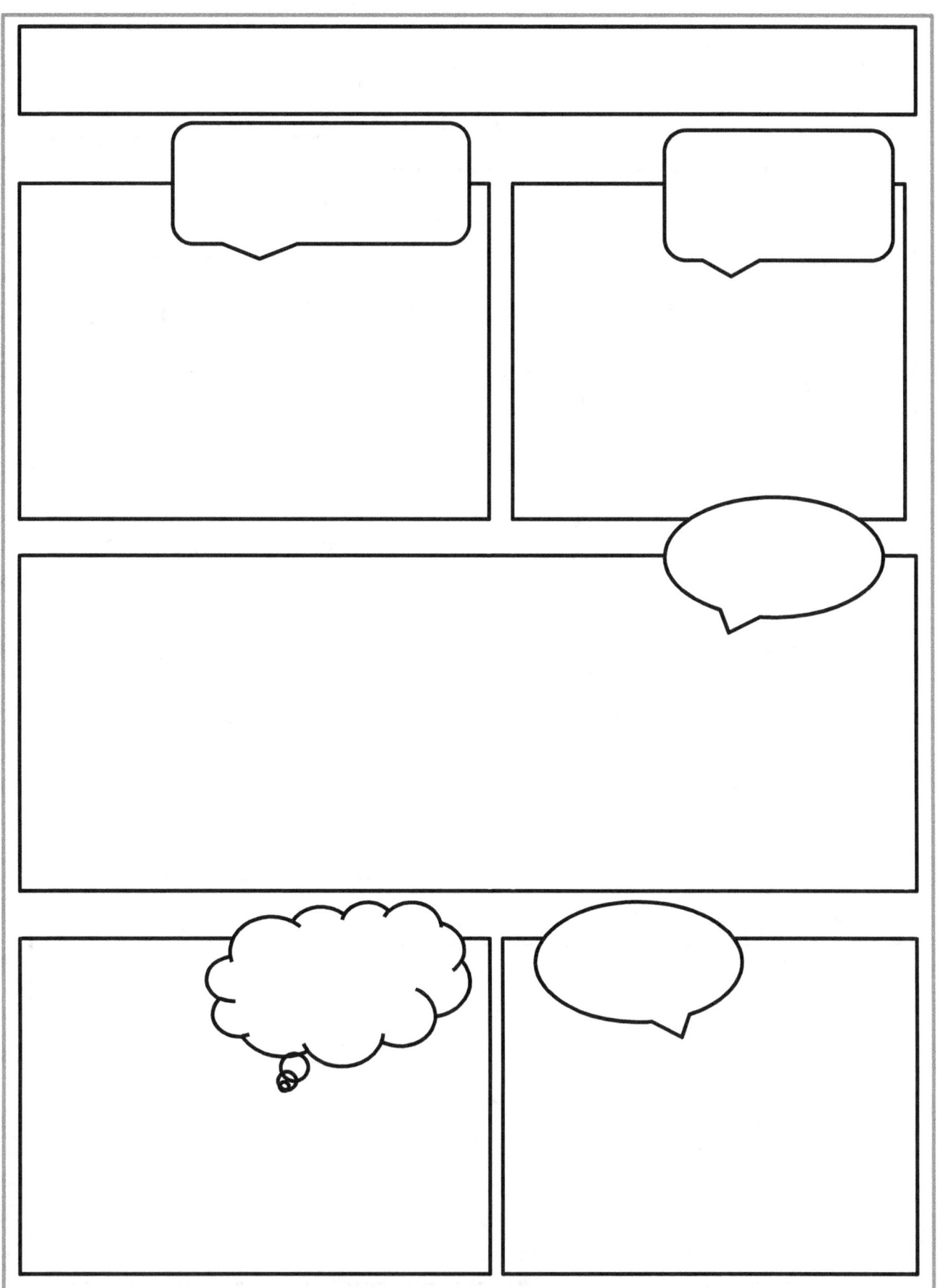

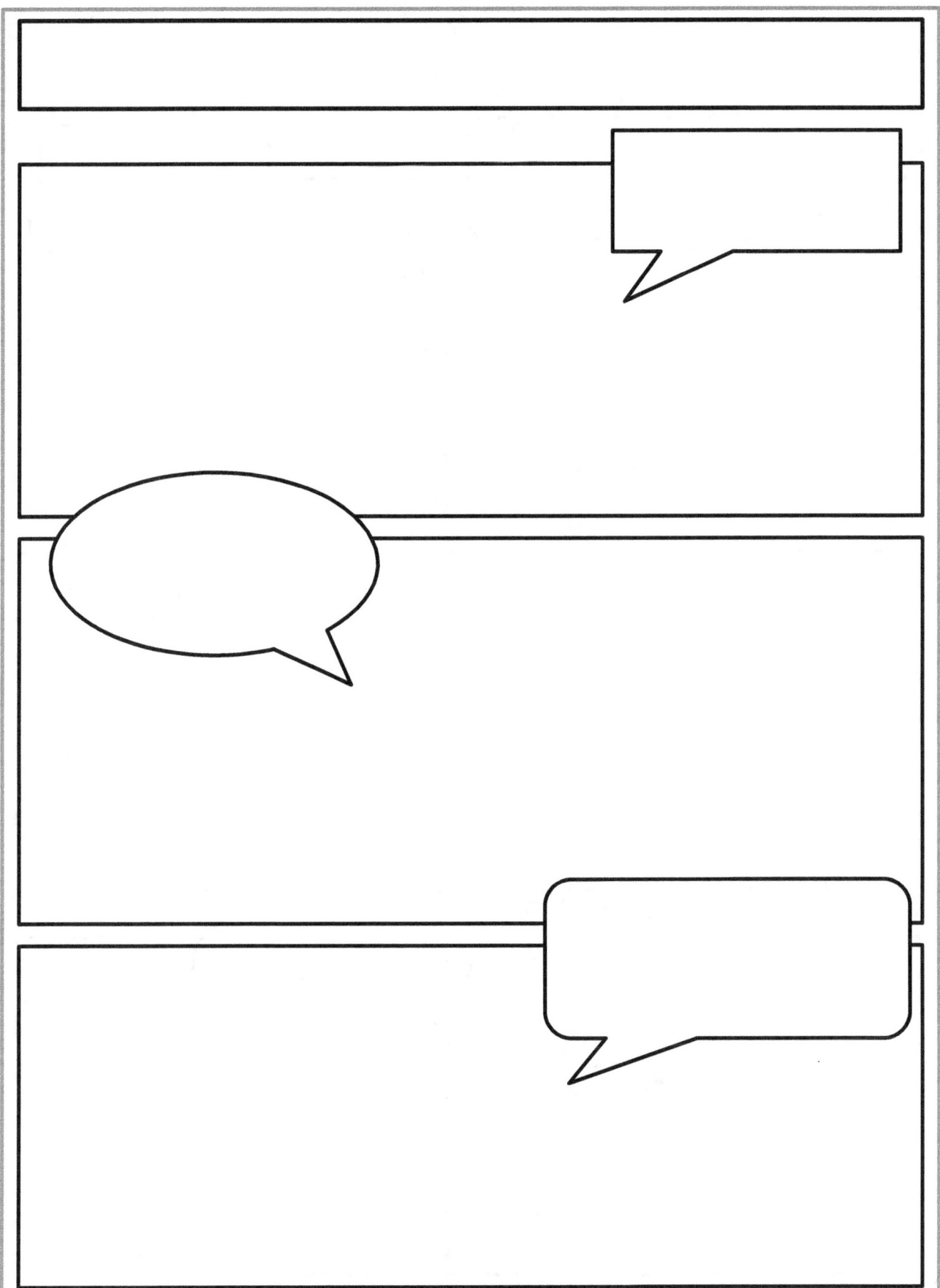

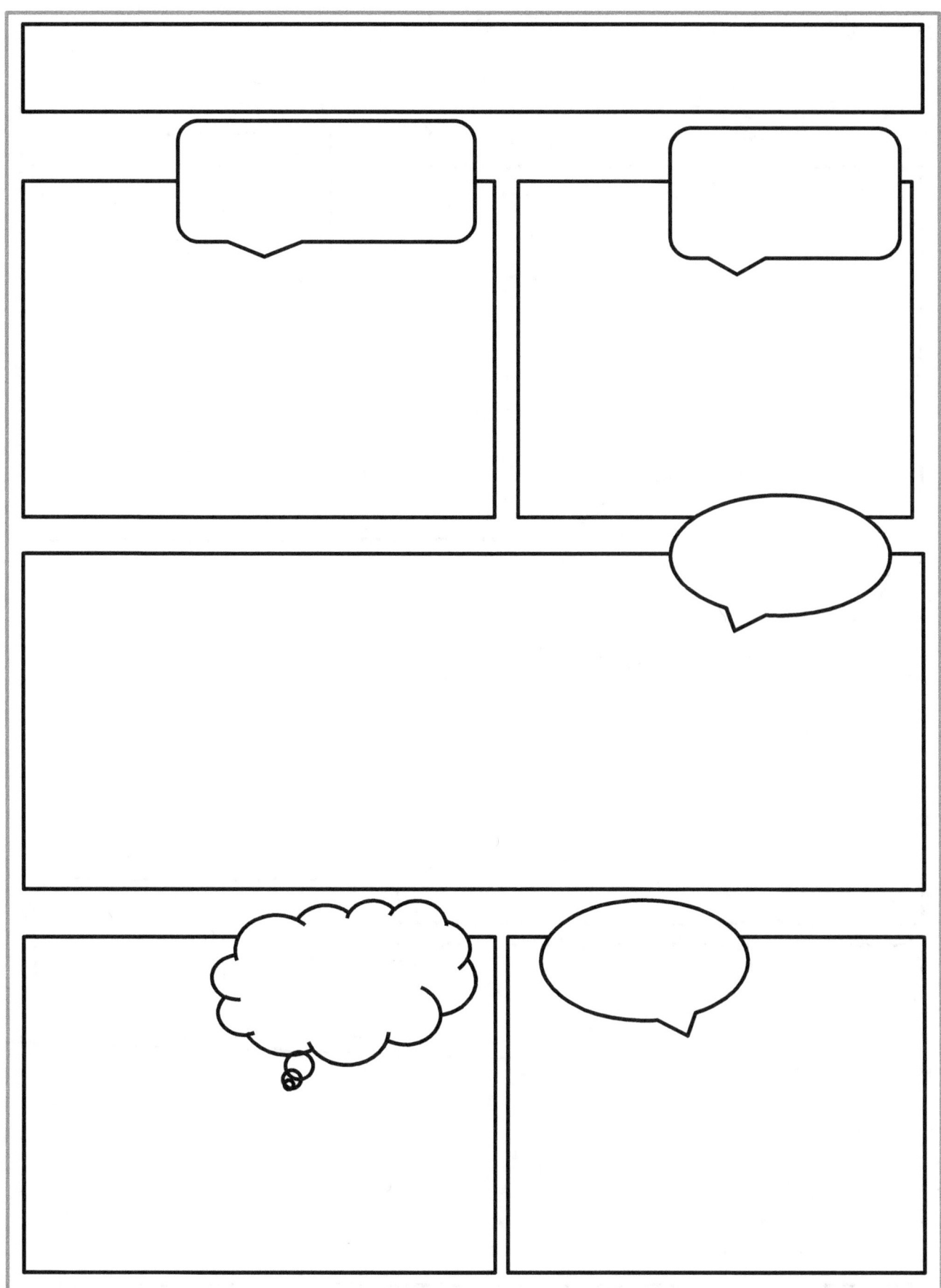

www.ingramcontent.com/pod-product-compliance
Lightning Source LLC
Chambersburg PA
CBHW081433220526
45466CB00008B/2377